The Eighth
American Saint

The Eighth American Saint

The Life of Saint Mother Theodore Guérin, Foundress of the Sisters of Providence of Saint Mary-of-the-Woods, Indiana

KATHERINE BURTON

WITH A FOREWORD AND AFTERWORD
BY MARY K. DOYLE

acta
PUBLICATIONS

THE EIGHTH AMERICAN SAINT
The Life of Saint Mother Theodore Guerin, Foundress of the Sisters of
Providence of Saint Mary-of-the-Woods, Indiana
by Katherine Burton
with a Foreword and Afterword by Mary K. Doyle

Updated and Edited by Gregory F. Augustine Pierce
Cover Design by Tom A. Wright
Text Design and Typesetting by Pat Lynch

Published by ACTA Publications, 5559 W. Howard Street,
Skokie, IL 60077-2621, (800) 397-2282, www.actapublications.com

Library of Congress Catalog number: 2006935394

ISBN 10: 0-87946-324-4
ISBN 13: 978-0-87946-324-3

Printed in the United States of America

Year 15 14 13 12 11 10 09 08 07
Printing 12 11 10 9 8 7 6 5 4 3 2 1

Contents

Foreword 9

Introduction 13

1   La Petite Providence (1806) 17

2   Sister Theodore of Soulaines 29

3   So Far, So Wild a Place 45

4   Music and Steam 59

5   Log Cabin on the Wabash 71

6   Living on the Love of God 83

7   The First Academy (1841) 97

8   Death from Pinpricks 111

9   New Missions 123

10 No Hidden Thorn 137

11 The Queen and the Mother 149

12 "Mend the Broken Platters" (1844) 161

13 "At Least, a Lock for the Door!" 179

14 Survival (1846–1847) 195

15 Security at Last (1847–1850) 211

16 The World Comes to Saint Mary-of-the-Woods 225

17 Another Teresa (1855) 241

18 Home in Mary's Month (1856) 255

Afterword 265

THE FIRST EIGHT SAINTS TO BE CANONIZED
WHO LIVED AND WORKED IN THE UNITED STATES OF AMERICA

St. Isaac Jogues (1607-1646): Jesuit missionary, first Catholic priest on Manhattan Island, first to preach the Gospel "a thousand miles to the interior" near Lake Superior, devoted to converting Native Americans, captured and tortured and held in slavery by Native Americans, martyred by Iroquois in New York State. Canonized June 29, 1930.

St. René Goupil (1607-1642): Jesuit missionary, surgeon in Quebec hospitals, captured by Iroquois, tortured and killed in New York State, first of his order in the Canadian missions to suffer martyrdom. Canonized June 29, 1930.

St. Frances Xavier Cabrini (1850-1917): missionary, first American citizen to be canonized, came to United States from Italy to help Italian immigrants, cared for the poor and sick and those incarcerated in jails, established orphanages, offered education to children and adults in several major cities across United States. Canonized July 7, 1946.

St. Elizabeth Ann Bayley Seton (1774-1821): foundress of the American Sisters of Charity, convert to Catholicism, first native-born citizen of the United States to be canonized, once married with family, endured tremendous personal hardships before devoting life to education and charity. Canonized September 14, 1975.

St. John Neumann (1811-1860): missionary, priest, fourth bishop of Philadelphia, born in Bohemia, responsible for bringing seven religious communities to the Diocese of Philadelphia, devoted much time to hearing confessions, visiting the sick, and teaching the Catechism to children. Canonized June 19, 1977.

St. Rose Philippine Duchesne (1769-1852): missionary, during height of civil unrest in France in the 1790s organized works of charity for the poor and offered material and spiritual support to priests in prison or hiding, opened convent school Missouri, served as missionary to Native Americans, often caring for their sick. Canonized July 3, 1988.

St. Katherine Drexel (1858-1955): born in the U.S., dubbed by journalist as the "millionaire nun," founded Sisters of the Blessed Sacrament for Indians and Colored People, now called the Sisters of the Blessed Sacrament, focused her work on the nation's poorest and most oppressed, founded Xavier University in New Orleans. Canonized October 1, 2000.

St. Mother Theodore Guérin (1798-1856): teacher and administrator in France, missionary, founder of the Sisters of Providence of Indiana and Saint Mary-of-the-Woods College, the oldest Roman Catholic liberal arts college for women in the United States, called by Paul John Paul II "a model of the best of womanhood." Canonized October 15, 2006.

DEDICATION

THIS EDITION IS DEDICATED
TO THE SISTERS OF PROVIDENCE,
ST. MARY-OF-THE-WOODS, INDIANA

The Servant of God,
Saint Mother Theodore Guérin
(Anne-Thérèse Guérin)

Foreword

&

The story of Anne-Thérèse Guérin, now known as Saint Mother Theodore Guérin, is one of courage, strength, perseverance, wisdom, and most of all trust in God. She was a pioneer on the American frontier, founder of a religious community, visionary for higher education of women, mentor to students and members of her community, and caretaker to countless people in need.

The few available photos and paintings of Mother Theodore depict her with a solemn, serious expression, which was customary at that time. I believe, however, that she was much sweeter in person. When picturing this outstanding woman saint in your mind, please imagine one of your own friends or relatives who exudes love and kindness. Mother Theodore also was known to have a fabulous sense of humor, so you can also imagine her smiling and laughing.

By the age of fifteen, Anne-Thérèse was fully caring for her ailing mother and younger sister after the loss of her father and two brothers. Ten years later, she entered the congregation of the Sisters of Providence in Ruillé-sur-Loir, France. Soon thereafter she contracted a serious illness that left her in fragile health for the rest of her life. Yet she went on to turn the entire city of Rennes, France, from a place of despair to one of hope, and she raised the educational level of the town of Soulaines while serving as superior to the schools there.

Upon the request of the bishop of the Diocese of Vincennes, Indiana, in the United States and the recommendation of her superior, Mother Theodore left her native France in 1840 to build a religious community and teaching institutions in the middle of a forest on an untamed continent.

She ventured on a 102-day grueling voyage across the Atlantic Ocean and into the American wilderness, and there she ultimately founded a new congregation of the Sisters of Providence, the first Catholic institution for the higher education of women in Indiana, elementary schools in Indiana and Illinois, two orphanages, and free pharmacies in Vincennes and Saint Mary-of-the-Woods. Through it all, she was loved and admired by her peers, fellow sisters, students, employees and the surrounding lay community.

Mother Theodore overcame insurmountable life challenges. She was undeterred by the separation from family, friends and homeland; drastic fluctuations and conditions in the weather; and devastating fires, disease and poverty. At least two superiors presented major difficulties for Mother Theodore and her religious congregation. One was distant and unsupportive. The other, though local, was demanding and controlling. In the early years there also was a sister in the community who, along with the chaplain, attempted to undermine the success of the infant congregation and the school. Mother Theodore treated all these people with the utmost respect, without compromising her responsibilities to those who most depended upon her.

Mother Theodore's legacy continues to this day with the vibrant community of the Sisters of Providence. Members of the Congregation work in inner city schools and among the poor, sick and aging. They also sponsor two college preparatory high schools, Guérin College Preparatory High School in Illinois and Providence Cristo Rey High School in Indiana, as well as Saint Mary-of-the-Woods College in Indiana, which is the oldest Catholic liberal arts college for women in the United States.

The Sisters of Providence motherhouse is located on more than 1200 acres of land in the town of St. Mary-of-the-Woods. There you also will find Saint Mary-of-the-Woods College, the Woods Day Care/Pre-School, the Providence Center, the home of the National Shrine of Our Lady of Providence, the White Violet Center of Eco-Justice, the Church of the Immaculate Conception, the Blessed Sacrament Chapel, the Saint Anne Shell Chapel, and organic gardens and orchards.

The story of Saint Mother Theodore Guérin is one that must be told. She offers as powerful a role model for today's generation as she did for her contemporaries in the early 1800s. Her example of holiness and leadership is timeless.

The Eighth American Saint was written by Katherine Burton and originally published in 1959 with the title *Faith Is the Substance*. It has been out of print for the last several decades, but the canonization of Mother Theodore on October 15, 2006, made it imperative that this book be made easily available to a new generation of readers. We have done only minimal editing to update the author's grammar, punctuation and spelling to a more contemporary style.

Burton masterfully weaved documented information about Mother Theodore into a compelling, intriguing and inspiring page-turner. She presented data from Mother Theodore's journals and letters in such a way that we feel we are witnessing first-hand the development of the Congregation of the Sisters of Providence in France and the path to the independent American community under Mother Theodore's leadership. I'm sure you will enjoy and appreciate this dynamic book as much as I do, and I am proud to be asked to contribute the new Foreword and Afterword.

Mary K. Doyle, M.A. Pastoral Theology
Geneva, Illinois

(Mary K. Doyle is the author of *The Rosary Prayer by Prayer* and *Mentoring Heroes*. She is currently writing a book on Saint Mother Theodore Guérin's relevance for today's Christians.)

INTRODUCTION

❦

C lose to the little town of Ruillé-sur-Loir, which lies midway between the cities of Tours and Nantes, in western France, there stands a small house, the first home of the Sisters of Providence. Built in 1806, it is made of stones that were gathered for the masons by the priest of the village, the children of his catechism class, and the young women who were the nucleus of his congregation of religious.

La Petite Providence lies outside the town, in a rough and treeless spot; its one long, divided room was large enough for the community of two, one of whom instructed the village children while the other visited the village sick and poor. Under its low attic, the rain and snow came in during the cold winters, and the hot sun beat on those who slept there long years ago.

By 1840, the Little Providence was still there, but a fine large convent— *La Grande Providence*—had been built for the congregation, which now had many religious in its ranks, teaching in its academies and free schools, nursing the sick poor, caring for orphans. It still held in all its dealings to its first motto: *Deus providebit* (God will provide).

In that year, six of its members left their home at Ruillé to begin the long, difficult voyage to the New World, to the frontier state of Indiana, midway across the United States. After a wearying journey from New York by steamboat and railroad, by canal and stagecoach, down the Ohio River by boat, then overland by stage, they finally came to Vincennes and then to Terre Haute, where they boarded a ferry to cross the Wabash River, and then went by wagon to their destination, a frontier settlement to which a few years ago Bishop Bruté of Vincennes had given the charming name of *Sainte Marie des Bois*—Saint Mary-of-the-Woods.

The convent they had hoped would shelter them was not, they learned, ready for them; there was not even a Little Providence. Instead their new home was two rooms in a farmer's house, the use of a cornloft for sleeping quarters, and a shed for kitchen.

From that small beginning in the Indiana forest has grown the present Congregation of Sisters of Providence, whose motherhouse is still Saint Mary-of-the-Woods. As of 2006, the 166th year since its founding, more than 5200 women have entered the Sisters of Providence, nearly 500 of which are members at this time.

Sisters of Providence are engaged in ministries throughout the United States, Taiwan, China and the Philippines in service to the poor, education, health services, and social and ecological justice. The charter of incorporation granted the Congregation in 1846 made it the first Catholic institution of the higher education of women in Indiana. That institution is known today as Saint Mary-of-the-Woods College.

The few acres originally bought by Bishop Bruté have grown today to over 1200 acres. Beautiful and ample buildings house the members of the congregation and their works, a shining proof of the vision, the patience, and the faith in the providence of God of their American foundress, Mother Theodore Guérin.

The work she so bravely opened and so successfully guided, continued to grow after her death in 1856. The beautiful Providence she built to replace the farmhouse convent was destroyed by fire in 1889, but the next year a new and larger convent was erected to house the religious. By 1924, Guérin Hall and a conservatory of music, as well as Le Fer Hall and a new infirmary, had been erected and dedicated. A new church had been consecrated by the apostolic delegate in 1907.

In the autumn of 1920, a colony of American Sisters of Providence went to China to work in Honan. They were six in number, thus commemorating the sacrifice of Mother Theodore and the five who came with her from Ruillé. After twenty years of work there, they were in 1943 interned in a Japanese concentration camp and some years afterwards were evacuated to Formosa.

When, in the summer of 1956, a celebration was held at Saint Mary-of-the-Woods of the hundred and fiftieth year since the founding of the congregation in France, it celebrated also the hundredth anniversary of the death of Mother Theodore. Archbishop Schulte of Indianapolis pontificated, and Archabbot Columban of St. Benedict's Abbey in Louisiana preached at the Pontifical High Mass. From Ruillé came delegates of the Sisters of Providence, and from Taiwan, to bring good wishes from the members in France and in the Orient.

Despite her busy life, Mother Theodore wrote many letters and journals of her voyages and her years in the New World, journals that became a valuable source of information on the history of the Church in the middle west and of Catholic education there. She was a pioneer of frontier education; in fact, until twelve years after she came, St. Mary's Institute was the only Catholic girls' boarding school in Indiana, and many Protestant families sent their daughters to the French nuns.

Booth Tarkington, whose mother had once been a student at St. Mary's Institute, wrote in the *Indianapolis Star* how vivid had remained her recollections of sixty years before at Saint Mary-of-the-Woods. These religious, Tarkington thought, must have been "women of exquisite manner as well as of distinguished education," who had brought to the New World from France something rare and fine—"for lack of a better word I shall call it distinction, a manner of simplicity and gentle dignity. It always springs to my mind whenever I delve for the true meaning of 'lady.'"

CHAPTER ONE

La Petite Providence (1806)

ℰ

Young Abbé Dujarié, appointed in 1803 parish priest of Ruillé-sur-Loir in the ancient French province of Maine on the border of Brittany, knew well that he had no easy task before him. But he was ready and eager to help with all his strength to undo some of the terrible damage that years of revolution and its aftermath had brought to France—and especially to this part—where there had always been a strong Catholicism, and where those who defended their faith met often with torment and death at the hands of the revolutionaries.

During the years of revolution, the clergy of France had been all but destroyed. Many were killed; some remained safely hidden through the efforts of loyal parishioners, who were in constant danger of losing their own lives for these acts of kindness; some went into exile in the New World or to England or Ireland. Those who remained hidden worked in secret to keep the faith alive, and among them was the young Abbé who was now heading the little parish at Ruillé.

Jacques François Dujarié had entered the seminary at twenty years of age, but before he could be ordained the tide of revolution had forced him to flee and hide. He became a peddler of linens; he worked in a weaver's cellar; he sold rice water in Paris. He was often suspected of being a cleric, but he was never caught. At last, after the fall of Robespierre, when a measure of safety returned to the land, he was able to finish his studies; in 1795 he was ordained, but secretly and in the loft of a barn, for there were still strong forces at work against religion. For some years he worked, still in secrecy and among people he trusted, until the Concordat of 1801 made it possible for him to come once more into the open.

It was clear, even then, that there had been more reasons than hate for this terrible civil war. In France, rule was still by privileged classes, though a new group was rising—the industrial workers and owners. For the peasants there was less than nothing; some of them were virtual serfs on feudal estates and their unhappy condition made them ready for revolt. Unfortunately, the revolt went too far and the good suffered with the guilty. Because too many of the great prelates had been as grasping as the great lords, the lesser men and women suffered too. Measures against professed religious were especially harsh beyond reason. Church lands were nationalized and religious were suppressed or put to death, while the clergy were required to take an oath of fealty to the state, which many refused to do.

One cruel group after the other came to power and each was wrecked in turn, but no matter who won the men and women of the Church always lost. Not in fact until 1801 was there any measure of safety for them; then a concordat was agreed on between Napoleon, who had the year before returned in triumph from his victories in Italy, and Pope Pius VII. This gave considerable freedom to the Church, but the fearful results of the past lawlessness were to last for a long time.

Especially in the first years of peace these results of the revolution were to be noted among the young people. The clergy and religious, returning from hiding and from exile, began rebuilding as best they could their broken churches and convents and rallied to rebuild the faith in their land. They worked to remake the moral as well as the spiritual life of the young, and they brought what material help they could; though the religious had little, those they helped had even less.

During those years there had been no attempt at education of any kind save for the wealthy. People who had been at first demoralized through fear had later grown indifferent to any practice of their faith. Their children, having known no other way of life than that of irreligion and hatred, were infected.

Abbé Dujarié knew that the starting point of his work must be with the children. He must aid them with food and shelter, and later persuade them to come to him for education in the rudiments and in the Faith. He knew he would need help in this, and also that he could expect none from his fellow clergy, who were busy with problems of their own.

His really great need was a corps of devoted women. But where to find them? The religious were scattered, and many of them had become secularized; it would be a long time before their congregations could reassemble. Their homes had been sold to secular buyers by the State; they had no money to buy them back or to buy others.

In the Abbé's parish were two young women to whom he appealed to aid him in teaching the children, at least the small ones. When they agreed, he suggested that he find for them a small house where they could teach and perhaps also come to live. But there was no house available that he could afford to buy, and so, when he took his catechism classes for a walk, he and the children picked up stones from the rocky soil and put them in piles along the road; a friendly farmer gathered them in his cart and dropped them on a small piece of ground that the Abbé had bought a few miles from his parish church. When the pile of stones was large enough, he hired masons to construct from them a little house, which he named *La Petite Providence*.

It stood outside the village itself, in an open space in the fields. He knew the site was too remote from the church, but it was all he could afford to buy. The first floor was divided into kitchen and refectory, community room and school room. Above these was a low attic, not high enough to stand erect in, which served as a dormitory.

There was no well, and the young women had to walk a long distance for water. Their food was poor—dry bread, skim milk cheese, grapes from their own vines, meat that the Abbé brought them.

The two young women wore a plain secular dress; they made no vows or even promises, and they were free to withdraw after a year if they wished to. They carried out whatever work the Abbé gave them to do, teaching and visiting the sick poor of the town.

In the beginning, the Abbé had not thought of establishing a religious congregation. However, he was aware that communities were springing up all over France—between 1802 and 1815 twenty-eight new ones were founded—and it was only reasonable that he should give thought to such a community, especially when other young women were coming to him with offers to help at the Providence. It meant that more and more children could be taught, more sick could be visited. The Abbé decided to form them into a religious group. He sent them for training to Madame de la Girouardière at Baugé, who had for some time been operating a hospital for incurables and whose own helpers were trained religious.

Six months later, the Abbé's protégées returned and definitely embarked on a life in religion, choosing a semi-religious habit of black with a white peasant bonnet and a veil like a peasant shawl, with a square black *piécette* and an apron. To each young woman the Abbé gave a name in religion, though as yet he did not appoint anyone as the community's head.

There were times when he was doubtful about the future of his group; the willingness was there and the devotion, but the organization was formless and amateur. However, they were now trained for their work, and it was clear that other young women would join them; in fact, as soon as it was learned that they were an established religious group, requests came from other parishes, asking for a few women to come to teach their children. The Abbé had to refuse, for as yet there were too few to do more than care for his own flock. Besides, they had no rule to guide them, only his written directives, and these were chiefly instructions on holy zeal and on charity.

Eventually the outside demand grew so insistent that he sent a few young women to nearby parishes. By 1809, they were teaching in eight schools. Further they could not expand, for they were too few, and the schools where they went to teach were too poor to pay anything to teachers who had so little themselves.

The Abbé had built for them a little chapel, ten feet by twenty, next to their Providence, and there the Blessed Sacrament was reserved. During the week, he or his curate sometimes came to say Mass. On Sundays, the young women rose before dawn and walked the three miles to the village church; Madelon, the rectory housekeeper, saw to it that they had a good meal before they went home. Madame Aubry, one of the affluent people in Ruillé, sent them back to Little Providence after Vespers with a supply of meat for the week; if the weather was bad, she kept them overnight in her own home.

Although the community continued to grow, they still had no real standing in the Church, no rule, no vows. For all his solicitude, the overworked Abbé could give them only limited attention. Yet they still had no head save himself, for among them he had so far found no one capable of taking full charge.

In the next year she came. The advent of one new member changed everything, and made certain the future of the group.

Josephine Zoé du Roscoät was a woman of almost forty years, of noble birth and excellent education, as well as of long experience in works of charity. Her family had been very wealthy, but like many others were in greatly reduced circumstances due to the Revolution; they had been fortunate, however, in that a faithful servant had concealed some family possessions and through their sale they were able to buy back a portion of their estate in Brittany.

The part of France from which she and Abbé Dujarié came, and many of the sisters of the Congregation were to come, had been staunchly Catholic since the fifth century. Following the Celtic invasion, English and Irish monks came to settle where the Druids had dwelt and where enormous monuments of those early days still existed. It was a land of mingled fact and myth, where Arthur had held his court and where Merlin wove his spells. It was also the land where Abelard was born and where St. Vincent Ferrer died. Not far from Ruillé stood the shrine of St. Anne d'Auray, the scene of centuries of pilgrimages and pardons.

The Bretons of the early nineteen hundreds had the faith of centuries in their blood. They were a dark, austere people, but one of deep spirituality and tenderness. From Brittany came many who were to play a part in bringing the faith to the New World. Bishop Bruté was born there, and so were many of the priests and religious whom he persuaded to come to his diocese in the wilderness of the middle west in America. Brittany was to furnish many members of the Ruillé group as it expanded into a large congregation. One of them was Anne-Thérèse Guérin, who was to open a branch of her congregation in the New World.

Mlle. du Roscoät had for some years taught music in a school that she and her mother had opened; the rest of her time she spent in work for the sick and the poor. For years she had wanted to enter a religious community, but her family objected. Her widowed mother wept bitterly at the prospect of being left alone. Her daughter had been considering various congregations when by chance she met Père de la Chapelle, one of the Fathers of the Faith (the name used by the Jesuits when they were suppressed) and he told her about this small group whose work he had been watching. He thought that she would be able to help them a great deal.

She agreed to have a talk with the Abbé, but after she returned home she had arrived at no decision; in fact, she had not even visited the convent. Some weeks later, she decided it was the will of God that she go there. She left her home secretly, knowing she could not face her mother's arguments. She came to Little Providence in bunting dress and with one change of apparel; she had sold her gold watch to pay her traveling expenses.

When she saw for the first time the actuality before her—the poor little house, the dormitory where there was hardly room for one more cot, the poverty and lack of everything, her heart failed her. Then she was taken into the chapel where there was the Blessed Sacrament and over the altar a little bas-relief of the Holy Family.

She had intended to tell the sisters that she could not become one of them. Instead, she found herself saying, "I have come to stay." Afterwards she said she knew she must stay when she saw the poverty of Bethlehem in the chapel where, before the picture of the Holy Family, glowed the little lamp that showed Jesus was at home in that small place.

Until Mlle. du Roscoät joined them, there had been no actual organization in the group. The sisters had taken no vows and could withdraw when they wished; they had no church approval, not even diocesan. With the advent of this new member, everything changed. The Abbé had been quick to see her value; he knew of her fine education and her years of social work. When he had given her the habit and the name of Sister Marie Madeleine, he decided the time had come to give real permanence to the Providence Sisters of Ruillé.

The members now took the three vows that were customary and also a fourth—devotion to the young and care of the sick. Hitherto it had been the Abbé who had appointed a member to act as superior; now the members were to choose their own head for a period of three years. With no delay they elected Sister Marie Madeleine, who became a superior almost before she was a religious.

The little community grew rapidly. The little stone house became impossibly small for the people who were crowded into it. Then, too, the tile roof was cracked in many places; rain and snow came in on the sleepers in the dormitory.

Abbé Dujarié rose to the occasion. He sold what property he himself still owned in Bas Maine. He begged funds in the parish and bought a field in Ruillé close to the parish church. There in 1820 he began the building of a new stone house, and the sisters, long cramped in their small home, watched its building with delight. Since it was close to the church, the long walks would be a thing of the past; instead of a dreary outlook on stony fields, they would now have a house that overlooked the River Loir. They would enter their new home with their circumstances much changed, and for the better. They had already named their new house *La Grande Providence.*

Meantime, Abbé Dujarié, seeing how well his sisters were progressing, devoted himself to a new project: the founding of a group of teaching brothers to take care of the boys of the parish. Their organization would be similar to that of the sisters, and the two groups would have joint funds; in other respects they would be separate.

He opened it with two young men whom he brought to live with him at the rectory. Their beginning was as simple as had been that of the sisters; he gave them one room for study and meals and prayers, a garret for their dormitory, and the parish church for their chapel. For spiritual exercises they had to depend on the Abbé. In addition to their hours of prayers and study, part of each day was spent earning a living by helping with the harvesting and grape gathering. They collected stones to build their own future monastery. Despite the hard life, eight young men entered the community within less than a year.

On Easter Tuesday of 1822, Sister Marie Madeleine left Ruillé to make a visitation of her small missions, now twenty in number. She had been away only a few weeks when word came that she was very ill of typhoid fever. One of the sisters hurried from Ruillé to nurse her, taking with her a letter from the Abbé.

"Worry about nothing," he wrote. "We shall be happy enough and well satisfied if our dear child lives and comes back to us in good health." Only four days later came the sad news of her death, followed by word that she had been buried in her family plot in the cemetery at Pléhedel. She was never to live in the fine new house into which they planned to move as soon as she returned to them.

The sisters she left felt her loss greatly, but it was no doubt the Abbé who missed her most of all and knew how great had been her contribution: within only four years she had built the Sisters of Providence into a community of true religious.

In September, the sisters moved into their new house, commodious and airy, and immediately elected a new superior. Their choice was Sister Cécile, thirty years old, who in the world had been Aimée Lécor, daughter of a peasant family from the Ile de Bréhat. She was a very different type from her predecessor. Her youth had been spent working in the fields and a life in religion had never entered her mind. But she had become a Franciscan tertiary, and in that group she met Mlle. du Roscoät, who asked her to teach a class of young children. She proved to be of great help there, for she understood the Breton tongue that many of them spoke. Eventually she followed Mlle. du Roscoät to Ruillé and entered the novitiate. She planned to become a lay sister because the Breton patois was all she knew well; her French was very imperfect. But Sister Marie Madeleine knew how deep her interior life was and how able she was as an administrator. When she lay dying, she told her nurse that she hoped the community would elect Sister Cécile to fill her place.

When Sister Cécile realized that she was being elected superior of her community, she was dumfounded and tried to refuse. She was finally induced to accept the office, but only because she had learned it was the wish of her dead superior. Father Dujarié changed her name to that of Our Lady, and she henceforth was known as Mother Mary. She had become the head of a considerable community, one now numbering fifty religious in twenty houses.

To the Abbé, hard pressed in many ways, it was a great relief to know that another competent woman was heading his young community, for much of his own time had to be given to his community of brothers, who were also increasing in numbers and now serving eight schools.

In November of 1826, the Sisters of Providence received royal approval. This gave them legal existence, and the Abbé now handed over the property to them as its legal owners. The Brothers of St. Joseph were then installed in a house of their own, the gift of the Abbé. But, unlike the sisters, who were now completely self-supporting, the brothers were often in financial difficulties; unlike the sisters, they brought no dowry with them, and as yet they had received no money for their teaching.

To aid the Abbé, who had so greatly aided them, the sisters paid for much of the brothers' maintenance since, being now incorporated, they could borrow money on their own assets. The debts, however, became at times a heavy burden; by 1830 they owed so much money that the Bishop of Le Mans decided to settle their difficulties by separating completely the two communities. The sisters assumed what debts remained, but in the future they were to be responsible only for their own bills.

In 1831, the Sisters of Providence at a general chapter voted to increase the number of their officers; in addition to a superior general, they were to have assistants, a secretary, a treasurer, and a mistress of novices. By that year the congregation had thirty houses.

Bishop Carron of Le Mans had watched over the sisters until his death; then the new incumbent, Bishop Bouvier, became their good friend. One of his first suggestions he made when he came to see them was that they build a chapel of their own, if they could possibly do so without going into debt. Hitherto they had used one of the rooms at *La Grande Providence* for that purpose, but it had become so small for their numbers that when all the sisters came home for a retreat they had to use the parish church, a very unsatisfactory substitute.

In March of 1835, Abbé Dujarié blessed the attractive little new building of stone, with Doric columns and a graceful facade. His sisters were sad when they saw how tired and ill he looked and noted that when he made the tour of the building he had to be supported by his curate. The next year, he relinquished his pastorate and returned to live at Le Mans with his brothers, who had now become affiliated with another group, Abbé Moreau's Congregation of Holy Cross. This move had to some extent been opposed by Abbé Dujarié, and it had been much regretted by some of the Sisters of Providence, who felt that they were losing a part of their family.

The sisters, in gratitude for all the Abbé had done for them in the past—they considered him their founder—assumed what debts he had and also paid him, until his death several years later, the sum of fifteen hundred francs a year as a pension.

When he died, there were two hundred and fifty-eight members in the Congregation; they lived in fifty-eight houses. They were still using the simple little rule he had given them, but in that year they appealed to the Bishop of Le Mans to formulate for them one better suited to their present status. He composed for them a rule, in which the fourth vow was retained, but they were now to make their vows for five years. Each boarding school, each house, no matter how small, was to have a free school attached to it. In addition, the sisters were to maintain pharmacies to supply with free remedies those who could not afford to buy any medicines.

At the motherhouse there had been changes, but the standard of living was much the same. The accommodations were rigidly simple, though they had seemed luxurious to those who had come from *La Petite Providence*. The sisters still slept on straw ticks and straw pillows; the curtains for their sleeping cubicles were very plain. The new rule allowed no luxuries and was insistent that there be no "carpets, waxed floors, gold frames or pictures of value."

Chapter Two

Sister Theodore of Soulaines

č

In 1823, the year after the death of Mère Roscoät, a new postulant came to Ruillé who was to be an important member of the Congregation in France and of even greater importance as a Sister of Providence in the United States. She was given in religion the name of Sister Saint Theodore.

Anne-Thérèse Guérin was born in Brittany, at Étables, a small town in western France, close to the Atlantic Ocean. In 1798, the year of her birth, that province was still suffering from the effects of the Revolution; allegiance among many people had become widely divided. Anne-Thérèse's own father, Laurent Guérin, was of a family which had supported Napoleon, while the family of his young wife, the Lefevres, was staunchly royalist. This made for enmity between the families, but it did not greatly trouble the young couple, who loved each other and married despite their parents' objections. They were very happy in their marriage. As a naval officer, M. Guérin supported his family well. Of four children born to the couple, the two sons died while still very young; the two daughters were to outlive both their parents.

Anne-Thérèse, the elder daughter, was baptized on the day of her birth, and following the ceremony she was consecrated to Our Lady. She was to recall, as one of her earliest memories, hearing her parents tell her that she was the Blessed Virgin's *petite fille*, that it was a high honor to bear that title, and that she must always live up to it.

Life at Étables was simple. In earlier years, under the old regime, both families had been people of property, but the Revolution had taken most of this. However, it was better not to have much money during those days; it did not look good to republican neighbors. As for rank, that too was something better ignored, and the Lefevres were of the lesser nobility. Anne-Thérèse had been shown, hidden in a trunk, a little cap that as only ladies of rank wore in former days.

"But we'll put it back in the trunk,' said her mother, "and keep it there as a memory rather than show it as a fact."

At Étables there was not much opportunity for an education, for it was one of the towns where the Revolution had thoroughly wrecked the schools. Madame Guérin was herself well educated; she taught her daughters to read and write, and she gave them instruction in religion when they were very small girls. When a young woman opened a school in Étables, Anne-Thérèse attended it for a year. She did not find it very interesting, perhaps because the method of education was too slow for her lively brain.

"Anne-Thérèse was not at school today," would come the report, and a few probing questions would elicit the fact that she had that day been roaming the beach or the hills—much preferable to Mademoiselle's routine. The following year a theological student, who was their cousin, came to live with them and learned of Anne-Thérèse's great indifference to learning.

"Let me teach her while I'm here," he suggested, and this tutoring proved a delight to the child; in that year of his stay at Étables she learned a great deal.

During her childhood and girlhood, the place she loved best of all was the seashore, and she grew to know it well. Her home was only a few hundred feet from the gray blue waters. By day she walked the sandy beach; at night she listened from her bedroom window to the constant murmur of the waves on the shore.

At her insistence, and especially because she was so well grounded in the catechism, she was allowed to make her First Holy Communion at the early age of ten. On that very day she confided to the curé at Étables parish that she wanted to be a nun some day. The old priest did not smile away this childish statement; he treated it seriously.

"Cherish that desire, my child," he told her, "and you will one day belong to God. It will come about—but only if you do not ever take back the heart you have consecrated to Him today." And Anne-Thérèse promised fervently that she would always hold to her intention. Some day she would be a religious.

During the next few years, the Guérin family saw little of their husband and father; he was with Napoleon in his various campaigns. When the Emperor returned to France before entering on his Russian campaign, M. Guérin asked to spend some weeks with his family before the forces set out for Russia. The leave was granted. The happy news came to Étables that he was on his way home. He was coming from Toulouse, and he had gifts for all the family with him.

He never arrived. Word reached his family of his death at the hands of brigands near Avignon. He had taken a shorter route than his companions in order to have more time with his family. He had a considerable amount of money with him, and evidently had been ambushed and slain and robbed of everything.

His death left Madame Guérin with little money and two children to bring up. Anne-Thérèse was now nearly fifteen, her sister Marie only nine. During this time of sorrow, the mother came to depend almost wholly on her elder daughter, and the young girl took up her task courageously, nursing her mother through a severe illness brought on by the shock of her loss, caring for the little sister, running the house.

Anne-Thérèse's education had to be given up entirely, for there was no money left. But she had inherited her mother's quick intelligence and her father's calm and thoughtful disposition, legacies which were to serve her well in lieu of a more formal education.

For some years longer, little remained for Anne-Thérèse to do beyond the duty nearest her—caring for her mother and her little sister. But her hope for a life in religion had never left her since the day she had confided her childish intention to the curé. She had, however, kept this hope from her mother and her young friends until one day, when a group of girls were discussing their future, they asked her about hers. "What kind of man do you want to marry?" asked one.

Anne-Thérèse was silent, and they urged her to speak up. She laughed them off, but finally, in answer to their teasing and evidently searching for words to convey her meaning in a veiled way, Anne-Thérèse said, "I shall marry a king."

Her startled companions stared at her, but, before they could press her further, she ran off, leaving the amazed girls wondering what she meant. Her mother's family were royalists, that they knew, and there was a king back on the throne of France now—but surely her aspirations did not soar as high as that. Yet they knew Anne-Thérèse was not a girl who made silly remarks. No matter what she meant, it was an extraordinary thing to have said.

Some weeks later, when the story came to her mother's ears, she asked her daughter to explain her strange remark. For the first time Anne-Thérèse spoke out frankly.

"My King is not on any throne of earth, Mother," she said, and then, as if she could no longer be silent, she blurted the truth: "I want to enter the convent, Mother."

The astute Madame Guérin had for some time realized where her daughter's thoughts were turning, but this was the first time she had heard them openly expressed. She began to argue with her. "Are you going to desert your family that needs you so much?" she pleaded.

"But, Mother, you are well now and Marie is fourteen years old. I would not be leaving you alone," she said gently.

Madame Guérin was not in the least won over by soft words or by logic either. Instead she turned to other methods of persuasion. She saw to it that young men came to the house to meet her pretty, brown-haired, vivacious Anne-Thérèse, and that she went to parties.

Later, when the townspeople became aware of Anne-Thérèse's desire, perhaps through her mother's remarks to her friends, one young man who had heard of this odd idea about wanting to be a nun asked Anne-Thérèse why.

"I feel I must do something for God," she said falteringly, "and for souls. It is the only way I can help."

"What can a woman do to help?" he asked with an amused smile. "Anyway, leave it to others—and marry me."

To his first question she had no answer ready; his offer of marriage she refused. But after he had gone, she began to wonder if perhaps she had been too bold in thinking she could really do something for God. She felt vaguely distressed, but she began to draw from her store of names of women who had done things for God, and this made her feel better. First of all there was Our Lady, greatly daring, greatly obedient. There was Judith, who had freed her people, and Esther who had delivered hers by her bravery and wit. There was Catherine of Siena, unafraid of the brilliant men who opposed her; Clare holding up the monstrance before the Saracens at Assisi; the great Teresa, tramping through Spain on her errands for God; Margaret Mary, who worked for God in her quiet cloister.

Anne-Thérèse would never be among those great names, that she knew, but she felt in her heart that there was a work ahead of her that would advance the kingdom of God—a small work, but nevertheless hers. What it was or where it would take her she did not know. But she was definitely certain that it was in the religious life that her own work must be carried out.

During the past years, her spiritual advisers had been of little help to her in this matter. When she spoke to them, it was of a life as a contemplative. They told her there was a much greater need in France of working for God in the world. Such a life was a form of prayer too. In fact, for such work the convent might not be really necessary.

However, the old priest who had been her confessor when she was younger did not say that to her. Some years before he had gone from Étables and was now stationed at Saint-Brieuc. Sometimes, when Anne-Thérèse felt bruised with opposition and misunderstanding and unkind words, she went to see him and talk with him. He listened and never tried to belittle her resolution; he urged her to be firm. She must wait until the call came. It would come, he assured her, but she must have patience.

Then, suddenly and unexpectedly and after years of opposition, her mother capitulated in the year when Anne-Thérèse was twenty-five years old. Madame Guérin came one evening to her daughter's room and sat down by her bed.

"I have decided," she said abruptly, "to let you go. I have resisted for a long time and now I say to you that you may go to the convent when you wish—and with my blessing."

No one was told why she had so suddenly given in to her daughter's desire, nor did Anne-Thérèse herself actually ever explain it to anyone. Once, years later, she said that her guardian angel had one day spoken to her mother, and that was how she had been able to enter the convent with her mother's consent.

There now remained for the happy Anne-Thérèse only the selection of the congregation she hoped to join. For years she had been certain this would be Carmel. That congregation with its ideals and life of contemplation had always drawn her. She decided to go to a nearby Carmelite monastery where she had friends and tell them of her intention.

One day, however, she met a friend from nearby Ruillé, who told her of a community there, the Sisters of Providence, and of its small but inspiring work and need of more members—especially those who could teach. Her friend painted it all in such glowing colors that Anne-Thérèse decided to visit there before she definitely made up her mind.

By that time it was the summer of 1823. Sister Marie Madeleine had died. The sisters were in their new home close to the parish church, and it was a new superior, Mother Mary Lécor, who interviewed her. Within a month, on August 18, 1823, Anne-Thérèse Guérin had entered there as a postulant.

During her first months, Anne-Thérèse was often lonely. She worried about her mother and her younger sister; she missed her little town and the seashore and her friends. But when a visit home showed her that all was going quietly and well, she returned to Ruillé and gave herself up completely to her new life and received her new name of Sister Saint Theodore.

During her first year in the convent, Sister Theodore had a very severe illness. Because the medical treatment was quite poor, she was left with impaired health. The medication had been so harsh that she was never in the future able to take any solid food, nor was she ever again entirely well. Her condition, however, did not impair her ability to work hard.

In order to speed her recovery, Mother Mary had sent Sister Theodore to the little town of Preuilly. There her active missionary life began, though she was still a novice. Religious were so badly needed that there was little time to give the recruits long training. Workers in the vineyard of the Lord to take care of the many neglected and untaught children were still all too few. From dozens of cities and towns came requests to Mother Mary to open new houses; that was why she sent her novices to staff some of them when they had been only a short time at the motherhouse.

When her superiors were fully assured that Sister Theodore had a true vocation, they allowed her to receive the habit canonically on September 6, 1825. Two days later, on September 8, 1825, in spite of her precarious health, she pronounced her vows. Some months after that she was sent to the house at Rennes as superior. She was in her twenty-seventh year.

There were many towns of France where it was unrewarding for missionaries to work, and Rennes was one of the most difficult. The morals of the inhabitants were bad, and many of the people were so rough and lawless that women had to stay off the city streets lest they be insulted. The bishop and clergy of Rennes, well aware that something must be done, decided to open a school first of all, so that at least the little girls might grow up better taught than the preceding generation. The clergy knew the teachers could not do a great deal, but they hoped the teaching of a few manual skills would allow the girls to better earn a living later. The schools would also provide the girls with the rudiments of education and some religious instruction.

When a building given by people of means in the city was ready, the bishop asked the Sisters of Providence to take charge. In 1821, the first sisters came there to teach. It proved a very hard assignment. Poverty the sisters could bear very willingly; they were hardened to that at Ruillé. They were also accustomed to children who were untaught in the most rudimentary matters. But the difficulty that faced them at Rennes was that it was all but impossible to do anything with these girls, for many of them were—in the full sense of the word—incorrigible.

When Sister Theodore arrived, she found that the sisters who had been at work there for five years were very disheartened. "We have tried so hard," said one of the sisters, "and we have been able to do so little. Sometimes I wonder if we have accomplished anything at all."

Mother Mary, who knew all about their troubles, had refused to be discouraged. The mission would not be given up so easily, she said, for there was too great a need at Rennes. Instead of calling back the sisters to the motherhouse, she replaced the superior with the newly-professed Sister Theodore, in whom she had great confidence.

The new superior, who was also trained as a teacher, had been in the pleasant little convent for only a day when she went to her schoolroom. The pupils had been assembled to meet her. Many of them were very young, and all of them stared at her, bold and unsmiling.

Sister Theodore smiled at them pleasantly and made a short welcoming speech. When she had finished, one of the older girls said in a loud rough voice, "Does she think she is going to turn us into nuns?" and the whole room rocked with laughter.

Sister Theodore called for silence and the room quieted down. It proved to be only a lull; the shouts and laughter began again. The new superior acted as if nothing unusual was happening. She simply waited until the students were weary of noise and were again quiet. Then she said that on the next day they would come together again and discuss the duties and work ahead. She made no accusations or threats of punishment. Then she left them quietly, having given, to their obvious surprise, no sign of displeasure or disappointment at their actions.

The next day she came again, and again they sat quietly before her and listened for a few minutes, Then, and evidently at a signal, they all rose, joined hands, and began to dance in a circle around the room, singing loudly. Since it was clear she could not establish order, Sister Theodore sat down. Finally, the children stopped their dancing and sat down too, obviously a little uncertain as to what to do next in the face of this lack of any show of authority.

When they were quiet, Sister Theodore rose and from the wall behind her took down a switch hanging there; she broke it into small bits and laid the pieces on her desk. Then she began to talk. She did not mention the girls' rudeness or noise; she merely told them of the plans she was making for their studies and the treats in store for them if they worked well.

Before long it was clear that she had won them over, no doubt because she had used persuasion instead of the severity they had come to expect. They did not become angels from that day, but they did turn from incorrigible little girls to fairly well-behaved ones. Sister Theodore kept strictly and faithfully every promise she had made them.

Her task grew easier when the girls began to realize that she really liked them. It was sadly apparent that in their short lives there had been little of the love or happiness or justice that even the smallest child instinctively expects from his or her elders, and the lack of which was at the root of much of the girls' bad behavior.

When later some of the clergy praised her for what she had accomplished, Sister Theodore said that nothing she had done was her own idea; she had simply applied to her new assignment part of the rule of her congregation: "A teacher who has the tact of gaining the hearts of her pupils can do with them as she pleases; her counsels, her admonitions, even her reprimands will be well received."

A few months after she came to Rennes, Sister Theodore had the school of several hundred pupils—none over fifteen and some much younger—

formed into good students. The religious instruction which they had once laughed at gradually became something they valued. One important result of this was that their parents, many of whom had, since the days of the Revolution, given up completely the practice of their faith—some through fear, some through indifference—returned to the Church in considerable numbers. It was an amazing thing, but a proven fact, that the community in which this school stood changed greatly for the better within a few years.

Sister Theodore spent eight years at Rennes. During that time she opened day nurseries which were of two kinds—free and paid. The money from the tuition in the ones paid for the free education in the others. Sister Theodore administered them all with equal care, but it was to the free schools that she gave her most loving efforts. She disliked begging, but she was willing to do it for the sake of helping these schools. And when she asked for funds, she tried to make people feel that giving it for such a purpose was a form of prayer. "Alms are semi-sacramentals," she would say earnestly.

When Mother Mary came to Rennes in the course of a visitation, she made it clear that it was not from mere duty. "I know that everything goes well under Sister Theodore's supervision, and I come to this house to rest," she said. She was happy that the clergy of the city were so satisfied with Sister Theodore, who had done such good work in a place where progress had seemed impossible and where now the Providence schools were landmarks of good will and efficiency.

At the end of eight years, Sister Theodore's reputation stood as high at Rennes as it had at Ruillé. In addition to her work as superior, she had been at various times sent to transact matters for her congregation in other parts of Brittany. At Rennes, of course, she was by this time not only respected and loved; she was a part of the city.

Suddenly, and from the clearest of skies, came trouble. Though innocent herself, Sister Theodore was to become involved in a mysterious situation that brought her misunderstanding and unhappiness. Word had come to the motherhouse, so ran the only explanation ever given on the matter, that Sister Theodore was completely out of sympathy with something the Mother General had felt ought to be carried through. Whether the remark was completely false or whether in some way a remark of Sister Theodore's had been wrongly reported, the gossip did great harm. Carried from one sister to another, and doubtless distorted as it went, when it reached Ruillé, Mother Mary professed herself overwhelmed to learn that someone in whom she had trusted so completely should fail to support her in what she considered a delicate matter.

The story most frequently told was that the trouble came about because of a sympathetic remark made by Sister Theodore at the time of the separation of the Brothers of St. Joseph from the Sisters of Providence. This remark was repeated later as a criticism of the action taken by Mother Mary towards the Abbé Dujarié, and Sister Theodore was reported to have spoken about the incident to some of the clergy. The story gained more credence when Sister Theodore, at home for a retreat, saw the old Abbé sitting alone in the little woods back of the convent, sad-faced and still brooding over the separation. She, loving and respecting him for his devotion to the community, went to the kitchen to bring him a bowl of hot broth to comfort him.

Abbé Dujarié was no longer the sisters' head, that was true, and it was also true that this separation had been a thing regretted by many of the sisters, who dearly loved the old Founder and knew how the situation had grieved him. Sister Theodore had not been alone in expressing sympathetic regret about it.

Whatever the trouble or how it came about, one thing was certain: matters grew worse instead of better between Mother Mary and Sister Theodore; the former was sometimes so harsh that she was actually unjust. The situation ended with Sister Theodore being recalled from Rennes and sent to be the superior of a small country mission at Soulaines, near Angers, where there would be only three sisters—herself, another teaching sister, and a cook.

The transfer itself did not especially trouble Sister Theodore, for she had always considered one office as good as another. From her first days in the congregation, she had willingly taken on any unpleasant task and been happy to help with the most menial work.

What saddened her was not that she had been taken from an important mission and sent to one considered very unimportant but that the mother general, whom she loved dearly, should have written her words of rebuke and actual distrust. At first she had accepted the accusation quietly and did not try to vindicate herself. But others were involved, and her spiritual director, Bishop de Lesquen of Rennes, insisted she give an explanation, which she did. It was received without comment at Ruillé, but Sister Theodore still felt the weight of her superior's displeasure.

The friends she had made during her eight years in the city also insisted she ask for an explanation, but she said she saw no reason in further discussion. "The transfer is to me a matter of simple obedience, and I shall follow the order given me," she told her friends again and again. But to Bishop de Lesquen, who had been very kind to her, she spoke more freely.

"How much I regret your going, my child," he said to her when she came to say goodbye and to ask his blessing, "and yet how happy it makes me to reflect on the amount of good you have done during your years in my cathedral city. That will last even if you must go." As she was leaving, he said, "I want you to bear in mind the fine phrase of St. Cyprian, that, 'it is impossible to exile a Christian because he finds his God everywhere.'"

When she reached the new mission in 1834, she found a letter from Bishop de Lesquen waiting for her. Again he urged her to be brave and to accept all this as in the providence of God. "My sisters and the priests of my household beg me to remember them to you," he ended, "and I reiterate, my very dear daughter, the expression of our devotedness in our Lord."

His letters did not cease to come; in fact, they were what gave Sister Theodore courage when she felt herself faltering. "So you are really enjoying your new position," he wrote in answer to her letter. "How happy I would be should I be consigned to a little corner of the earth where I could live unknown.... The city offers advantages but it is no less true to say that in the country a person is more alone and that everything leads to meditation…. If in the road we travel we make some false steps, we must not be too discouraged—a great many saints have made them too!"

One thing was very clear: the bishop of Rennes was completely on Sister Theodore's side in the matter that had brought about her sudden demotion. He openly called it a weapon of calumny that had defeated her, but he wrote that of course this had been used even against our Lord, as well as against St. Francis de Sales and many others.

In one letter the bishop made it clear that he knew who the calumniator was, for he wrote: "Not only has the author been wanting in justice and charity but also in truth…. If I do not now make strong remonstrance to your superiors, the only reason is respect for authority. Had I been consulted I should not have failed to ask for your return to Rennes. If any doubts of you are entertained where you have been sent, simply request any disaffected persons to write to me. They will get full and entire satisfaction. I shall not give you a complimentary certificate but a conscientious one."

Sister Theodore would not have been human had she been able entirely to conceal her sorrow at what had happened to her, but she never spoke of it to the two sisters who were with her at Soulaines. She put all her efforts into the new assignment.

As the bishop had prophesied, Soulaines proved a very happy place for her. It was a small town and did not have the terrible poverty of Rennes, nor was the matter of discipline paramount. This mission brought her one new duty, however—nursing. When such work was demanded of the sisters, they were sent to take a course in nursing and basic medical training, in order to give their patients trained care. In keeping with this practice, Sister Theodore was given a similar opportunity under Dr. Lecacheur. In later years this course was to stand her in good stead.

The school in Soulaines that was in Sister Theodore's charge grew rapidly. With the funds it brought in she was able to open a free school. There were only two teaching sisters and the work was heavy, but Sister Theodore loved to teach. Her favorite subject had always been mathematics, and she taught that at Soulaines so well that when the school inspectors made an official visit two years after she came to the town they were greatly delighted with the work of the pupils. "We shall report it to the Board of Education," they told her, and soon afterwards a medal of honor was voted to her.

Word of this award came to her unexpectedly. She was dusting the community room when several gentlemen from the Academy of Angers came to announce it. She was ready to receive it then and there, but the visitors insisted she must receive it publicly and in the presence of the mayor and the curé. To her very evident embarrassment, that was exactly how it was presented.

When Sister Theodore went from Soulaines, after six years there, she left a fine impression behind her. In part this was due to the successful schools, in part to the good nursing. Another reason had to do with a certain M. de la Bertaudière, the grand seigneur of the town, a proud old man with the autocratic ways of the old regime and a very wealthy man still, even though some of his estates had been confiscated during the Revolution.

Soulaines had been anxious to have a new church, since its old one was all but beyond restoration. "Monsieur," as he was called, quite as if he were the only prominent person in town, had agreed to build it, since the people were too poor to do it themselves. Not long after Sister Theodore came to Soulaines, something had gone wrong about the plans and Monsieur withdrew both his good will and, much worse, his offer of financing the building. The whole town had discussed for months this one thing: how to prevail on the temperamental Monsieur to change his mind.

When several people suggested that Sister Theodore be sent as an intermediary, the curé decided to place the problem before her. She was quite understandably taken by surprise. "But I am a newcomer," she protested, "and surely ought not to interfere in a matter which concerns the village." Then she laughed. "Besides, what can a poor nun be expected to accomplish?" If she thought this ended all argument, she was mistaken. "But it is because Monsieur likes you very much, that we all know," said the curé.

Sister Theodore shook her head. To her that was a very strange reason. Eventually, however, she agreed to see what she could do, and after long and careful thought as to what to say, she went to call on Monsieur. She found him at first unwilling even to talk about the unhappy matter, but it was soon evident that he had been deeply hurt, rather than insulted, by the remarks of some of the townspeople.

"It is for the glory of God that I wanted to build this church, Sister—and some think I was going to do it for my own glory," he said, not in anger but with deep sorrow.

She gave him her sympathy and then spoke of the fine plans already drawn up. She had seen them and knew it would be wonderful to have them transformed into a beautiful edifice for honoring God that would replace the shabby place in which the people now worshipped.

In the end, her eloquence moved him to carry out what there was little doubt he was very anxious to do. "Very well," he told her. "I'll build it and at my expense. You can tell the committee to go ahead."

When Sister Theodore left Soulaines in the summer of 1840, the new church was rising. It gave promise of great beauty, with its graceful façade and the fine marbles brought in for its interior. In the cornerstone, on the memorial notes buried within it, was the name of Sister Theodore Guérin and below it the thanks of the grateful town of Soulaines for her aid in building their church.

Her sojourn at Soulaines lasted only six years, but the people there kept a deep love for her in their hearts, and long after she had gone her influence on the school and the little dispensary remained. As for Sister Theodore, she spoke always with deep affection of her beloved people at Soulaines. She did not want to leave at all. She felt as much at home there as she had at Rennes. It was only that another call had come for her services, and so she made ready to depart.

CHAPTER THREE

So Far, So Wild a Place

℮

In 1839, there came to Ruillé-sur-Loir an ecclesiastic from faraway America, Celestine de la Hailandière, vicar general of the See of Vincennes in the state of Indiana, who had come to France to secure teaching brothers and sisters for the diocese. At his earnest plea, the Congregation of Holy Cross planned to send six brothers and Abbé Sorin as superior. Now he had come to ask the Sisters of Providence to give him sisters who would establish a motherhouse and a school in Vincennes. He had been promised a group of Alsatian sisters, but it had been found impossible for them to go. He was hoping he would be more fortunate at Ruillé.

He had been sent by Bishop Bruté, head of the See of Vincennes, who four years before had himself come to France and returned to the New World with nineteen priests, including four Eudists who were to found a college at Vincennes. The bishop had been in dire need of help. When he, often called the most learned man in America, had come reluctantly from his beloved college of St. Mary's at Emmitsburg to the Indiana wilderness, he found in all his diocese only one priest whom he could claim as his own and two others who had been lent him for a year by the bishop of St. Louis.

The number of his clergy was now augmented by the group from France; the diocese, due to constantly increasing immigration from the East, had grown rapidly. At the time he came to France to ask help, his See included not only all of Indiana but also a large portion of Illinois. There was need of many more religious to establish schools there, and since he was too worn out to go himself a second time Bishop Bruté sent in his place one of the priests whom he had some years before persuaded to come to America.

Monsignor de la Hailandière, after his arrival in France, had gone first to Strasbourg, where he was to meet members of the Picquet family, a considerable number of whose relatives lived close to Vincennes, at Sainte-Marie in Jasper County, Illinois.

This settlement in the midwest was one of the most interesting of its day. It was composed entirely of members of one very large French family. The Picquet family had lived through several revolutions. By 1837, seeing that the Catholic situation in France was still far from good, they decided to seek a home across the sea; there they would plant a colony and develop it into a sort of Christian democracy, as various other groups had already done. Their plan, however, was unique in that it was to be built entirely by one family.

Joseph Picquet, a young man of nineteen, was sent to report on prospects and find a suitable location. When he returned home two years later, he had found the location and evidently also earned the complete confidence of his elders, for he came back to America with purchase money for thirteen hundred acres of prairie in Illinois. The family soon followed and built their colony, which they named Sainte Marie in honor of Our Lady. Now Monsignor de la Hailandière reported to those of the Picquet family still living in France that their relatives in the New World were flourishing.

He went next to Ruillé to see Mother Mary and to tell her of his plans, hoping that she would give him some of her sisters for Vincennes. Since she had never considered extending her congregation overseas, she hesitated to give him an answer; if she did so immediately, she knew it would be to refuse. Yet she felt that perhaps this was the will of God, so she said she would have to ask him to wait for his answer until the community came together the following week for a retreat. Then they would discuss it.

"But I can tell you now," she said, "that there is only one person I would trust to head such a mission—and that is our Sister Theodore."

"Whom I already heard about in Rennes," Monsignor de la Hailandière said. "They told me that she is no longer there."

Mother Mary shook her head. "She has been for some years at Soulaines," she said briefly.

When the community gathered at Ruillé for the retreat, they learned about the possibilities of some of its members going to Vincennes. Mother Mary told them what Monsignor de la Hailandière had told her about this diocese of Vincennes in Indiana, of its rapid growth, its many immigrants both French and German coming there from the East. He was seeking sisters to teach his French parishioners, of whom there were a great many, since Indiana had been from its beginning largely populated by the French.

The community listened to all this with deep interest, and when Mother Mary asked who would volunteer if they did decide to send a group, many gave their names. Sister Theodore's name was not among them. It was not that she was unwilling to go, but she felt too humble to be worth choosing and also knew that her continuous poor health might be considered a serious handicap.

Later, when the council decided favorably on the proposition, Sister Theodore was greatly surprised when Mother Mary came to tell her that she wished to send Sister Theodore with the group going to America; more than that, she wanted her to be their superior. Would she be willing to go?

"If you feel you cannot go, we cannot open the mission," Mother Mary said flatly.

Sister Theodore looked at her superior in utter disbelief at first. When she saw how serious Mother Mary's expression was, she asked for time to consider the matter. The words of the rule had come to her mind: "The sisters must be disposed to go to any part of the world." For some days, Sister Theodore spent much time in the chapel in prayer before the Blessed Sacrament. Then, on August 24, she went to her superior. "I am willing to go if you wish to send me," she told her, and her face was quiet and the expression in her eyes showed certainty.

She went back to Soulaines, where people stopped her on the street to say how they had missed her. Monsieur took her to the new church to show her how much work had been done during the few weeks she had been away.

She would not see it completed, she knew, but she decided not to tell him or her other friends just yet that she was leaving. It would be some time before her departure and she would tell them about it a little while before she was to leave.

What chiefly troubled her about this new mission was that its success or failure would depend on her. She was already forty-one years old, perhaps too old for pioneering; she had never been in really good health since she was a postulant. On the other hand, there were no ties of family to hold her. Her mother had died the year before; her sister Marie was happily married.

More than once during those last months at Soulaines, Sister Theodore's courage failed her. She was tempted to tell Mother Mary that she could not go, but she was held back by the fact that on her depended the establishment of the mission. The group could not go if she withdrew. She had all but completely made up her mind to accept when she learned she would be given the title of superior general for the new group and any other houses set up in the United States "until such time as the bishop of Le Mans and the bishop of Vincennes shall otherwise jointly decide." Again her courage failed her.

This time she decided to write to the bishop of Le Mans for advice. He answered reassuringly that our Lord did not choose the powerful of earth for His apostles, but humble working people: "Let us then consider ourselves nothing, but let us be ready for anything. Since you have been chosen, think of nothing but preparing yourself in the best manner you are able; bring to it a good will and rely constantly on help from above."

Bishop Bouvier had already told Monsignor de la Hailandière he considered Sister Theodore an excellent selection and hoped she would go. She was a wise, prayerful woman, refined by suffering, well trained as a teacher and a nurse.

One day in July, sad news reached Monsignor de la Hailandière: Bishop Bruté had died a month before. He would himself now be bishop of Vincennes, for he had been named auxiliary with the right of succession. Before he left for home, he went to Paris and there, in August, he was consecrated.

When he first came to France in 1838, Monsignor de la Hailandière had received the promise of a community of Alsatian sisters to send a colony to establish a mission at Vincennes. Their spiritual director was Pére Mertian, a relative of the large Picquet clan, who had promised twenty-five thousand francs to defray the expenses of their founding. Later, when these sisters could not go, the bishop was told that this sum of money would be transferred towards the purchase of property for the Ruillé sisters for their new mission.

Before he learned that the Alsatian sisters could not go to Vincennes, Monsignor de la Hailandière, while visiting his family near Saint-Servan, had called at the home of friends, the Le Fer de la Mottes. He was delighted to learn that one of the daughters was interested in the religious life.

Irma le Fer de la Motte was a brilliant girl, well educated and eager to be of some use in the world. "I have heard about you," she told the Monsignor, "before this meeting with you. Now I have heard you preach and they were right in what they said about you: you talk of nothing but America."

He looked at her seriously. "We need young women like you in the New World. Why don't you join these Alsatian sisters, of whom I have been telling you, and come to America with them later?"

"But I am happy here," she said, "perfectly happy. It is only for God that I would ever give up my life here in France, and even if I went it would be only as a lay auxiliary." She looked at him hesitantly. "I do know that God is worth some tears and heartbreak—but I wonder does He want mine?"

Eventually she agreed to join these sisters, but only as a lay member. When the sisters found they could not go to America, he persuaded Irma to go instead with the Sisters of Providence, but first of all to go to see Sister Theodore at Soulaines and discuss the American mission with her.

She and Sister Theodore were immediately drawn to each other—the eager young girl and the woman refined by years of spiritual stress and hard work. When she left Soulaines, Irma had decided to enter the novitiate at Ruillé and make a year's novitiate there before joining the group going to America.

Although she felt this young woman would be a wonderful acquisition, Sister Theodore worried about her; she looked so frail and delicate that she did not think Irma could ever share the hardships of pioneers. But the young girl had said stoutly that she was really very strong and that she was going to pledge herself for Vincennes as soon as her novitiate at Ruillé was completed.

In the spring of 1840, Sister Theodore told her friends at Soulaines that she was leaving them. At the beginning of July she said goodbye, to the unhappiness of the whole town, from Monsieur to the smallest child in her classes.

Monsieur de la Bertaudière had been especially sad to see her go. "Now you will not see the church finished," he said sadly, "the church that is yours and mine. But perhaps some day you will come back and see it," he added hopefully. She promised to try, but she knew there was little chance of that, for she felt she was leaving France for life.

She went to Ruillé to prepare for the long journey and the new life in a new world. Two professed and two novices were to go with her—Sister Vincent Ferrer, who had held various offices in the community and was to be her assistant, Sister St. Dominic, Sister Mary Xavier, and Sister Marie Liguori. Mother Theodore did not think Sister Dominic was strong enough for the hardships of Indiana and asked for a replacement. Sister Basilide, the new appointee, agreed to go with one proviso: that her going would not mean her complete separation from the congregation in Europe. She was assured that the Ruillé sisters, with the consent of the bishop of Vincennes, could return at any time if they so wished, but Ruillè would not recall them. Even so, the contract was not yet drawn up between the diocese and the community, for Bishop de la Hailandière wanted Sister Theodore to see all the possibilities of America first.

However, the new mission, Bishop Bouvier of Le Mans and Mother Mary had decided, was to be independent of the motherhouse at Ruillé;

the new house would have its own head and she would be superior general over all its institutions. Only the bishops of Le Mans and Vincennes, acting together, could replace her.

The ties uniting the two houses thus separated would be those of mutual sympathy and affection, and of counsel. Whatever help was given would be financial and personal.

Sister Mary Xavier and Sister Marie Liguori had entered the community at Ruillé in May of 1840 and received the habit on July 12, 1840, the day they left Ruillé for America. Consequently, they were to make their novitiate and first vows in America at the expiration of the time set by the Rule. Sister Mary Xavier was a warm-hearted young woman with so quick a temper that later her superior was to call her "Fagots," which means "fire-starter." The other, Sister Liguori—the "Marie" was usually dropped—was the youngest of them all, well educated and for several years secretary for her father, who was a notary of ecclesiastical affairs for the government.

Irma le Fer de la Motte had expected to be one of the party, but when the time for leaving drew near she was taken ill and it was clear she would not recover in time to go with them. Mother Mary had been very dubious about her value as a religious at all.

"You will see, my Theodore, that she is good for nothing but to love God," she said. But Sister Theodore wanted this young woman in her group and promised the disappointed Irma that when she was well enough the new community would be very happy to welcome her among them.

Sister Theodore, on a short trip to Soulaines to settle certain matters there, went to say goodbye to the doctor who had given her medical training when she first came there. He was very troubled to hear she was going so far away. "It is like hearing that a friend has been condemned to death," he said. "And you are far from well, Sister. Think of the hardships of the journey and then of the rough life in that wild country."

"Well, I had never thought of going to America myself," said Sister Theodore, "and I am still surprised to know that I am actually going. I did want to work for souls in other lands, but I always thought of going to China or Russia—and instead it is to be the New World."

Later, when she wrote to say goodbye to her sister Marie, she had to repeat these words, for Marie had wept at the thought of her sister going away—"so far and to such a wild place."

"I am certain it is the will of God for me to go there," Sister Theodore told Marie, but the latter remained unconvinced. "You will be unhappy so far from home, and in a place where the language is different and the customs too," Marie answered.

"I know, I know all that. I am even now torn between a desire to get to work there very soon and the knowledge that my heart will all but break when I leave. I do love you all and Ruillé and Soulaines and all my beloved France. But I am sure it is God's will for me, Marie—of that I am certain."

The new bishop of Vincennes had long since returned to his diocese. He had promised that he would try to have the new house ready for the sisters when they arrived there. He was returning to a heavy task, he well knew, for now he had the entire burden of the diocese on his shoulders, and this burden would not be light, for the country under his care was still, for much of its extent, pioneer country. For many years French hunters and trappers had been the only white men there, sharing the woods and rivers with the Indians. Later the English came in and there was greater rivalry than before and less peace.

In 1800, the Indiana Territory was organized, and sixteen years later it was admitted to the Union as a state. Settlers flocked in, even though at the time it was still largely Indian country. Little by little, the narrow trails of the Indians, which had crisscrossed the country, disappeared and widened into roads on which the first mail routes were located. In 1820, the first stage coach rattled from Louisville into the little settlement of Vincennes.

It was a rich country from which the Native Americans had been driven, one of hills thick with tall timber, with veins of coal and sandstone, with sugar maples and fine black loam. It was little wonder that more and more settlers came.

In 1810, when Bishop Flaget was consecrated bishop of Bardstown,

Kentucky, his diocese included Indiana. When Indiana was made into a separate diocese in 1834 and named Vincennes, Bishop Bruté was appointed as its bishop.

There had been a resident pastor in Vincennes previously. In 1823, young Father Champomier arrived there, but eight years later he withdrew in discouragement. He had worked hard. He had even managed to complete the shell of a cathedral. Next had come Father Petit, a Jesuit from Kentucky, and then Father Lalumière, who was still in the town when the new bishop arrived.

Bishop Bruté had made the long journey reluctantly from his Baltimore college, his chief baggage "a boat load of books." He was a man of unbounded love and zeal, as well as of great learning; his English was imperfect, but the good he was to accomplish was very great.

He found the people of his diocese, and especially of Vincennes and the area about it, poverty stricken and indifferent, but Father Lalumière and he were at first able to take care of the few Catholics. Before long Irish and French and German Catholics came pouring in, and the bishop found himself in need not only of priests but of money. From the Leopoldine Society in Munich and the Society for the Propagation of the Faith in France he received goodly sums. From France also came the priests he had persuaded to come. It was said of him that he accepted only the best, and these were excellent. Among them were Father Petit and Father de Saint-Palais. He had one Englishman, Father Edgar Gordon Shawe, a convert.

However, most of his priests were Bretons like himself, men who were willing to share his life of hardship and loneliness. One of the most brilliant who had come to him had been Father de la Hailandière, a successful lawyer who had been appointed a judge when he was only twenty-four years old; a few years later he resigned from the bench and entered the seminary at Rennes. Bishop Bruté had asked the bishop of Rennes to name a priest who would make a good vicar general. Bishop de Lesquen had suggested Msgr. de la Hailandière, who accepted the offer.

When they first came, only Father Shawe of all his men spoke English;

but they were all young and learned it quickly. In their parishes were French people who helped them. Strangely, the man who never learned it even fairly well was de la Hailandière, and of him the disappointed Bishop Bruté wrote later "He knows little English and makes no effort to acquire it."

The year after his arrival in Indiana Bishop Bruté had bought eleven acres from the Thralls family, Germans who had come from Kentucky and owned a great deal of acreage across the river from Terre Haute. On this tract of land he built a small frame church. He sent Father Buteux, another of the group from France, to be pastor for the Catholic families living in the area, including Terre Haute, which was now growing into a thriving town, although it had few Catholics. The bishop gave the name of Saint Mary-of-the-Woods to the new parish.

Some people thought it rather a foolish place to put a church, having the idea that a larger one at Terre Haute would have been more sensible, but the bishop said confidently, "Wait, only wait. Some day there will be sisters here and a school. Then you will see fine things accomplished at my *Sainte Marie des Bois.*

He had been very much disappointed to learn that the Sisters of Charity of Nazareth, who had had a school at Vincennes for eight years, had that very year been forced to withdraw. Poverty and indifference were the reasons they gave; these had driven young Father Champomier away too. Ill health, due to hardships, had also been responsible. Two sisters had remained, however, at Bishop Bruté's earnest request, and he persuaded Mother Rose White to send him two of her sisters from Emmitsburg. All these were of course only a loan until he could find a permanent religious community to take over.

The four sisters who made up the whole number there now opened a school for boys and girls opposite the cathedral, and before long they had eighty pupils. The bishop was happy, but his joy was overshadowed by the knowledge that his teaching sisters were merely lent to him. He had asked the Sisters of St. Joseph and the Religious of the Sacred Heart to come, but they had so few members and were so badly overworked that they had to refuse. It was then that he decided to send his vicar general to France in his place, remembering his own earlier and very successful trip. He hoped that Monsignor de la Hailandière would do as well in securing women religious as he himself had some years before with priests.

When that ecclesiastic returned to Vincennes as bishop, he found himself a busy man. One of his first acts was to hurry with the building of the house for the sisters on the tract of Thralls land where Father Buteux already had built his little cabin home and his little frame church.

He was greeted by the sad news that the church had burned down while he was away and that Father Buteux was saying Mass in his one-room cabin until the church could be rebuilt. When the bishop wrote to Sister Theodore at Ruillé to give her the best directions for their journey, he mentioned the burned church but said he would build another—"for everything is done quickly here. Five years here is like a century in France, as you will see." He said he had already begun the building of a brick house for the sisters. "Busy hands have begun work on the house in which you are to live." He added that he realized it would not be ready when they came, but he would find shelter for them meantime. He thought they would also find postulants waiting for them, and Father Buteux would function as their chaplain.

At Ruillé, Sister Theodore had received a letter from Mother Mary telling her it would be impossible for her to be at the motherhouse when the group set out for America, for she must remain in Brittany where she was making a visitation of the houses. It was mainly an affectionate letter, but it showed Sister Theodore that she had again incurred Mother Mary's displeasure. Sister Theodore was fairly certain she knew why: she had not considered Sister Dominic, Mother Mary's selection as nurse for the group, strong enough for pioneering a mission. Sister Theodore asked for a replacement, and Sister Basilide was chosen. Sister Olympiade had been added to the group by Mother Theodore at the request of Bishop Bouvier, also to the displeasure of Mother Mary, who had intended to dismiss the sister from the community as she was only a novice and somewhat difficult in disposition. But Bishop Bouvier thought it a wise choice, and Sister Theodore thought so too; she knew the qualities of the young sister, who had been with her at

Soulaines. Sister Olympiade had an indomitable will and great powers of endurance; she was a fine cook and a good seamstress.

Mother Mary had said goodbye to the group going to America before she set out for Brittany. It was a bitter disappointment to Sister Theodore not to have Mother Mary's blessing in person when they set out on their long journey. A second disappointment was the fact that Irma was not coming with them; Mother Mary felt definitely that she was not yet well enough to travel.

"But my heart will go with you over the waves to your mission at Vincennes," said Irma, when they embraced and said goodbye, "and as soon as I am well I shall come to you."

On July 12, 1840, three of the little band set out for Le Mans from Ruillé to receive the Bishop's blessing before they took to the ship. They had received the blessing of the Lord in the chapel of the motherhouse, and they had embraced their sisters for the last time. Sister Theodore's tears fell fast as they left, and part of her sorrow was because the hand of their Mother had not been raised in blessing at their departure.

They traveled all night in the carriage; nothing broke the silence save the sound of the wheels and the horses' clattering hooves and an occasional stifled sob. The night seemed very long and they slept little. At dawn they reached Le Mans, alighted half asleep at the Providence house, and were greeted with affection by their sisters. Waiting for them were Sister Vincent and Sister Basilide, who had been making farewell visits at their homes.

When they went to call on Bishop Bouvier, he gave them his blessing. He told Sister Theodore to write to him whenever she wished and about whatever she wished. Several days later, Canon Lottin celebrated Mass for them and gave them Holy Communion; then they left Le Mans by stage. An all day journey brought them to Lisieux, where they spent the night and picked up Sister Olympiade and two friends from Soulaines, Monsieur and Madame Marie, who were to go with them to Le Havre and who promised to take care of all expenses until they embarked on the ship for America.

When the stage reached Honfleur and the sea came in sight, Sister Theodore felt a strange emotion sweep through her, so strong that she almost fainted. Why this was so she did not know, for the sea had been an accustomed sight and she had spent all her young life close to it and loved it.

At Honfleur, they went in a steamboat to Le Havre, only to learn that there would be a delay of several days before their ship could sail. The Maries now said goodbye, after having assured themselves that the sisters were in good hands. A religious community, the Ladies of St. Thomas, had invited them to stay at their convent until their ship the *Cincinnati* sailed.

The sisters carried with them various farewell gifts, some of which they had packed unopened. One, sent by an old friend of the Congregation, the Comtesse de Marescot, which was marked "confections," they thought they might as well give away unopened. They decided at least to look at the contents, however, and when it was opened they found layers of orange leaves covering candies, and among the candies lay pieces of gold, three thousand francs in all—as much as Sister Theodore's entire purse contained.

At last, on July 27, the hour they had both hoped for and dreaded arrived. The sails extended, one after the other, as the wind swelled them. The land grew dim to the little group at the rail, until first Port Francis disappeared, and then the last bit of land faded.

Sister Theodore, leaning against the cordage, watched the shore of her country flying away from her until it was only a line on the far horizon. She stood there thinking of all she was leaving—her convent home, her sisters, Soulaines, her own sister Marie. Then she turned and saw her sisters in tears, for their thoughts were like her own. She forgot her own grief in comforting them.

The captain was very kind to the sisters. He gave them his own room to use during the day, making them understand by gestures, for he spoke no French. There were only fifty-eight on the ship besides the crew; the sisters were the only cabin passengers.

Others sometimes came up to them, but since they knew nothing of each other's language they could not carry on a conversation, though their friendly interest was clear on their faces. One of the passengers was a rabbi with a long beard and so venerable a face that he seemed straight out of the Old Testament. One group was a family of Germans, six brothers and a sister, all going to settle in America, and there was such a tender love between them that it was a joy to behold. There was a Thomas Brassier, a Breton, with his family of six, who were emigrating, and Sister Theodore promptly engaged him to come to Saint Mary-of-the-Woods and work for her.

At first, all the sisters were seasick except Sister Basilide, who took care of them. By the third day they all, even Sister Theodore, felt well enough to go on deck and see the coasts of Ireland and England. The weather had been a little rough at first, but later the sea was smooth and quiet as the Loir River.

They had been on board five days when Sister Theodore began to write in her clear fine hand a journal of their voyage to the New World.

"The moment of separation and of death had come at last," it began. "We had to leave all." But even above these words of sorrow she had written firmly, *"A la plus grande gloire de Dieu"* ("To the greatest glory of God").

CHAPTER FOUR

Music and Steam

ፘ

The voyage was very long; the ship did not reach the shores of the United States until September 5. Although steamship travel was by that year fairly common, much more speedy, and much more comfortable, the sisters had chosen to go on a sailing vessel because it saved them a considerable sum of money.

The weather had been variable, but for the first weeks the quiet seas reflected blue skies and sunsets beautiful beyond any they had seen on land. Once, looking over the expanse of sea, Sister Theodore said to the others: "Oh, I feel so happy just to know that all this is His and that I belong to Him," and then she added reflectively, "What will our God be in our true country when even in our exile He shows Himself so great, so magnificent, so powerful!"

The sisters found the days interesting. There were always ships in sight; once they counted twenty-five on the horizon. They strained to see if any bore the flag of France, and when one came in sight Sister Theodore found she loved it more than she had realized. Her eyes filled with tears that blurred the symbol of her home.

Once a huge fish was caught by harpoons—a sea hog, said the captain. It took six men to haul it in, and the crew ate for a week of its meat. The sisters tried it with some misgivings but found it very palatable; it tasted like pork and not at all like fish. One day a great whale followed the ship, spouting as if in a rage at this puny vessel that was getting in its way.

All these things Sister Theodore faithfully chronicled in her journal. She wrote of the calm weather, the wonderful nights with the moon rising from a dark sky, the great clear stars, the aurora borealis streaming across the heavens.

The sisters found it more pleasant on deck than in their tiny cabin or the captains room or the dining room, though they appreciated his kindness in inviting them there. There were no napkins on the table at meals, no spoons, only the blade of a knife and a fork to use for all needs. The captain carved and then filled the plates with what the sisters selected from the various bowls and platters. As for his own plate, it was a sight on which the sisters gazed with awe; he filled it with fowl, beefsteak, an egg, stew, toast, and cooked prunes! They were never able to season their food with what he advised for everything and himself used plentifully: mustard and black pepper.

On August 5, a storm broke and every sister was seasick. Poor Sister Theodore was merely sicker than usual, for her companions knew that every day of the trip she had been ill; she was the worst sailor of them all. Besides, she suffered from an inflammatory fever that made her so ill that at one time her worried sisters actually feared she might die. She had been troubled too, but chiefly because there was no priest on board and no opportunity to receive the sacraments.

The weather improved, and so did Sister Theodore. The storm had been unexpected, they learned, for the ship had some days before passed the banks of Newfoundland, reputedly the source of bad weather, and there the water, green as bottle glass, had been very quiet. They had been glad to know they were nearing their journey's end, but on August 15 they were sad they could not assist in celebrating the great feast day of the Assumption of Our Lady. They had the roar of waves instead of church bells, the shouts of sailors instead of the chants of the choir.

On the last day of August, another storm broke suddenly while the sisters were sitting together on deck. One sail was all but carried away before it could be furled; the masts bent like reeds. The ship seemed to be floating in a sort of mist produced by the spray of the sea as the great waves dashed against it. The captain and his crew, drenched with the sea, took no time to rest or sleep.

From amidships, the sisters heard the sound of cries and lamentations, but they knew they could do nothing, and so they remained on deck as long as the captain allowed them to stay. The rabbi came up to them, his face showing his fright, and stared in utter surprise to see them sitting there quietly.

"How can you be so calm?" he asked in broken French. They tried to explain: they had said their prayers, they were in God's hands. He shook his head and staggered away.

"It's all in his own psalms," said Sister Olympiade in some surprise, and they decided to include him in their prayers.

The storm left as suddenly as it had come, and when land came in sight on September 5 the sea was calm. The sisters stood at the rail, watching the shore come nearer and nearer, saying thankful prayers that they were safely at the end of their long journey and praying for confidence and success in the life ahead.

When, at dawn, the ship entered the bay leading to New York City, the sisters were amazed at what they saw. This was not the wilderness they had expected. Here were gardens, fine homes, tall trees, lawns sloping to the water's edge, a country as fresh and smiling as France in June.

All about them were ships—coming, going, some of them fast little steamboats whose bows seemed to be deriding the slow sailboat. But the *Cincinnati* went peacefully along, her pilot steering carefully among the many craft. By five in the afternoon they were anchored in the bay.

All about them were people looking eagerly towards the shore, where no doubt relatives and friends were waiting their coming. It was sad for the group of religious to know that the arrival of the *Cincinnati* would bring no one of their family to welcome them. There were other religious houses in America, but no Providence; there were plenty of people, but no sisters to be glad they were coming. Suddenly Sister Theodore felt apprehensive: suppose they found no friendly face in this foreign land, no one who understood their tongue?

Happily she was wrong in her fears. When customs officials came aboard, with them was Dr. Doane, the head of quarantine, who greeted them kindly and in French, explaining that he had worked for some years in a French hospital and was well acquainted with religious orders in France. He brought them refreshments—biscuits and milk and fruit from his own orchard, a great delight to the sisters who had suffered for forty days from very poor food and even worse cooking.

He asked who was to meet them and they explained that the bishop of Vincennes had promised to have someone at the boat. They were feeling very downhearted, for it was clear that no priest was meeting them, but Dr. Doane tried to cheer them up. "Don't worry," he told them. "Before long you will be surrounded by numerous friends very happy to see you. I am informing the bishop of New York of your arrival and his vicar general is a Spaniard who speaks French fluently."

Though they were told they might leave the ship, the sisters decided to wait until someone came for them. When no one appeared, they spent the night on the ship and were still there at noon next day, increasingly troubled about their plight. The fine weather was gone; rain fell in torrents. They could hardly see the shore through the mist.

Early in the afternoon they were all on deck when they saw a small boat coming towards them with an elderly man in the stern who called up to them that he was Father Varela and that he had come to escort them to a shelter for the night. Dr. Doane had told him of their arrival, and the bishop had sent him to take care of them.

They were to come down to his boat, he told them—a hazardous act, they realized, as they looked fearfully downward and knew they must descend by the rope ladder swinging along the ship's side. Finally Sister Theodore summoned up her courage.

"Come, if we have to die, let us die, but say nothing," she told the others, and led the way down the ladder, trying to be brave so that they would be too. Rain fell and waves broke about them as they went down, one after the other. Their faces were pale when at last they all stood on the deck of the little vessel. But they had made it.

Father Varela took them first to the quarantine station on Staten Island, where Dr. Doane was waiting for them. He put them before a big hearth fire to dry them off; then they were taken by ship to the Brooklyn ferry dock, a ride of half an hour; from there Father Varela took them by carriage to hospitality at the house of Madame Parmentier. To the tired, homesick religious, the five days they spent there were ever afterwards looked back upon as days in heaven.

The Parmentier family, they learned, had settled in Brooklyn in 1815. André Parmentier had been a noted horticulturist in France who had been able to put his profession to good use in America. He had set up the Botanical Gardens in New York City; his methods were new and contributed greatly to the beauty of the city. When he died in 1830, his wife continued to live in her Brooklyn home. She devoted herself to welcoming bishops and missionaries, priests and religious who had just come from Europe, many of whom she sheltered before they went on to their assigned stations.

Next morning, Sister Theodore and the others renewed their consecration to the missions at a church to which Madame Parmentier drove them. It was a wonderful occasion for them: Mass and Holy Communion after fifty days of deprivation.

During the next days their hostess took them to visit landmarks in New York. They went to Mass at St. Peter's Church on Barclay Street and found it a fine edifice, its walls dazzlingly white, its pews of solid mahogany, its galleries with three tiers of seats, arranged like a theater. There were many men as well as women in the congregation, all of whom were very devout.

Madame Parmentier took them about New York in her carriage. They thought it a beautiful town, but even its finest houses seemed very severe and sombre, almost depressing. The walks of pressed brick they thought handsome, and the carriages as elegant as any in Paris. What chiefly amazed them was that all the women wore bonnets.

"We did not see one woman who was not wearing a bonnet," noted Sister Theodore in her diary. "Even the milkmaids wear them while milking the cows. Milk is carted around in quite a stylish conveyance drawn by two horses, and the men who distribute it are dressed as if for a wedding. It is impossible," she wrote, almost with awe, "to have any idea of the extravagance of the Americans without having seen it."

They were taken to call on Madame Gallitzin, superior of the Religious of the Sacred Heart, who told them she was just leaving to open a house in St. Louis, not far from Vincennes. They went to call on Bishop Hughes, now in charge of much of the work of the diocese, for Bishop Dubois was very ill. They told him they had been advised not to wear their religious habit in New York, but that so far they had met with no trouble. He said he was certain they would not. He counseled them, however, to wear secular dress when they crossed the country westwards.

The one sad thing was that apparently no one from Vincennes had come to meet them. No money was waiting for them, and this was a very important item. Mother Mary had advanced the funds for the voyage. These were to be repaid by the Diocese of Vincennes when they got to New York and this money would be used for their trip west—"and one must have money to travel in America," said Sister Theodore ruefully.

Meantime, at Madame Parmentier's home, the sisters studied maps and went over routings, looked at textbooks, priced school supplies, and even learned a little English. Sister Theodore was able to read English but did not understand it enough to carry on even a simple conversation; the others knew even less than she.

Father Varela had not forgotten them. He came to call on them several times, offering them every kindness and service in his power. The French sisters were very grateful for his interest in their welfare in spite of his manifold duties. They saw at firsthand the demands that were made upon the limited time of a vicar general, who was constantly called upon to welcome religious coming into a missionary country.

Five days after they arrived in New York, word was brought to Sister Theodore that at Philadelphia a Mr. Frenaye, who handled all business matters for the bishop of Vincennes, was waiting for them, and they prepared to go there. With them to the train went their new friends, Madame Parmentier, Father Varela, Mr. Byerley, who had helped them with their luggage, and a young man who spoke French and would escort them to Philadelphia.

They thanked the people who had been so kind to them, who had treated complete strangers as their good friends. Then they went to the ferry to take the train on the other side of the river. Standing together on the deck, they noticed a small ship over whose stern was gaily waving a flag—the flag of France! Perhaps that would be the last sight of home for a long time, and Sister Theodore gave it a salute from her heart. Then she said to herself resolutely, "The true country of a Christian, but above all of a religious, is heaven." It was a fine quotation and they were true words, but as she looked at the flag disappearing she was afraid that she spoke them with her lips and not with her heart.

They rode to Philadelphia on the South Amboy and Camden Railroad, opened only a few years before, the first rail route between New York and Philadelphia. The locomotive, the John Bull by name, was imported from England and was the first the sisters had ever seen. It was amazingly large and the coaches were too, seating at least forty people. The train went like lightning, past fields and villages with white houses and green blinds, along a canal where they saw boats pulled jerkily by a horse that walked along one bank. They were glad they did not have to travel so slowly. The train, they were told, went twenty miles in a single hour. The sisters were not at all alarmed by going so fast and greatly enjoyed the new experience.

In Philadelphia they were met by Mr. Frenaye, who said that no word about them had come from Vincennes. He did know that religious were expected, but he had nothing more definite than that as to their journey west from the bishop of Vincennes. However, Mr. Frenaye would be able to advance them the funds needed.

He suggested they call on Bishop Conwell, and that prelate made the sisters very welcome; however, he knew nothing as to how they were expected to reach their destination. Mr. Frenaye had assured the bishop that the sisters could travel west alone, but Sister Theodore was unwilling to set out without further directives from Vincennes. Bishop Conwell then suggested they stay with the Sisters of Charity, of whom he had already asked hospitality for them. He wanted them to write the western bishop as to what they were to do, for he too thought it hazardous for a group of women religious to start across a country when not one of them could understand its language.

The Sisters of Charity received them very hospitably, but neither the superior nor her seven religious knew any French. Somehow they managed to understand one another, however, and when they met in the little chapel it was clear that in the most important thing of all the women were on terms of complete familiarity and unity.

During Mass at the cathedral next morning, Sister Theodore was amazed at the number of communicants, especially the great number of men, and she admired the reverent silence of the congregation all through Mass. The faith and piety of these Americans made her think sadly of the indifference of many in France.

When it was learned that there were French sisters at the convent of the Sisters of Charity, many French people in the city came to call and the sisters enjoyed good talks in their own language. The visitors admired their habits; Sister Theodore had already decided they liked their own much better than those of the Sisters of Charity—"black serge and a sort of little lute-string cap not worth two sous," she described it in her journal.

The sisters loved Philadelphia, with its straight streets and houses of red brick with snowy marble stoops and iron balustrades. "Except for public monuments," wrote Sister Theodore, "I do not think I have seen anything in Paris that approaches the richness and splendor of this Queen City of America."

Even though Sister Theodore spoke so admiringly of the city's houses, the thing that roused her greatest interest was the waterworks, to which some of the French people had taken the sisters. She set down very detailed descriptions of this mechanism which brought water to all parts of the city: "By pumps through subterranean pipes, water is forced to a height of 120 feet, kept in enormous reservoirs, filtered and then passed through thousands of small pipes that resemble the arteries of the human body and distribute the water to the farthest points of the city."

At last a letter had come from the bishop of Vincennes, who regretted not having met them in New York. It was not lack of foresight on his part, he assured Sister Theodore, but it was partly due to a misunderstanding on the part of the priest who was to have been there and partly to the fact that the bishop had not been able to send one of his own priests: they were so overwhelmed with work that they could not get away. He promised that the money that Mother Mary had advanced would be paid in full when they reached Vincennes; meantime Mr. Frenaye would take care of their expenses.

The bishop also hoped that during their stay in the East they were picking up some knowledge of English, and he too suggested they wear secular dress on their travels, since it might be really dangerous to go through some parts of the country in a Catholic habit. Sister Theodore read this with dismay, for it meant a considerable extra expense, which would cut deep into the sisters' diminishing supply of funds for emergencies.

"A bientôt," the bishop ended. "Come quickly—yes, at once. If you delay, the expense will be double, for the river may be closed since we are already well into September."

Fortunately Bishop Conwell had produced for them a priest who was going to Vincennes—Father Chartier, who would look after them and interpret for them. They said goodbye to their hostesses and set out for Baltimore by boat and train. In that city they were met by Sulpicians, who took them to the Baltimore house of the Sisters of Charity. These sisters knew little more French than had the sisters in Philadelphia. But they did know enough of the language to produce some very amusing errors.

In the evening the superior asked the visitors something that sounded like, "Are you coachmen?' and when this was finally untangled, to the great amusement of all, they learned that they were merely being asked if they wanted to go to bed! Next day, they were taken to the cathedral, a fine building with many side altars and beautiful paintings that had been sent to Bishop Carroll by King Louis XVI. The archbishop was away, but the superior of the Sulpicians had been delegated to greet them. Father Deluol was a witty and charming man, happy to talk in French with his compatriots—"and he has retained all the vivacity of a Frenchman," noted Mother Theodore proudly.

They said goodbye to the hospitable sisters, who sent messages by them to take to their house in Frederick, where they were to spend a night. In that city they were met by Jesuits, in their familiar wide-belted cassocks and small four cornered hats, who took them to see their beautiful church, its marble mantle of great artistry, its tall vases of alabaster.

At the convent of the Sisters of Charity, Mother Rose White, who had been one of Mother Seton's first companions, was superior. She spoke French and told them many stories of the early days at Emmitsburg and of the privations endured there, so harsh that any present ones would seem a luxury by comparison. It encouraged Sister Theodore to hear this story told by an experienced pioneer religious; if they had lived through such strenuous days, surely she and her companions could too, she said. Mother Rose White told her that at one time, and at the anxious request of Bishop Bruté, when other congregations had withdrawn their members, the Sisters of Charity had sent several of their members to him so that his children might have teachers.

These religious followed the French method of financing a free school for poor children with funds from their academies for paying pupils. Sister Theodore herself planned to use this method. She listened carefully to explanations of teaching methods in this country and decided to use some of them. Already she had learned one thing very important in this new land: for the success of an academy, music was an imperative. "No piano, no school,"

Mother White said succinctly and from the depths of long experience.

"Such is the spirit of the country," wrote Sister Theodore in her journal. "Music and steam!"

CHAPTER FIVE

Log Cabin on the Wabash

ꝭ

At last, on September 18, with their French-speaking fellow traveler, Father Chartier, the sisters set out on their journey of a month, by railroad, steamboat, stage, and canal to Indiana.

They took the stage to Wheeling, having engaged the entire vehicle, which seated nine people. The sisters found it very different from a French diligence; it had a square top, cross seats, and oilcloth curtains at the sides, which were the only protection from rain or fog.

For two days and two nights they traveled the old National Road to the Ohio River, passing through beautiful scenery, wild and very mountainous, for they were crossing the foothills of the Alleghenies. The seacoast cities had revealed to the French religious a world of civilized living, even of opulence. Here was something very different; here was nature unspoiled, mountains and valleys and wide meadows with no human being in sight, no homes or farms. The road was often narrow, with rocks overhanging it; giant trees, half uprooted, sloped towards it. Sometimes they skirted precipices down which they dared not look. The horses toiled up the hilly roads, but they rattled down them with lightning speed.

One thing Sister Theodore noted especially was the large number of trees that had fallen. "Like corpses they lie awaiting burial," she wrote. "I cannot tell you the sad feelings that take possession of the soul at the sight of this death in the midst of life." Someone at Baltimore had told the sisters that these mountain roads were infested with bandits, but to their joy "the merciful hand of the Lord has preserved us from accident and harm."

After a while, they came to occasional log cabins and fields of corn that they had already learned was often the only staple grain used to make bread. "It is the chief article of diet for these people, whom our French Republicans call 'the happy Americans,'" she wrote, after sampling corn bread for the first time.

The stage had been hard traveling, but at least they were the sole passengers. The river boat on which they now embarked was very crowded, and passenger space was limited. They could get no berths and were obliged to sleep on straw pallets on the floor of the main and only public parlor. The alternative was to sit up all night, and they were too weary for that. In the room were at least thirty women. There was a stove there also, which made the hundred and fifty miles of voyage down the Ohio River a very unpleasant experience.

At one point the boat ran aground—Father Chartier said resignedly that the boats often did—and this made the trip take four days longer. But the scenery on the Ohio was beautiful, and the sisters thought it little wonder that French explorers had called this stream *La Belle Rivière*. The water was clear; on the banks were hills covered with trees, often festooned with vines. Here and there a village nestled in its valley. Sometimes they passed a burned or wrecked ship and said a prayer that they might not meet with such tragedy.

When they reached Cincinnati, Father Chartier went to tell Bishop Purcell of their arrival, and that prelate came promptly in a carriage to take them to a convent. To their delight it was again a Sisters of Charity community, and they felt as if they were among old friends. More than that, they learned they had been expected; their stay had been arranged for by the sisters in Baltimore.

The travelers were now on the borders of Indiana; their weary journey was almost over. They were given a good dinner and a good bed, but what made them happiest of all was that after seven long days they were at last able to change their clothing.

Next morning in the chapel they heard Mass and received Holy Communion. Later they attended a High Mass at the cathedral. But this was a very different church from the ones they had so far seen in Baltimore and New York and Philadelphia. As Sister Theodore looked about her, she could hardly restrain her tears at sight of the poverty, the complete inadequacy. Never in her life had she seen so poor a church—and this was a cathedral.

Next morning, they were on another boat, a much better one, and the following day they reached Madison, where they had been told to wait until the bishop of Vincennes would meet them. They were now within eighty-five miles of Vincennes.

They waited for two days at an inn—"nearly dying of lonesomeness"—before the bishop appeared, two gentlemen with him, and it would have been hard to tell which was the bishop. The sisters looked with amazement at his incongruous appearance; the last time they saw him he was arrayed in the purple of a prelate. Now only the episcopal ring which they knelt to kiss told of his office.

He was very apologetic. "The priest in New York to whom I wrote about you somehow missed you," he said. "I am sorry about it but glad you are here at last." He told them he must go to a new mission immediately. They were to go on to Vincennes without him. In two weeks he would be back and in the meantime their chaplain, Father Buteux, would meet them and see that they came safely to their own mission, a settlement close to Terre Haute. This surprised Sister Theodore, who had expected the house and school to be in Vincennes.

"It will not be your own house that you will occupy at first," said the bishop, and he seemed to be having difficulty in explaining. "Yours is not as yet ready, but we have arranged accommodations with the Thralls family for the present."

The sisters continued their journey down the Ohio, after giving heartfelt thanks to Father Chartier for all his kindness. Since they had plenty of time, Sister Theodore decided to stop in Louisville to see Father Perché, a missionary priest she had known at Rennes. She took with her Sister Basilide, leaving the other religious with Sisters of Charity in the town.

Father Perché was away from home, but in his place they met Father Badin, a veteran missionary, who had been in that area for some fifty years. He had fled from France in the days of revolution and been ordained in the new land. There he remained. He told them stories of the early days, how he had labored for almost two years without seeing one other Catholic priest; now there were forty there.

The women enjoyed their talks with Father Badin, for he was still filled with Gallic verve and could tell very dramatic stories of his exciting adventures as a pioneer. Then too he was so holy a man that they felt better for having talked with him. In the course of the conversation it was discovered that one of their group, Sister Olympiade, was his cousin!

He also explained something that had puzzled them. The Sisters of Charity whom they met in the midwest were an entirely different group than the Emmitsburg sisters. The community of sisters with whom they were now staying was a Kentucky order, and their title, "Sisters of Charity," bore the addition "of Nazareth."

Their hosts were obviously very poor, but it was also clear that they considered poverty merely one of the facts of pioneer missionary life. They served their guests a supper of dried herring, boiled potatoes, and corn bread, and only later did the visitors learn that the fish had been an extra in their honor. There was nothing poor about the hospitality, which was the essence of the community, and Sister Theodore found herself thinking how much of the spirit of primitive Christianity these American Catholics had — the charity that St. Paul so emphasized for his people.

In the morning, Father Badin came to the chapel to say Mass and give them Holy Communion. It was for Sister Theodore a birthday gift, and a wonderful one. She was that day forty-two years old.

They said goodbye to the sisters and the old priest, and he told them they had given him great happiness: to talk about his dear France with people who had so recently been there.

Once again they embarked on the Ohio River, going now by a series of canals, for at that point the river was full of rapids. The locks fascinated Sister Theodore, as had the waterworks in Philadelphia, and she watched the mechanism with deep interest.

When the six locks were behind them, the stream was very quiet. It was so clear that the little tree-covered islands were as distinctly reflected as if other woods were planted in the water.

At sunset they came to Evansville, but a sudden heavy fog made it necessary that they remain on the boat until morning. From this point they were to go by coach. Just before it left, a priest came hurrying up to them and introduced himself as Father Anthony Deydier. He told them they had been long and eagerly awaited. Since there was time, he took them to his little log rectory to talk with them. He told them that he was one of the priests who had come at Bishop Bruté's plea. While he was talking the sisters were looking at him in dismay. His appearance seemed beyond ordinary poverty. He was so wretchedly dressed that had it not been for his collar one might have given him alms thinking him a beggar. His coat was old and torn and so were his shoes; his trousers were badly patched; his shirt was in rags and his clerical collar hung by a few strips about his neck.

At last Sister Theodore could no longer bear this in silence.

"Your housekeeper does not mend for you very well," she said.

"Oh, I haven't any," he said lightly. "No one has in this part of the country."

"But who cooks your food and makes your bed?"

"Oh, that is simple enough. We make our own beds and a baker brings us corn bread every day. Our log hut serves as church and school, so you see there isn't much housework to do. We are often away on missionary journeys, and then we sleep anywhere—under a tree sometimes. Here at home we put a mattress on a bench and it makes a good bed."

He changed the conversation to talk of Saint Mary-of-the-Woods, its lovely location, in the very midst of the forest. Sister Theodore, who during the past few days had grown somewhat apprehensive about all these forests and by the fact that they were not to be located in Vincennes, asked him,

"Father, are there families with children living near there?"

"Well," he said, as if considering, "not too many or too near right now—but they will come. This is a big country and it is growing fast."

When the stage was ready to leave, the sisters said goodbye to him. He waved gaily to them from his hut under the huge trees, and it was very clear that he was far from being an unhappy man. But Sister Theodore looked at the other sisters and said, "Can that really be a temple of God and the home of His minister that we have just seen?"

At Vincennes they went directly to the convent of the Sisters of Charity, where the bishop had arranged for them to stay until Father Buteux would come for them. There with relief they donned their habits again, and put away, they hoped for the last time, the secular garb they had traveled in. Then they went to the cathedral to give thanks for their safe arrival.

Even from the outside the church had little to recommend it, but once they were inside the structure they could hardly believe their eyes. Even the poor cathedral at Cincinnati had been a fine house of God compared to this one.

"*Mon Dieu!*" whispered Sister Theodore as she stared about her in amazement and sorrow, and thought how their barn at Soulaines had been better adorned and more neatly kept. Somehow this proved the last straw, this half-finished utterly bare church. Sister Theodore wept bitterly as she knelt there.

Next day she examined the building more calmly. It was of brick with large windows, but most of the panes were broken. The roof had something on it that looked like a chimney in ruins but which was obviously meant to be a steeple. Inside, the poor altar was of wood, with a worm-eaten railing around the sanctuary; the bishop's seat was an old red chair that no French peasant would have allowed in his best room.

As a city, Vincennes seemed to Sister Theodore not very different from Louisville. The river on which it was built was navigable only in the summer and early fall, the sisters learned, and the streets were all but impassable in winter. The Eudists from France had a house there, a very good one—"but not yet paid for," they told her sadly. It was heartening to the sisters to see again these good Bretons, who had been their near neighbors at Rennes and were able to give Sister Theodore news of others she had known in France. It was only when she spoke of her own future school and her hope that it would soon be ready that there came again the uneasy and uncomfortable silence she had noticed when she spoke of Saint Mary-of-the-Woods with Father Deydier.

By this time Sister Theodore was herself growing uneasy about the situation into which they were entering. She was not worried about her ability to establish a school; after all, she was a superior with sixteen years of teaching behind her and she had with her five capable women, four of whom could function as teachers. She was beginning to wonder, however, where were these children who were to come to their academy? Would they come from Evansville with its ragged pastor, or Vincennes with its poor shell of a cathedral? Unless she was greatly mistaken, she was beginning to be afraid that the sisters would be settled in forest country—and would there be any academy girls there or near by? And, if not, where would they get the funds to open a free school?

Her sisters were all capable and thrifty women, reared in the French tradition, who could promise not to be a drain on the diocese, but they must be located in a place where they could fulfill their vocation. Some of their schools in France were in populous cities, some in rural areas among villagers and peasants, but no region seemed to them to present so deserted an aspect as did midwest America. Their work would call upon all their resources of faith and courage.

When the bishop arrived in Vincennes, she spoke with him of her fears. He had come home before Father Buteux could be notified about coming for them. The bishop only smiled when she wondered about the possibility of bringing pupils to such isolated places as she had seen.

"They will come," he said, but his confidence was greater than hers.

"You will do very well at Saint Mary's," he assured her. "The spot was chosen by Bishop Bruté and has his blessing on it. You will find it a very fruitful place for souls."

When she still looked dubious, he said gently, "Look, Sister, all American communities start out like this, especially our academies and boarding schools. Besides, I could never afford to buy for you even fifteen square feet of ground in a city."

"Instead we go to a forest to instruct I know not whom," thought Sister Theodore, but she did not say it aloud.

While they were still at the bishop's house, a priest came in and was introduced as Father Buteux, their chaplain and already pastor of the settlement where their school was located. The next day they were all to set out for their future home, and he would accompany them.

On the way out of the bishop's house, Sister Olympiade slipped a little as she came down the steps. Father Buteux cautioned them all to be very careful about the steps of this house. He had himself fallen down them last winter. It was easy to see why one could slip; the steps were made of badly rotted wood and shook even under slim Sister Theodore. But Father Buteux said that despite its dilapidated condition the house was a very friendly and hospitable place. "The bishop's home is a store where all his priests come to get what they need. All he has is ours," he said simply.

A storm delayed their departure for several days, but at last, on October 20, at ten o'clock on a starless rainy night, they took the stage for Terre Haute. Their own final destination lay across the river from that town. As they went along, the road grew steadily worse and soon a heavy rain was falling. Several times they had to change their route because a bridge had been swept away by the torrent.

Sister Basilide, who had been ill, was placed on the floor of the stage and wrapped in a heavy cloak so that she could sleep; whether she did so was doubtful, for the coach rolled unmercifully. The sisters grew accustomed to the sudden jolts, but suddenly one, much worse than the others, threw them all to the floor of the coach on poor Sister Basilide. They learned that the stage had upset in a deep mud hole.

Everyone managed to get out and were directed to a small cabin nearby. The owner came out to help the driver, while the sisters were made comfortable by his wife. She brought them bread and coffee, but she could not talk with them for neither knew the other's tongue; she merely smiled at intervals as they sat getting dry at the roaring hearth fire. The woman was smoking a pipe, a custom they saw for the first time that night and which fascinated the Frenchwomen.

The stage was finally lifted out of the mud and the travelers climbed in again and went on their way to Terre Haute, where they planned to spend the night at an inn. Before long the road became so impassable and they were so wet from the water that splashed in through the floor of the stage that at last they had to give up and seek shelter at a farmhouse. Here they spent the rest of the night before a fire that the kindly owners of the house built for them. In the early morning they started out once more and reached Terre Haute in the afternoon. It was too late to cross the river, however, and they went to the little inn for the night.

In the morning they went to Mass in the little church and found Terre Haute a fairly large town with many houses. After breakfast they started to cross the Wabash River in the conveyance that had been sent for them from Saint Mary's, a wagon rather than a carriage, and evidently made for the rough roads of the area.

Since Saint Mary's was only four miles away, they expected to reach there by early afternoon. Instead, this short distance included a five-hour wait for the ferry. Other wagons had got to the wharf ahead of them. The river was high and the current strong, and so it took some time to get each wagon across.

Once over the river, the sisters found themselves on a road that was in part under water; the horses plodded through the mud, plunging into deeper water, while the sisters clung with all their might to keep from being shaken out of the wagon. The water rose still higher until the road was all but swallowed up. It seemed to them they were crossing a large pond.

Finally Father Buteux climbed down and waded ahead to sound the depth of the water with a pole. Soon it was too deep for safety and he had to climb back with the driver. By that time the horses were all but swimming and the wagon had a foot of water on the floor. The sisters looked out on what was a sea full of tree tops. And they had two miles still to go!

Sister Theodore could feel no fear at the prospect. "When one has nothing more to lose, the heart is inaccessible to fear," she wrote later of this alarming adventure. Now she watched the water pouring in on them and said nothing. The driver urged the horses along and managed to pull them through to dry land ahead. But before long they met with water again, this time so deep that nothing was visible of the horses except manes and heads. Evidently the steeds were cheered at the sight of more land ahead, for they went through at a gallop, all but filling the wagon with water. No one cared, for now they were on terra firma and the horses were again completely visible.

A little later, Father Buteux said solemnly, "You are now in Saint Mary-of-the-Woods. Some day I shall tell you its romantic history." But what the sisters wanted most just then was to be dry and have a roof over them again.

"All this is my parish" he said, as the wagon cut deeper into the forest. The sisters were wondering when their mission would come in sight, when suddenly the wagon stopped. "Come down, Sisters, we have arrived," said Father Buteux briefly, and they all obeyed him.

In the gathering darkness of the forest they saw that they were standing on the bank of a deep ravine. There was no house in sight. He led them down the steep bank, over a rough log, and up the opposite side. They saw a clearing and logs ready to be sawed into firewood, but the glowing dusk made even the clearing dark and fearsome. They could see no village, at first not even a house, but Father Buteux pointed to what was apparently a building of some kind.

He seemed to be hesitating as to what to say. Then, in hearty tones, as if to produce courage in his amazed companions, he said, "There is the farmhouse where you are to lodge until your own brick convent is ready," and he waved vaguely in the direction of the forest. "The postulants are waiting for you there, and a room has been prepared for all of you."

Sister Theodore could not tell what her sisters were thinking, but she felt they must be as dismayed as was she. Suddenly there came to her a vision of another house—the tiny cottage of the first Sisters of Providence in far away Ruillé—*La Petite Providence*, even smaller than this. It was a vision that gave her a sudden spurt of courage, and she turned to Father Buteux with a smile. Her first thought had been that this new home compared poorly with the stables in France where the cattle were sheltered. Now she thought not only of their own Little Providence, but of an even smaller Providence—the one at Bethlehem.

When he saw her reassuring smile, Father Buteux smiled too and led them to a little log cabin hardly visible in the darkness. So far none of the sisters had said a word, for they had agreed not to speak until they had visited the Blessed Sacrament.

By the light of the lantern he carried, they saw a single room, a very poor room. As they entered the low door, the rough boards that formed the floor were unsteady under their feet. Nothing in the room showed it was a church until they saw before them in the shadows the little pyx that held the Host.

There was no tabernacle. The altar was three boards resting on two stakes driven into the ground. On the planks was a blue cotton cloth. For a moment Sister Theodore was really overcome: the Lord of the Universe in so poor a place as this!

She knew that God was there, as surely as He was in the proud cathedral in Paris or in their own little chapel, clean and simple, kept shining with devoted love, at Soulaines. She knelt with her sisters about her. They were at home, for He was there before them. They knew now that they would have a place to rest their heads almost as poor as the place where His head had first rested.

Perhaps, thought Sister Theodore with deep humility, it was an honor

He had accorded them. When she came from the cabin chapel, she bent and kissed the ground of their new home in the land of promise. "Leave thy lands, thy relations, the house of thy fathers," the Lord had said, and they had done so. They were ready now to begin their apostolate.

Later, Sister Theodore was to refer to this moment as that of her conversion. She was tired and cold, disappointed, and all but afraid, yet some new order of thinking seemed to be invigorating her. A definite realization came to her that instant that was never to leave her, an infused grace that entered her soul as she knelt for the first time in the little log cabin chapel of Saint Mary-of-the-Woods.

Chapter Six

Living on the Love of God

ℰ

Father Buteux led the way to the farmhouse, and there warm hospitality awaited the weary travelers. The fried chicken that was to have been their noon meal was reheated for them. The roaring fire in the big hearth dried their garments, and the strong hot coffee cheered them as they gathered with Joseph Thralls and his wife and children around the rough table. At one side were the four postulants, who had been waiting for more than a month and whom Father Buteux had taken in charge until the sisters came.

It was all so warm and friendly, the room glowing with firelight, the faces smiling about them, Father Buteux talking, now in French, now in English, that for a while the newcomers could forget the darkness of the forest outside.

When they were shown the place where they were to sleep, they found it a long low attic with ten straw-filled ticks for the ten members of the community. The bishop had assured Sister Theodore that her own house would soon be ready, and she could only hope it would. For that night she was too weary, as were her companions, to do anything but sink on the straw ticks and go to sleep.

In the morning Sister Theodore learned that very little of this farmhouse had been set aside for her community, only a fairly large room and an attic and a shed to serve as kitchen. The large room would have to be refectory, recreation room, infirmary. In the attic, which was really the corncrib, everything had been moved out to make room for the straw ticks, which were placed so close together that the ten who slept on them had to walk over ticks until they came to their own.

Sister Theodore made ready to greet the new postulants as best she could in her few words of English. One of them was a French girl, Josephine Pardeillan, from Alsace; she had arrived earlier and had been living for some time with the Picquets at Sainte-Marie. Two others came from Vincennes—Frances Theriac and Genevieve Dukent. The fourth, who had also been for some time in Vincennes, was Mary Doyle. She had been Sister Gabriella, a Sister of Charity of Emmitsburg, whom Bishop de la Hailandière had persuaded to leave her own congregation and join the Sisters of Providence.

Sister Theodore was not happy about accepting ex-members from other congregations; in fact, the rule forbade it. But in this case the bishop had acted before the sisters came, without reference to her judgment, and she was not sufficiently established to take a stand. Then, too, it seemed that in Mary Doyle they had a valuable acquisition. She was about twenty-five years old, well educated in French and English, a good musician, and reputed to be an excellent teacher. She knew the locale well, for she had taught at Vincennes for almost three years. She was what Sister Theodore needed most of all: an English teacher. To learn English was a vital need for the French sisters, and Mary Doyle was willing to teach them.

Daylight had made many things clearer to Sister Theodore. She now learned that though her community was in crowded quarters they were much better off than Father Buteux. Early in 1838, Bishop Bruté had erected a small church on ground he had bought at Thralls Settlement and placed it in the charge of Father Buteux, whose parish included Terre Haute. This little church had served his small flock well until it burned down.

"So you see, like your home, mine too is only temporary," he said to Sister Theodore.

Later she was to learn more about this priest. Born in Paris, he had been brought up in a wealthy home in that city; he had received a fine education from the Eudists, had been ordained, and could no doubt have gone far in ecclesiastical preferment had he so chosen. In fact, the archbishop of Paris had offered him the pastorate of a church in the city in order to keep him. But Father Buteux had desired one thing only: to answer the call of Bishop Bruté and go as a missionary to America. Here she saw him, sharing his poverty with the other pioneers and with a flock, he told her, scattered over an area of sixty miles.

When the sisters went to Mass, they saw the full reality that the dim light of the night before had not made very clear. Evidently Father Buteux slept and worked in the small space that was also used as a church. At one end was the makeshift altar they had seen the night before; they saw the plainness of chalice and paten, the cotton altar cloth, the faded piece of calico that was the altar cover. At the other end of the twelve by fifteen cabin was a pallet with ragged blankets where Father Buteux slept, and also two small tables, one loaded with books, the other with a few dishes. There was a trunk, a bench, an old chair. In this small compass he said Mass, slept, ate, and worked.

Perhaps to see an American-born priest who had been brought up in such a pioneer environment would not have been so startling, but for the elegant priest from Paris to be living like that was indeed an amazing sight. Later, when Sister Theodore ventured to speak of his poor surroundings, he looked at her for a moment as if he did not understand. Then he laughed aloud.

"My dear Sister," he said, "I can tell you in all honesty that I have yet to learn the meaning of trifles and privations—do believe me. And after you have been here for a while you will understand better what I mean."

Later, telling this to her sisters and remembering Father Deydier's smiling response to a similar remark, Sister Theodore said soberly, "Is he really to be pitied?" and answered herself, "I do not think he is."

During the morning the sisters went to look at their own future home, so deep in the woods that it was invisible until one stood directly in front of it. It was a brick building, not very far from the Thralls's house and the log cabin of the chaplain. It was surrounded by oaks as tall as those of Brittany, as well as by a profusion of walnut trees and beeches, of maples and pines.

To reach it they had to go down one of the ravines, for their house stood on the other side of the declivity.

It was a two-story building with high arched windows on each side of the wide front door—a very good building. But it was clear that it was far from ready for occupancy. Plastering had just been begun, and it was all too evident that it would take some weeks for this to dry—and winter was at hand.

Father Buteux said he himself was overseeing the work and Mr. Thralls was helping the workmen with the plastering and carpentering. The priest was doing even more: on their second day he brought the sisters a big load of firewood that he had chopped for them.

Later on their first day at Saint Mary's, the newcomers took a walk in the forest, with the young Thralls chattering about them, running to bring them nuts or colored leaves. Already the trees were red and gold with the colors of autumn, and the fallen leaves of other years made a soft pathway. They had needed this one day to recover from their weariness, and they enjoyed it thoroughly. On the next day they turned to a consideration of the work ahead and its problems. They set up their simple housekeeping effects. In the shed that was their kitchen Sister Olympiade made soup of bacon and salt beef and learned how to make the universal bread—corn meal loaf and corn pone.

At the end of October, their baggage arrived from the East, in fine condition due to the efforts of Mr. Byerley, who had covered every box with pack cloth. Their books were uninjured, their little statues unbroken. To their delight they found a large jar of Chablais preserves, sent by their friend Madame Parmentier, and a jar of butter. These they shared with the Thralls, who in turn brought them pawpaws, persimmons and bags of nuts and showed them where to find the best grapes.

Their physical needs taken care of for the present, Sister Theodore turned to other matters. One was that of students, for she still wondered how she could find children to teach in this seemingly endless forest. Would pupils actually come there? And where would the sisters find the sick for whom they were to care? No doubt there were some, but they were scattered over so wide an area that she despaired of ever reaching many. "Questions numberless and persistent," she wrote in her journal.

She began to arrange the order of the day for her community in accordance with the rule of the congregation and to instruct the postulants. Mary Doyle was proving her value in teaching them all English and in interpreting the instructions that Sister Theodore was giving in French.

At the end of October, the bishop came for his first visit to his new community. He greeted them joyfully, and it was very apparent how happy he was to have them there. He assured them that their own house would soon be ready and their troubles over. Sister Theodore, however, had been thinking matters over and had decided they could not possibly wait until then. The present overcrowding made even the simplest community life all but impossible, and it was apparent the new house would not be ready for them until spring. She had learned that the Thralls had another house nearby to which they would be willing to move. She persuaded the bishop to ask Mr. Thralls to sell him the house they were now partly occupying. When the bishop hesitated, she offered $200 from her own small store. This evidently persuaded him, for a few days later he announced that he had bought the Thralls' house and the acreage about it for $1,800. And so the Sisters of Providence came to almost immediate occupancy of a motherhouse.

The other matter—that of establishing their academy elsewhere—she also discussed with the bishop, but on this point she found him adamant. "No, Sister, Bishop Bruté chose it and we must follow his wishes in the matter—and, besides, he never made a mistake. 'Only be patient,' he used to say. 'I have seen the wilderness blossom more than once.' You will see he was right about this too. It will blossom some day, and I want you to stay as the gardeners."

The bishop had heard the other sisters call their superior Sister Theodore. Before he left them, he said to the community, "From now on, let us call her Mother—for that is what she is." And with delight the sisters began to use the new title.

As soon as the Thralls had moved to their other home, the sisters hastened to make the house as nearly like a convent as possible. They were able to limit now the number who slept in the corncrib. The shed was no longer used for cooking. Soon they had folding beds to replace the straw ticks, an old bureau, a table and a dozen chairs, a stove, pots and pans. They bought unbleached muslin for sheets, an expenditure made through Madame Parmentier, who proved then and in later years an excellent buying agent for their household needs.

They chose one room to serve as chapel. There the Blessed Sacrament could be housed in a place infinitely better than in the church, which was at one end of the chaplain's cabin. That cabin had been so small that it was proving impossible for all the sisters as well as the Thralls and the few other Catholic families in the neighborhood to go to Mass together. Some had to stay outside the door, and as the weather grew colder this had become impossible.

The sisters arranged the new room with the small statues of Our Lady and St. Joseph, brought from Ruillé, placed on the old bureau that was to serve as the altar. Over it they hung their crucifix, and on a table they put their beloved books—the works of St. Francis de Sales, St. Teresa, St. Alphonsus Liguori, the *Christian Perfection* of Rodriguez, and others, all with "Providence de Soulaines" written on the fly leaf.

On November 29, Mass was said there for the first time and the Blessed Sacrament was reserved by Father Buteux. Then they prepared for their first retreat. The bishop was sending them as retreat master Father Augustine Martin, his vicar general, a Breton who before he heeded Bishop Brutés call had been for eight years the chaplain of the Royal College at Rennes.

At the end of the retreat came a renewal of vows by the professed. Then Father Martin announced a gift from the bishop: the community was to be permitted Benediction each Thursday in their new chapel.

After the priest had gone, Mother Theodore wrote Father Martin a letter of thanks. He wrote in return that she must continue to have courage; it would be needed — that he saw clearly — but he assured her that the rewards would be great: "And pray for this poor missionary sometimes and for the stray sheep he must run after through deserts and forests and at the risk very often of losing his own way."

By this time Mother Theodore knew well the larger hazards of her work, but she was also aware of some of the smaller ones. She was, for instance, learning the meaning of American pride. The sisters had secured a young woman, evidently very poor and with no education whatever, to do their washing. At noon the girl sat down with the community at dinner, and when Mother Theodore suggested gently that it would be better if she did not take her meals with them Mother Theodore felt a sudden chill in the air and saw a deep sense of insult on the young woman's face and on the faces of the American postulants as well.

She was to learn that the word "servant" was enough to make any hired girl quit on the spot, something that seemed very strange to the French nuns. But they accepted it, as they accepted the fact that Father Buteux and Bishop de la Hailandière expected an academy to flourish in the forest.

Mother Theodore could wait, she decided, for the spirit of the new country was so different from anything she had known. Already she was realizing the depth of her love for the faraway country of her birth, which was feeding and clothing these missionaries in the New World, building churches for them, giving them aid without which the lot of the French missions would have become intolerably hard. She had learned, for example, that it was through the Picquet family in France that money had been provided to pay for their land and to build their new brick house.

One postulant left because of ill health, but two more came in December. There were twelve to provide for now. The sisters had plenty of meat and cabbage, and wood for their fires. Neighboring farmers had promised to help clear a garden space for them, and the Thralls had left them a cow and several pigs; they had plenty of chickens. They began to feel a sense of permanence and a sense of being at home.

In that month, the neat brick house that was to serve as a home for Father Buteux was completed. The sisters made it ready for him, and they arranged a room in it for visiting clergymen; its first occupant was the bishop, who came to spend Christmas with them. He reached Saint Mary's in time to celebrate the Midnight Mass in the sisters' chapel in the farmhouse. The sisters sang with happy hearts the noels they had learned as children in France.

Next day, sleigh bells jingled in the frosty air. The Catholics came from all around through the wintry woods to attend the Mass of Christmas with the sisters at the new little altar in the woods.

Then the joy of Christmas was dimmed. The day following the feast, Mother Theodore, who had come without difficulty through the terrible trip to Saint Mary's and had been enjoying a good health unusual for her, was taken very ill. The bishop, who was still at the convent, sent for Dr. Baty of Vincennes, and when the doctor examined her he thought she was suffering from brain fever. He remained at Saint Mary's for eight days, treating her, but when he left he was not certain she would live.

On January 18, Mother Theodore was so low that the Last Sacraments were administered and the prayers for the dying recited. The bishop, who had been called back to Saint Mary's because of her serious condition, was as deeply troubled as were her sisters. All shared a common thought: if she were gone, what would become of the new mission?

The bishop went to the chapel and remained for a long time before the Blessed Sacrament. When he returned to the sisters his face was much brighter. "I do not think your Mother will die," he said briefly. Then he blessed them all and went on his way.

The bishop was right. Mother Theodore recovered. No doubt the strength of the prayers for her recovery helped, but her convalescence was very slow, even with Sister Olympiade's devoted and skilled care. The ceremonies of vesture were set for February 2, 1841, and the three professed met at her bedside to vote on the candidates. Mother Theodore was too ill to attend the ceremonies at which the bishop presided, assisted by Father Lalumière, the first priest ordained for the diocese of Vincennes. The ceremonial was carried out as nearly as possible to the way it was at Ruillé.

There were sixteen members in the community now. Two of the first postulants received the habit. Sister Olympiade made her first vows. The bishop gave a fine talk, filled with his hopes for the community and its future work.

On February 15, Mother Theodore was for the first time able to come to Mass with the community, to their great joy. Her health now grew increasingly better, even though she was recovering, as the bishop put it, "with disconcerting slowness."

Before he left, Father Lalumière had told Mother Theodore that later he would bring his niece to the novitiate and also that he would make the community a gift of two hundred and fifty acres of land near Fort Wayne. He said that he was merely the agent in this transaction; Our Lady was the real donor. All that was asked in return were the prayers of the community on the work the priest was doing.

Mother Theodore, when she realized how very ill she was, had promised a statue of the Immaculate Conception for the convent chapel if she recovered. When there was no money to buy it, she turned to her old friend in Soulaines, and "Monsieur" wrote promptly that he was sending her one. He was very happy to secure the statue for Mother Theodore, even though it required a trip to Paris to select it. He reminded her to be very careful in having the box unpacked, as the hands were detachable and separately wrapped!

Spring came at last, their first spring in their new home. It was heralded by a long, hoarse whistle from the banks of the river, for the ice had broken and this was the signal that announced that navigation on the Wabash had begun again. The air grew balmy; trees were green with early leaf. At the convent doors, wild flowers bloomed, and in the forest farmers were tapping the maple trees for sap. The sisters from France saw for the first time the beauty of Indiana in April, with plum and hawthorn blossoms making the air sweet and the bright plumage of birds everywhere.

At Saint Mary's, they rejoiced in the variety the season brought, for the winter had been a time of monotony. Their greatest excitement had been the arrival of letters from France, and these were read again and again. These letters brought about an odd custom, carried out in a spirit of sacrifice but a source of difficulty to later historians of the sisters' early days: when they wanted a certain favor very much, they burned some of these treasured letters as an offering to God of their dearest possessions.

Fortunately many of these letters survived. Letters from Mother Mary, from the bishop of Le Mans, from the curé of Soulaines, were nearly all preserved. The curé wrote that people were still sad about the departure of Sister Theodore and that some refused to believe she was really not coming back. " 'She gave us clothing,' one will say," wrote the curé, "or, 'She gave me wonderful medicine when I was sick and was not afraid to come in the rain or through the mud either.' " If Sister Theodore could only see the beautiful church now, which they owed to her intercession. But, fine as it was and much as they loved it, sometimes the curé felt sad to think that they had such fine marble and gold leaf when he knew that in America the sisters were poor and had such a very plain house of God.

Many people had asked him to write to her that she must be sure to come back for the blessing of the church—did she think that perhaps she could? Then, too, there were several young women in his parish asking about the possibility of coming to her as postulants.

Not all the postulants had been a success. One had gone back to her family, too homesick to continue; a few others had been sent back as poorly fit for the religious life. Those who came now were all Americans, and this meant that they were in many ways different from the postulants to whom the sisters had been accustomed in France. A spirit of independence characterized them all, an excellent thing, Mother Theodore was realizing, provided only that it did not go too far. From the beginning, she had admired the honesty and the uprightness of the Americans.

Sister Liguori, who wrote in a very fine hand, had begun in the winter evenings to make a copy of Mother Theodore's journal of their voyage to America to send to Ruillé. It was then sent in turn to Bishop Bouvier, the Maries, the Comtesse de Marescot, Monsieur Bertaudière, and their other benefactors. Months later, letters came back commenting on the journal. Though all admitted it was an excellent account, they were far from certain they liked this strange region to which their Sister Theodore had gone, and they felt her place was in France. "Come back from that land of savages—oh, how gladly we will receive you," wrote Madame Marie.

The letters were a joy to read, but they wakened no desire to return in those who read them, even when Madame Marie wrote, "Dear Sister, we beg of you do not stay where the climate is so severe. Does God ask the sacrifice of your life? I cannot think so." She added that they really needed her back—"and in Indiana others could do the work but here it is you alone who are necessary."

M. de la Bertaudière wrote that he was sorry to hear of her serious illness—"you who are half a doctor yourself." He too hoped she would get back for the dedication of the church next year and also that the statue would reach her soon. He wrote of what was happening in France, that everyone feared they were on the eve of a general war, and if so they would have the combined forces of Europe against them—"unless Louis-Philippe makes himself very meek and bends very low." If the king did not have to defend the land against foreign powers, he might well find another danger facing him—revolt at home.

The French sisters retained their love and their deep interest in the country they had left; most of them were royalists and their sympathies lay with such a regime. And even though politics were not discussed in the community, Mother Theodore led prayers against this danger of war in the land of her birth. When it was learned that the danger had been averted, at least for the present, she had prayers of thanksgiving offered.

From Bishop de Lesquen of Rennes, who had been so kind to her, came word that he had resigned his see; he was eighty-two years old and tired, and besides he thought these last years of his life ought to be given to thinking of his last end. He wrote to his friend—"our Sister of the woods"—that the distance that separated them could not weaken the sentiments of the heart "which can leap over space." He was deeply interested in what she wrote about the new mission and it did not surprise him that she had met with difficulties. He asked her to remember always that "if the labor affrights you, the recompense spurs you on." He was glad that her bishop in the New World took such care of her and her community, and he hoped the Lord would bless her a thousand times—"as also your holy companions and your dear children."

The space for a kitchen garden had been cleared in early spring by Thomas Brassier and his sons, the family who had been with the sisters on the *Cincinnati* and to whom Mother Theodore had sent money to come to Saint Mary's to work. The space was planted with potatoes and cabbage, lettuce and turnips. This would supplement their other food, although all food was cheap. Eggs were twelve cents a dozen; flour, five dollars a barrel; and chickens, a dollar a dozen. Of course, there was not a great deal of money either, and the purchase of a desk or a table was a really important event.

While Mother Theodore had been recovering from her illness, a new postulant had arrived from Pennsylvania, a young widow sent by Mother's friend Father Varela in New York. Madame Parmentier knew her well too and felt that in Mrs. Anne Moore the community would have a worthy member. She had been at Saint Mary's for only a short time when it was clear that they had been right about the young woman's value. As Sister Gabriella, she was to prove a very valuable member of the Sisters of Providence.

In April, Mother Theodore was well enough to go to Vincennes to shop for things difficult to get at Terre Haute, such as tulle for the postulants' bonnets. She had another reason for the trip: she was still not completely well and wanted to see Dr. Baty again. He assured her that she might resume her duties, but he warned her against overexertion.

When she went to call on the bishop, he told her that Father Martin was very anxious to open a school in his parish at Logansport, but money was lacking and so were sisters. She knew she could not help him as yet and was very sorry. Her trouble too was lack of money and the fact that as yet there were only four professed sisters.

"We need so many things, and all of them necessary," she told the bishop. "We want more fruit trees to add to our orchards. We need farm tools and new habits. We have bought a new horse, though, with the elegant name of Mignon, and it cost a good deal. And we must pay the men who work for us. And we must buy food."

She thought the bishop did not look very pleased with her quick refusal of Father Martin's request, though he said nothing. She was sorry, for she wanted to please the bishop. She felt he had done his best for them, and she knew that demands on him were heavy, that money was hard to come by and becoming increasingly so. Then, again, he had paid all their expenses so far, although he had not reimbursed them the money that Mother Mary had advanced for their trip. He had sent them postulants. More than once he had made the difficult trip to Saint Mary's, even though he was a very busy man. When Mother Theodore was ill, he had written her reassuringly; when she was well again, he had written how happy the news made him.

"Do you know why I have so great an interest in you?" he wrote. "It is because God loves you so much. It is His grace, His work in you I love, His designs I admire…. Let nothing frighten you. Draw from those designs the conviction that should ever deepen in us that in the eyes of God there is nothing of worth in us."

Already on several occasions Mother Theodore had noted the unusually great difficulties the bishop had to encounter, and the small chance he seemed to have of carrying out the plans he had made for Saint Mary's. When she faced the isolated situation of her community and the unlikelihood of success in working there for souls or setting up a school, she had suggested to him that the sisters return to France. This brought from the bishop violent objections. He said that the words, "We could return," rang in his ears and made him unhappy. She and her community and their future were in his thoughts continually, and he knew his plans would work out. He begged her not to be discouraged. "Let us live on hope—but above all let us live on love of God," he wrote.

She promised to try. In a long letter written to Mother Mary some months before, she had asked that Ruillé keep the mission very specially in their prayers. The little American community needed those prayers. It was not the icy winter Mother Theodore feared nor the possibility of material hunger. "Those will not really ever be my crosses," she wrote. "I foresee others much heavier. But heaven is the price of all, and Calvary is the way."

CHAPTER SEVEN

The First Academy (1841)

❦

Despite her promise to Bishop de la Hailandière that the sisters would stay, Mother Theodore continued to feel uncertain of her own ability as administrator. One reason for this was the advice of the community's chaplain. It was not that Father Buteux was growing uninterested in his work at Saint Mary's; on the contrary, he was far too interested.

He had been greatly concerned with the preparations for the new school, just as he was in all matters pertaining to the women religious. A learned and zealous man, he had taken very seriously the fact that the bishop, when he appointed him, had given him some authority over temporalities also, although that had been intended to cover only the time before Mother Theodore came from France. In fact, up to that time the priest had the four postulants completely under his direction.

When the French sisters arrived, members of an organized group, with a definite rule and with their lives governed by their spiritual superiors, he saw his influence diminish. It was also true that his ideas of the powers of a chaplain were very inaccurate, just as his ideas for religious life were not only austere but sometimes very unusual. He assumed that he was to be with the community members for hours of individual spiritual direction, to take recreation with them, to supervise their trifling everyday needs. He would complain if he thought the cook put too much cabbage or turnip in the soup; if the sisters wanted so small a thing as an extra handkerchief, he thought they ought to ask his permission.

It was against Mother Theodore that, as time went on, his greatest criticisms were directed. In fact, it was these criticisms that helped make her feel she was unworthy of being at the head of her community.

In the summer of 1841, she spoke again of being replaced in office, a suggestion which greatly upset the bishop, who thought that after her last visit to him he had convinced her that the community was doing very well under her leadership. He reminded her that she had said on that occasion, "Though all should leave, I shall not." Now she was suggesting that she wanted to do exactly that.

"I do not want to leave," she protested. "It is only that I do not feel qualified to be at the head."

"No one could do it better than you," the bishop said earnestly. "And if you hold your office for no better reason, do it to help me, for I am in the midst of a great amount of business of all kinds. I shall confide in you by telling you that I feel a sea of bitterness rising against me every way I turn."

Mother Theodore had also written to Ruillé in regard to her fears about her capability and had asked Mother Mary to replace her with a really competent head for the American house; she felt herself very inadequate. The reply had been that the council refused to consider this at all; Mother Mary wrote they had decided that the suggestion was made only because of Mother Theodore's own deep humility. They knew from others that she was doing very well and advised her to cease worrying about it.

Mother Theodore was no longer asking to be replaced, since both her congregation and her bishop were against it. It was true, too, that she was beginning to feel stronger in her position; she saw that perhaps some of her early hesitation had come from being in a new and strange land, where she knew little of the language. Moreover, her long and severe illness had made her uncertain of her value. Now her work was progressing and she felt, for her, unusually well. Workmen were finishing the house begun the summer before. The grounds were being cleared and walks constructed, with Mother Theodore supervising it all; in fact, more than once she and her sisters had lent a hand with the actual work.

Mother Theodore went to Louisville and to Cincinnati to procure books and furniture for the academy. In those cities she visited schools so that she might get a better idea of methods of teaching, for she knew that she must combine American with French ideas if she hoped to make a success of an academy.

During those busy days of preparing her sisters for their future work of teaching, she did not neglect their spiritual training. Her meditations were always carefully thought out, though they were always simple and full of practical application.

"Sisters," she would say, "some of us have homely faces. But we have our consolation: all the beauty of the king's daughter is from within." They must preserve, she told them, even if they were not beautiful in features, a pleasant countenance: "We cannot change our features, but we can change our expressions. Cold looks repel, but a genial manner links us to the apostles and evangelists whom our profession obliges us to imitate."

Often her talks were on the Holy See, for if she had any special devotion, those who knew her said, it was this. She took such pride in the Church's sovereignty that it was as if its needs were her own personal concern, and many of her prayers were directed to asking blessings on the vicar of Christ.

She had other devotions—to the Holy Spirit, to Our Lady, to the Holy Infancy, and she loved the tradition of guardian angels. This last she had brought with her from Ruillé, where the religious carried out the lovely custom of saluting the guardian angel of whomever they met. It was a devotion, she said, excellent for religious teachers, because their own duties to children were in so many ways like those of the guardian angels.

St. Anne, too, she loved dearly, and the great Teresa; but the deepest and most tender of her devotions was to the Sacred Heart of Jesus, for there she saw best exemplified the providence of God—their own title, their own aim.

Almost from the time the sisters came to Saint Mary-of-the-Woods, Mother Theodore had established a devotion to Our Lady. "We began the month of Mary as solemnly as possible," she wrote in her journal in May, 1841, and it was a devotion that was to spread from their convent to Terre Haute and to other towns. Later the sodality of the Children of Mary was founded at Saint Mary-of-the-Woods. This organization was the first of its kind in Indiana.

At first, the Sisters of Providence wondered whether they would meet with trouble if they wore their habits when they went to other towns. They knew there was much prejudice against vowed religious in the middle west, especially among some of the immigrants from the eastern states, where bigotry was rife and associations working against the Catholic Church were vociferous and slanderous. When Mother Theodore and a companion went to Terre Haute for the first time, however, they decided to wear their habits and found they caused no disturbance at all.

The French and American members of the community were becoming well acclimated to each other, but small differences in customs were sometimes harder to overcome. "Today we did our washing for the first time in the American fashion," ran one letter to Ruillé; and another, "Here they make soup of oysters; it is deplorable. And they eat potatoes boiled in the skins." On one thing, however, all the letters were in agreement: the land was as fair as that of France, and thanks to the country air they were all very well.

The sisters now turned all their thoughts and efforts to their academy. In July, the boarding school was to open for a trial term; then there would be a vacation, and if all went well the school would reopen in September. Despite Mother Theodore's doubts it was evident that pupils were going to come to their forest. For some months, inquiries had been coming to Saint Mary's, many of them from Protestants, asking when the sisters would be ready to accept boarding pupils.

July 2 had been the day decided on for the opening, but they were not ready and postponed it to July 5. On the day before that, the first pupil arrived, Mary Lenoble—"whom we cannot help keeping even though we are not yet ready," wrote the annalist. Mother Theodore was glad that the name of their first pupil was that of Our Lady. It was a good omen.

The academy was blessed on its opening day by Father Buteux. Another pupil had arrived, and classes were opened in French and English. Sister Vincent was appointed superior of the school, and on her faculty were Sister Aloysia, who had been Mary Doyle, and Sister Marie Joseph, who had been Josephine Pardeillan. Sister Thérèse, who had come as a postulant from the Picquet colony, was to be cook.

Four more pupils came on the second day, and still more during the week. Among them were Ann Law from Vincennes, whose father was Judge Law; the two daughters of Joseph Richardson, a pioneer from New York; Kate Dowling, daughter of the editor of the *Wabash Courier*; Mary Farrington, daughter of Terre Haute's most prominent business man. Nearly all the first pupils were Protestant. Even though the parents of these girls might not approve of the Catholic Church, they did approve highly of French academy training. As for the Catholics, most of them were too poor to afford a private academy for their children.

All the new pupils, Catholic and Protestant alike, walked from the new school to the farmhouse chapel, going through the woods and across the little bridge over the ravine to assist at the Mass and the chant of the *Veni Creator Spiritus* that marked the opening of the academy at Saint Mary-of-the-Woods.

When at the end of July the students went home for vacation, it was clear that Mother Theodore's fears had been unfounded and that there would be no dearth of pupils. The school was off to a flourishing start.

In August, and before the fall term of school opened, Mother Theodore prepared to go to Vincennes to attend a very important event.

At Vincennes there was great excitement when the cathedral was at last ready for consecration. For months, Bishop de la Hailandière had been intent on finishing the edifice left uncompleted by Father Champomier, the first pastor of Vincennes, and Bishop Bruté, its first bishop. One difficulty had been that the trustees had been debating how the work was to be done and how the money was to be raised, until one day Bishop de la Hailandière presented them with a *fait accompli*—but only on paper. The plan called for a bell tower, a rectory, and a good school, all of them necessary for a cathedral, he told them. They merely stared and shook their heads when they contemplated what this would cost.

All the bishop had in hand was $1100, left by the will of Bishop Bruté, to use for plastering the building. When this was done there was no money to do anything further, and none had been offered. Finally, in 1840, the trustees gave the church and the property to the bishop to do with as he pleased. His hands freed, he used funds collected from abroad to begin rebuilding and repairing.

First of all, it was necessary to rebuild the sanctuary wall, which was in danger of collapsing; then he transferred Bishop Bruté's remains to a crypt prepared for them. By April of 1841, Bishop de la Hailandière was already at work making plans for the consecration. When the work was entirely finished and the steeple in place, he planned to hold the first synod in his diocese.

Mother Theodore, who had been invited to attend the ceremonies to be held on August 8, was almost too late, for she had wanted to make sure that the Brassiers finished storing the hay in the recently built barn. Then she and Sister Aloysia set out for Vincennes to see what the bishop had in his invitation called "the very great day of which you have never in your life seen the equal." He had added, in his prudent way, "To avoid expense take the little carriage and the smallest possible amount of luggage."

Mother Theodore thought of the cathedral as it had been the day she had looked at it with a sad heart because it was so desolate and so poor. She was greatly surprised at what she now saw—a graceful tower, nice windows, a well-painted interior, a good altar.

The ceremonies were impressive. So many people came that Father Petit and Father Larkin stood on elevated pulpits on the grounds explaining to the overflow outside just what was going on inside. Bishop Purcell had come from Cincinnati to celebrate the pontifical Mass, and next morning he preached at a memorial service for Bishop Bruté.

Afterwards, when Mother Theodore met Father Petit, she reminded him that eighteen years before she had been present at a retreat he had given at Ruillé. When she met for the first time Father Benoit of Fort Wayne, deputed to go to France on a special mission for the bishop, she secured from him a promise that he would go to see Mother Mary at Ruillé. Then she hurried home for the opening of the retreat, to the closing days of which the bishop had promised to come. The bishop always enjoyed a few peaceful days at St. Mary's in the quiet of the forest and convent after his crowded days at Vincennes. "Here all is calm, here all is well," he once wrote to Father Martin. "The few days I am spending here almost make me forget I am a bishop."

Unhappily, though, all was not well at Saint Mary's itself. The bishop knew from other priests of Mother Theodore's difficulties with the chaplain and discussed the matter with her.

"I thought I had made matters clear to him, but I evidently did not," the bishop said. "He is exceeding his duties when he tries to form your novices. He is your chaplain; he is here to administer the sacraments and nothing more, excepting a weekly instruction to the community. And now he tells me he feels he is too much restricted here. I think I shall remove him."

This was not exactly the solution Mother Theodore expected. "But you must remember, Monseigneur, when we first came here we were promised daily Mass in our own chapel. If you remove the chaplain, we might have to depend on neighboring clergy, and there are none very near us."

"Don't worry about that," he told her. "The brothers are sending another group soon, and with them will come several priests from France." And then he began to smile broadly. "And someone else will be with them," he said. This news he had saved for the end of his visit, and now he looked at her face to see the delighted surprise he knew would be there when he told her. "Irma will be with them."

He was right. Mother Theodore's face lost all its worry and was filled with joy. This was her dearest wish, her great hope—to have Irma le Fer de la Motte with her in America; of late Mother Theodore had grown afraid that perhaps Mother Mary would never let her come. Now she was coming to join the Saint Mary's community at last.

The matter of Father Buteux was left unsettled for the time, but one thing the bishop did settle before he left the convent. An unhappy rumor had been going about the diocese that Father Buteux was trying to withdraw Sister Aloysia and the other American sisters and have them form a community of their own, something which would spell disaster for the present community, since they were very dependent on the English-speaking teachers for the new academy.The bishop knew this was more than mere rumor. Father Buteux had spoken about it to several of the clergy when they came to see him at Saint Mary's, and they had brought it to the bishop's attention.

Mother Theodore had herself been of two minds about Sister Aloysia from the day she found her awaiting the arrival of the sisters at St. Mary's. She had been uneasy about taking as a member one who had belonged to another congregation, but the bishop had accepted her. Sister Aloysia had given as her reason for wishing to enter the Sisters of Providence the desire of the bishop to have her do so because the French sisters would have a strange language and different customs to contend with and she could be of assistance. Her own congregation, the Sisters of Charity, were well supplied with members; she had withdrawn honorably, and so her going was not really a defection. It was very true, too, that she had proved to be an excellent teacher. When the academy opened, she had been the only teacher who spoke English without an accent. Then, too, it was she who taught the young sisters English and was interpreter for the American postulants. Whatever doubts she had had at first, Mother Theodore later had been inclined to agree with the bishop regarding both the young sister's teaching ability and also her earnestness in the religious life.

But not long before the bishop's visit, Sister Aloysia had suggested to Mother Theodore that perhaps she could be given extra duties and serve, as she put it, "as a medium between community and people." This the bishop turned down entirely, for it would in a way place her above her superior. Instead, he suggested Sister Aloysia be considered next in rank to Mother Theodore and to this the latter agreed, hoping it would also satisfy Father Buteux.

In France, Irma le Fer de la Motte had long been waiting for word that would grant her the desire of her heart—to go to America as a missionary. The permission had been slow in coming. Since she had been too ill to sail with the first group, she had remained at Ruillé to complete her novitiate, as Mother Mary had insisted. The newly-named Sister Francis Xavier had been willing to wait, but as time went on she wrote to Mother Theodore, "Shall I remain in France? Shall I ever go to America? I know not. God knows and that suffices. He is my guide and it is not necessary that I know the road." Then she added wistfully, "But sometimes, thinking of you and Vincennes, my nature resists."

She had been vested in December of 1840 and sent immediately to the house in Brest, a good community with twelve members. When Bishop de la Hailandière heard that, he said indignantly, "They have stolen our Irma." By sending Sister Francis to a mission, Mother Mary clearly planned to keep her in France. When this was realized at Saint Mary-of-the-Woods, there was consternation. Mother Theodore had been counting on Sister Francis to come soon and had hoped that several others would come with her, as she had asked Mother Mary more than once. They were urgently needed for teaching. Irma, who was a talented and skillful artist, would be especially valuable.

Mother Theodore decided to write Mother Mary very straightforwardly. The bishop felt and so did she that Sister Francis belonged to Vincennes. She knew that Mother Mary had been of the opinion that this novice, on account of her youth and health, would be of no value at St. Mary's. Mother Theodore knew this would not be the case, and she urged that the young religious be sent as soon as possible to Vincennes. In fact, she asked not only for her but for at least two others to help with the new and growing academy.

Bishop de la Hailandière wrote an equally firm and definite letter to Mother Mary, with the result that the exasperated superior wrote that Sister Francis could decide for herself what she wanted to do with her future. Troubled by these conflicting opinions, Sister Francis asked for advice from Bishop Bouvier, and after considering the matter he wrote that he was inclined to tell her to go and suggested she come to see him. By the time she came, he was definite in his opinion: he thought she ought to go to America.

"She is borne on wings of love," he wrote to Mother Theodore, and said he had made the arrangements for her to leave with Père Moreau's brothers when they sailed for America with Abbé Sorin.

Sister Francis made her vows before she left France and was permitted to make them perpetual. She left for Honfleur by stage and ship with six brothers and one priest from Holy Cross at Le Mans and also with a Monsieur Dupont, who was known as the Holy Man of Tours. They sat next to each other in the stage, saying their beads together and making the Way of the Cross. He talked beautifully of God while the bumpy stage rolled through the night, Sister Francis told Mother Theodore later.

When they reached the ship, Madeleine Berthelot, a young woman who was to serve as cook at the seminary in Vincennes and to be Sister Francis' companion on the voyage, did not appear. Fortunately, five women religious of the Sacred Heart were sailing on the *Iowa*, and so Sister Francis was able to sail.

The religious were in lay garb. Sister Francis had on a black bonnet and a long shawl, which hid her habit and made her look less like a religious. She looked very frail and young in her sombre garb as she stood on deck, gazing towards the dark ocean and all but seeing there the land of America for which she had been longing.

Despite continuous and severe seasickness—once the women with her actually thought she was dying—Sister Francis enjoyed the trip. There was Mass frequently in a little cabin used as a chapel, and somtimes one of the priests read to them.

When the *Iowa* reached New York harbor and Sister Francis stepped from the ship, Father Sorin behind her said softly, *"Voilà, ma soeur, vous êtes sur la terre d'Amerique!"* And she stooped to kiss the ground.

On the dock to welcome her was Mr. Byerley with a letter from Mother Theodore. He said he had been watching daily to be sure to meet her ship.

"But where are the other two?" he asked in surprise, expecting other Divine Providence sisters.

Sister Francis was equally surprised at his question. "I am the only one," she said, and then told him she had been invited to go with the other women religious to their convent on Houston Street.

She was made very welcome and, though she had not expected to do so, she remained for six weeks because there was no one to go with her on the long journey west. The stay did her good, for it brought back her strength, depleted by seasickness; during those weeks she also had a fine opportunity to practise English with the Sacred Heart sisters.

When Madeleine Berthelot reached New York on a later ship, Sister Francis prepared to go with her to Saint Mary-of-the-Woods. Madeleine was a robust girl who could take good care of her frail companion, but the Sacred Heart religious were loath to see Sister Francis go, for they had grown very fond of her. "How would it be possible not to be won by so charming a person?" said the superior to Madame Parmentier.

The little group started out, Sister Francis in secular dress. Father Bellier, a Eudist, in whose care she and Madeleine had been placed, had chosen the cheaper and also slower route from Philadelphia by canal and rail. It was an uncomfortable trip at first, most of it spent wedged among coffee sacks and trunks, but Madeleine took fine care of her charge, even sticking a candle in an apple so that Sister Francis might have a light at night when she could not sleep.

Father Bellier, also in secular garb, proved a fine entertainer. He would often take out his guitar and give the passengers a French song in which some of them joined. But it was a great relief to the young women when at Pittsburgh they embarked on a steam vessel and had a tiny cabin of their own.

On November 9, after three weeks on the way, they reached Vincennes at last, and Sister Francis said goodbye to the others. Bishop de la Hailandière said he would himself conduct her to Saint Mary's. He drove to Terre Haute with her in a little open carriage, thus saving the twenty franc stage fare, he told her. When the road was very bad, he got out and walked and she drove, trying to guide the horse around stumps and holes while he trudged silently along beside them. At last, at seven in the evening, they heard a lovely sound: the bell of Saint Mary's ringing the Angelus. A few minutes later Sister Francis was in Mother Theodore's arms.

Mother Theodore led the tired girl first to the chapel where she knelt, not so much to give thanks for a safe arrival as to offer all the rest of her life to God. That, she told Mother Theodore, was what she had wanted to do at Ruillé; now at last she could make that vow as a missionary in America.

Mother Theodore thought Sister Francis looked frailer than she had ever seen her, but no doubt that was in part due to the rigors of the long voyage. There was no doubt as to the complete happiness of the young religious.

"Sorrow has mysteries like the sea," Sister Francis said as they walked to visit the academy next morning. "To sink into its depths may mean certain death, and sometimes I have felt that too. But one day I read that one must remember that some come back with pearls and corals in their hands, and I felt better. I had sorrow when I thought I should never come here. Now I know the joy."

Mother Theodore told the newcomer a little about the academy in the woods, for she had seen Sister Francis look in amazement at the great trees and the solitude about them. She told her something about the American pupils too, so different from the French girls whom they had both taught.

"You will understand them better after you have known them for a while," she said. "They have great pride and are very independent, but once you have their hearts they will do anything to prove their devotion to you."

In this case the newcomer did not have to wait long for affection. Some of the children came running up to greet Mother Theodore and one, after looking at the smiling young sister beside her, reached up to kiss her. For a moment the young French religious looked confused, and then she bent and returned the caress. Mother Theodore was delighted at this quick response to a demonstrativeness that was very different from that of the more reticent children of French convent schools.

Later, when Sister Francis had more time (there was never a great deal, as she was soon to find out), she told the community of her adventures—of M. Dupont and the Sacred Heart sisters in New York, of Madame Parmentier and Mr. Byerley, of people on boat and train who had been very kind to her. Mother Theodore, looking at the lovely dedicated young face, could easily understand that kindness and marveled that the community at Ruillé would let her go on this journey without reassuring themselves that she would have a companion all the way.

Sister Francis had brought with her letters from old friends, one a note from Canon Lottin who had helped Bishop Bouvier write the Ruillé rule that in 1843 was to receive preliminary approval from Rome. He wrote how interested he was in the new mission: "I have become quite American myself since the sisters adopted the New World as their home. If a revolution comes again and drives me out of France, I shall take refuge at Saint Mary's. Do not smile. Stranger things have happened." He sent as a gift a nail shaped like those of the Cross and wrote that he had touched it to the original relic in the Church of the Holy Cross at Rome.

Only a few days after Sister Francis arrived at Saint Mary's, another recruit came, brought by Father Buteux. She was a very different type but, like Sister Francis, an intellectual. Already the newcomer from France had seen that the Indiana postulants were, as she wrote the novice mistress at Ruillé, "not chosen from any other class than that from which Jesus chose His disciples."

The newcomer, Eleanor Bailly, was a well educated young woman who was born at Mackinac in 1815. Her father was of distinguished French ancestry and a wealthy fur trader; her mother was an Indian princess of the Ottawa tribe; both were staunch Catholics. Eleanor had lived at Baillytown, on the Calumet in Indiana, where the Bailly family were the only white people. The children of the family were sent to Detroit to boarding schools, and after their education was completed they became a part of the social life of the city. Several of the Bailly girls were married, one to a cousin of the artist Whistler, another to a well known civil engineer in Chicago, Francis Howe.

The family visited Chicago at intervals, but their home was in Baillytown, a well known and welcome stopping place for missionaries en route. The whole Bailly family had long devoted its efforts to the welfare of the Indians. Mass had been celebrated on their dining room table by Father Badin, Father de Saint-Palais and others. One of the daughters often acted as interpreter, translating service and sermon for the Indians and even serving in the unusual role of interpreter for confessions.

These two young women, Irma from the Old World, Eleanor from the New, were different in many ways. One was never really healthy; the other was vigorous and strong. One was delicately lovely; the other was tall and darkly handsome. One had the gentle piety of her French forebears; the other had the hardy faith of the frontiers. But both Sisters of Providence were to accomplish much good for their congregation and for the people among whom they worked and taught.

CHAPTER EIGHT

Death from Pinpricks

ℰ

Almost as soon as the Terre Haute newspaper published the announcement of the academy's opening, pupils had begun to enter their names. At first the applicants had been girls who lived in the vicinity, but when the winter term opened girls came from greater distances. Four came from one small Catholic colony in Edgar County and another from Pittsburgh. Early in November, Mother Theodore wrote to Bishop Bouvier that the school had nineteen boarding pupils, mostly non-Catholic, and that already any prejudice of the Protestants among them had greatly diminished. Most of the girls, she said, were in their early teens and were preparing for high school work. But again she spoke, as she had before, of her one complaint against these New World children—their pride and independence, so different from French girls of the same age.

Since they were American children, she encouraged them to celebrate the great national holidays at the school. Some of the students had relatives who had been a part of the early years of the republic, and the girls were themselves a very patriotic group, willing to fall in with her suggestions.

At the first celebration of Independence Day the following year, Mathilda Richardson read the Declaration of Independence and Ann Law was oratress of the day. A stage set under the trees was decorated with evergreens, and there reader and oratress held forth. The school sang "Hail Columbia," and the chaplain ended the ceremonies with Benediction. A dinner was served to the students and their guests. There were many toasts—to liberty, to Mother Theodore, to the sisters, to the young ladies, to the heroes of the Revolution, to the friends of the students at home. Then the young ladies took a ride to the river and, as the *Wabash Courier* chronicled it, "the banner gracefully waved over their heads its stripes and bars and plainly told them that they were indeed independent.... At early candle lighting time the young ladies returned to the domain where they concluded the celebration with a cheerful dance." The paper did not mention the fact that since there were no boys as partners some of the girls served in that capacity, distinguished by diamond-shaped bands on their right sleeves.

On this and on lesser occasions, Mother Theodore made it plain to her students that she considered patriotism a duty next to religion and insisted that they become thoroughly familiar with the history of their country and its great leaders.

In other ways, the school retained very French characteristics, even to the afternoon collation of bread and sugar and tea, the fine needlework, which later many of the girls put to use in embroidering for their own homes, the long walks in the woods, the close surveillance. There were few amusements, but the sisters showed a great deal of ingenuity in devising games for recreation and outdoor diversion.

It did not take Mother Theodore very long to realize that despite its inaccessibility her school was going to prosper. She was beginning to learn, in fact, that nearly everything was inaccessible in that part of the country and that remoteness did not daunt people in the least; that even Saint Mary-of-the-Woods was not too isolated.

It was also true that the little school was very simple, its furnishings were restricted to necessities, its lighting and heating very primitive; but the pupils were girls of pioneer stock and were used to privations. They did not expect anything better. Even the clothing and supplies they were asked to bring were simple—six summer and three winter dresses, a few towels and napkins, "a fine and a coarse comb and a small drinking cup."

The simplicity of the life did not trouble their parents either; what they wanted for their daughters was an education in the basics and in the graceful arts, and these they expected the sisters to supply. They evidently felt the sisters did, for the academy was soon going so well that Mother Theodore hoped to open a day school the following year. Already more Catholics were coming to the settlement, and obviously they were the poor for whom a free school would be needed.

As for the sisters from France who had at first found the climate very different from their own, they were becoming adapted to it and were in better health than they had been the year before. They had of course all suffered from a sickness known locally as "Wabash ague," which produced chills and fever in the unfortunate victims. They were, however, less troubled by this than were those who lived close to the river and the valley; the school's location was high above the stream and was evidently a much healthier site. At the time no one realized the cause of this enervating sickness; it was due to the swamp mosquitoes.

By the autumn of 1841, Saint Mary-of-the-Woods was a different place from what it had been when the little group of religious first came there. Even the newer arrivals among the postulants could not imagine how it had looked when the French sisters first saw it. A considerable space in the forest surrounding the original buildings had been cleared. The farm now boasted an excellent field of corn and wheat; the apple trees were bearing well, and the vegetable garden gave a fine supply for their table. Berries and grapes were in such plentiful supply that the postulants were kept busy picking them.

When the Thralls farmhouse, now the motherhouse, became over-crowded, an open porch on the south side was enclosed and made into a chapel. On the other side of the house a wing was added to give space for the rapidly increasing membership. An altar was built for the new chapel. A little bell that the bishop had given them and blessed in September now rang the Angelus three times each day. A space was ready on the altar for the statue that M. de la Bertaudière was sending them; it had reached New York and would soon be in its place. When Father Buteux said Mass on the morning after the chapel was ready for use, the sisters received Holy Communion from the little pyx that had been on the makeshift altar in the log cabin on the night the sisters first came.

When Sister Francis saw how many things were needed for the new chapel, she wrote home to solicit them from her relatives and friends. Her brother, who was a priest, sent a box of articles donated by the ladies of his parish, among them a monstrance and a quantity of incense to replace the cheap resin substitute that was all they had been able to afford. M. Dupont, who had prayed with Irma during the night on the stage from Ruillé, sent several chalices, one of which the community gave to the Holy Cross brothers, who were now living at Saint Peter's, one of the settlements where the bishop owned land.

The brothers had not been able to stop off at Saint Mary's when they came through Terre Haute. They had written that they were sorry, and Mother Theodore was sorry, too, for she had a gift for them—a team of oxen and a wagon. Later she had these driven to their mission, and Brother Vincent sent profuse thanks, again repeating how sorry he was it had not been possible to stop to see them: there had been time only to water the horses at Terre Haute and go on. The oxen were so gentle, he wrote, and so useful—"a good part of our prayers are yours, but on condition that you give us a share in yours."

When the statue from France arrived, it was placed in a niche above the altar. It was larger than they had expected it would be, but it fitted in well. It was in pastel colors, a presentation of Our Lady as a girl, her arms outstretched, a look of loving devotion on her face. Now that she was here, the chapel was complete.

Sister Francis had proved her worth immediately. She was put in charge of the novices; she taught drawing and Latin. She worked hard to improve the English that she was learning very rapidly, aided in part by her six weeks in New York, but she never became fluent in the language.

The study of English had been one of the first things Mother Theodore put into practice for her French sisters. From the beginning, a few prayers were recited in this language, even though it was still strange to the newcomers. Mother Theodore herself made good progress, and by the end of the year was able to talk with the American postulants without an interpreter. The bishop, despite his own lack of facility in the tongue, urged her to have the French sisters speak it as much as possible to one another. He asked Father Petit to translate for them the Litany of Providence and a long prayer to St. Joseph, and both these they recited daily. Father Petit also wished to translate the rule into English, but the bishop refused to give him a copy. Father Petit, a Jesuit who was a great help to the bishop, had himself brought them the translated prayers and stayed at Saint Mary's for several days. Evidently he had been deeply touched by the precarious situation of these French religious in their forest home, for before he left he gave them an address on the text: "Fear not, little flock." It was on love of vocation and was very encouraging; it heartened Mother Theodore greatly for some of the hard days that lay ahead.

From the time she landed in New York, Mother Theodore had studied New World methods of teaching. By the time she opened her academy, she knew much about American educational demands. She had learned, too, how eager were these Americans for a fine education for their daughters, something as true of the little western settlements as of the cities of the East. They wanted not only the usual basics but also the graceful arts—drawing, music, embroidering were considered essential to the curriculum of an academy of girls. In these subjects lay a much greater appeal than in simple sewing or cooking or any form of home industry.

Nearly all such education in the fine arts was at the time in the hands of religious groups. In the East there was the growing public school system, but in the part of the country to which the Sisters of Providence had come this was as yet untried. There were a few rural schools where a smattering of reading and writing was taught and enough arithmetic to keep accounts, but that was all.

In the East were academies, both day and boarding, for boys and for girls, but even as late as 1834 Bishop Bruté had found not one such school in his diocese. Of the Sisters of Charity of Nazareth who had come there as teachers, only a few remained; the others had been recalled to Kentucky.

While she was still in the East, Mother Theodore had studied carefully the teaching methods of Mother Seton's congregation and that of the Religious of the Sacred Heart, schools that the Parmentier daughters had attended. At Louisville, she had noted the methods of the Sisters of Charity. The Nazareth Sisters had been recalled from Vincennes, leaving only the remainder of the group of Emmitsburg sisters that Bishop Bruté had begged on a temporary basis from Mother Rose White. Their small school was still well maintained, but Mother Theodore noted in her journal that "the two sisters with their twelve pupils are going from the beginning of the day to the end and are worn out."

Mother Theodore was well aware that the right textbooks were very important and that these must be books fitted for American students in an American environment, even when the French method of teaching was employed. In the carefully drawn prospectus for the academy when it opened in 1841, the circular named English composition first of all, then rhetoric, natural philosophy, chemistry, botany, mythology, biography, astronomy, as well as French—a truly ambitious series of courses considering the few number of teachers. As for school equipment, she used the kind she had used in France—maps and charts and also a blackboard, articles that were not as yet in general use in American schools.

In the matter of tuition charges, Mother Theodore and the bishop had decided to charge one hundred dollars a year for board and basic academic classes; extras cost various amounts, ranging from French at ten dollars per term to music at thirty. The matter of finances was a very important item to Bishop de la Hailandière, who was sometimes very nervous about expenses. "I have no money," he would write to Mother Theodore. "Not a cent. Be sure not to go to any unnecessary expense."

A few weeks after this caution, he would apparently be in funds again, no doubt because he had received his annual appropriation from the Society for the Propagation of the Faith; at that time his diocese was receiving from that organization the largest amount allotted to any diocese in the United States.

When funds arrived the bishop would send all manner of welcome articles for the new school—dishes, chairs, irons, lamps, and two "sophas," one of which was to be for his own use when he came to Saint Mary's, the other "a common one for general use."

Father Buteux was still at Saint Mary's and still insisting at intervals that Mother Theodore give up her office and allow someone to replace her, preferably one of the American sisters, although it was clear that none of them was trained for such a task. As for the bishop, when this was presented to his attention he simply ignored the suggestion.

By this time Mother Theodore was herself grown very uneasy about Sister Aloysia. It was clear, even to one not of a suspicious nature, that the newcomer was planning to take over completely, utilizing the position given her by the bishop and Mother Theodore to act as the latter's assistant. Sister Aloysia, however, was by this time aware that she was being thwarted in this attempt by some in the community who had grown very wary of her.

Alleging that she was not well and needed treatment for her lungs, Sister Aloysia said that Mrs. Williams in Terre Haute was willing to take her in so that she might be nearer a doctor until she was better. Despite Father Buteux's urging, the bishop refused to permit this and wrote to Mother Theodore to refuse the request, adding, "What could she find there really except the attention of people of the world?"

Sister Aloysia gave up her plan and remained at Saint Mary's, but the pleasant attitude she had shown at first was gone. She grew increasingly annoyed because her position of authority was lessened and she was now merely a teacher like the others. She began to show odd symptoms. She would faint frequently at recreation and several times went into a sort of trance from which she refused for hours to be roused. Sometimes at night she would wake other sisters and say she was afraid: she heard rappings at the doors.

Father Perché stopped at Saint Mary's one day while on a missionary journey. Having heard about Mother Theodore's strange novice, he asked to talk with her alone. When he came back to Mother Theodore, he looked troubled. "I think she is possessed, Mother. You must send her away or she may do real harm here."

Mother Theodore knew that Father Perché was a man of great spirituality, and also of great common sense, not given to flights of fancy. She decided that, despite the bitter winter weather and her own poor health, she would go to Vincennes, lay the matter before the bishop, and give him Father Perché's opinion. She had one other troubling matter to lay before him about the same religious. Sister Aloysia had been secretly talking to some of the postulants, suggesting they leave with her and form a new and entirely American congregation.

Mother Theodore and her companion drove in their little buggy, well wrapped in a buffalo robe, one holding an umbrella while the other drove, for the weather of early winter was very inclement. When they reached Vincennes and the bishop, Mother Theodore's long explanation of her reason for coming found him not too gracious. He had of course seen only the good teacher in Sister Aloysia and her value to the struggling community because of her command of English—that necessary commodity for Saint Mary's. Then, too, Sister Aloysia was his own selection; he had sent her to Saint Mary's, had been for some time her spiritual director, and had always shown a decided preference for her. Mother Theodore was herself well aware of Sister Aloysia's value, but not to the extent of seeing her disrupt the community.

Despite his irritation, the bishop said he would come to Saint Mary's very soon and try to settle the matter. When he came a few weeks later, he studied the entire situation, heard a full account of all the trouble Sister Aloysia had caused and was still causing, and concurred with the decision of the council that she must no longer remain. Some of the sisters had been very devoted to her, for there was no doubt that Sister Aloysia had an engaging personality, and they took this decision badly, as did the postulants to whom she had talked about forming a new congregation. But when she left Saint Mary's, no one went with her.

In February of 1842, something else happened, also a result of the difficulties with the dismissed Sister Aloysia. A letter came from Mother Mary, usually so infrequent a writer. It had been written in December, when matters were at their worst, but it had not arrived until the situation has been cleared up.

Mother Mary had received, she wrote, a long anonymous letter, mailed from Cincinnati, stating that the Sisters of Providence at Saint Mary-of-the-Woods were in great trouble and were, in fact, actually suffering. What was chiefly the trouble was the present head of the community, and the writer thought that perhaps a change of superiors was urgently needed to save the community from further difficulty.

The letter showed clearly that Mother Mary, although not strictly entitled to exercise jurisdiction over the American community, was conscious of a definite responsibility towards the French sisters, four of whom had been subjects of Ruillé. The bishop's failure to approve the rules and to stabilize the Indiana community still kept the ties between Ruillé and Saint Mary-of-the-Woods binding.

Mother Mary wrote reproachfully to her daughter: "Is it lawful for you to hide from me circumstances that weigh heavily on your sisters? I want to know everything, my dear Theodore, tell me the whole truth." And she asked that each sister write her a separate letter "about all that concerns herself in particular."

"Have you any new missions?" the letter asked. "Where are the Brothers of St. Joseph—also thrust into the desert to perish from hunger? On what do you live? Do you plant wheat? Do you make butter? Have you milk? But it is useless for me to ask—you tell me nothing."

This alarming letter was immediately answered by Mother Theodore in fourteen closely written pages. Her superior's long complaint, the result of an anonymous letter taken very seriously by its recipient, drew from Mother Theodore remarks that were more severe than usual. She spoke sadly of her heaviest cross—that she displeased her Mother—and then went on, "But, my dear Mother, if the favor of being again your daughter must be bought by exciting your compassion for sorrows we do not suffer, then I must renounce it…. I do not recall having hidden from you knowingly any of our sufferings. It is true that our whole life is one of sacrifice. Who would doubt this? Strangers to the manners and customs, to the religious opinions and especially the character of the people about us, lost in the deep solitudes of Indiana, buried alive as it were in this huge tomb—without a doubt, humanly speaking, our life is miserable. Obliged to have business relations with a people of whose language we are ignorant and who are noted for their skill in driving sharp bargains. Having in our own home American children, that is, strangers not only to our way of acting but even to ordinary Christian conduct, quick to condemn everything contrary to what is done in this country, so proud, so contemptuous—certainly all this puts one to death daily, as it were, from pinpricks. My dear Mother, you know all this so well that you forewarned me of it yourself before I ever came to America."

Then followed a detailed account of their relations with the bishop, with Father Buteux, their present financial condition, the health of the sisters, their food and what it cost, the religious spirit among the postulants—"to which Irma le Fer contributes so much"—plans for their future, successes and failures, the gradual learning of English. This long letter, with confidential letters from every professed Sister, was mailed to Ruillé.

The decision of the bishop and the council regarding Sister Aloysia had been no doubt very necessary and for the good of Saint Mary's, but for a time it caused great harm to the growing academy. Sister Aloysia had gone, when she left the convent, to Terre Haute, to the home of her friend, Mrs. Williams, and there spoke at length of the harsh treatment she had received at Saint Mary's, where she said she had been desirous only to work for the good of the community and to help build up the school.

Word came that Sister Aloysia was opening a school herself, with the assistance of Mrs. Williams. The one promise she was making to parents of prospective pupils was that the teaching in her school would not be as poor as she had found it at Saint Mary-of-the-Woods!

As time went on, Sister Aloysia's reputation as a teacher drew a number of pupils from Saint Mary's. People felt sorry for her because they thought she had been badly treated, and Mrs. Williams spoke everywhere in praise of her protégée. Sister Aloysia's bad influence, instead of diminishing, grew as the months passed. In the year following her forced departure from Saint Mary's, she had drawn away more and more prospective pupils, until by October of 1842 the Sisters of Providence had, as Mother Theodore wrote unhappily to Mother Mary, "ten pupils, not one of whom pays a penny. We keep these, however, for it would make a very bad impression to have our school closed. Our enemies would triumph."

Some weeks later an answer came from Mother Mary, one of her infrequent letters. "It seems to me you would do well not to receive these ramblers from other congregations," she wrote. "Generally speaking, they are good only to create disorder."

Mother Theodore agreed with all her heart, but she knew it had not been so simple as that: the Bishop had accepted Mary Doyle even before the group from France had arrived at Saint Mary's. The young woman who was to become Sister Aloysia had been already there and waiting.

CHAPTER NINE

New Missions

c

At Christmas of 1841, Father Perché had come to see the community and he brought fine gifts: two new postulants, one Irish, the other German. Both of them spoke English, and so were real treasures. While at Saint Mary's, he gave a fine talk to the sisters on the formation of the religious spirit.

Father Perché was delighted with the school and happy to know that what was now called Saint Mary's Institute was being founded along the lines of similar institutions in France and that its primary object was to be the higher education of women. The charter that the Sisters of Providence were to be granted a few years later showed clearly that this had been its early intention, for the state charter granted Saint Mary-of-the-Woods all rights and privileges of chartered institutions to conduct schools of higher education and to do all to promote the study of the arts and sciences. It had seemed strange to some when Mother Theodore had announced this as the plan for their future, when as yet some of the pupils were all but ignorant even of the basics of education.

To Father Perché, however, it did not seem so, for he saw that she was building for the future. "You are advanced in your view, of course, Mother," he told her, "but later years will show that your view was the right one.'

She asked his advice in regard to opening another mission; Mother Mary's letter had made it clear that she thought the community should have more houses, but the bishop felt it was too soon. Father Perché agreed with the bishop. "You have done so much already in the short time you have been here," he said. "Your improvements have been made with good taste and good judgment. It is not that I think you would not succeed with another house, for I am certain you would."

His reason for waiting, even if other towns and settlements were urging her to come, was that the religious spirit of her community, still in the process of being formed, might well be injured if she sent her sisters away from the motherhouse too soon. "I have seen this happen in other communities," he said, "and so I advise you to go slowly."

Since the bishop and Father Perché both held like opinions, Mother Theodore decided to wait a few months longer. Then came a request which she decided to answer.

Early in the spring of 1842, the Sisters of Providence of Indiana opened their first mission in the United States, at Jasper, a German settlement some fifty miles from Vincennes, where Father Joseph Kundek was pastor to about fifteen families. He had written more than one letter to Mother Theodore, appealing for a school and sisters to staff it; he could provide for them "a suitable house and maintenance," he wrote, but that was all. That was enough for Mother Theodore, who knew that in these poor Indiana parishes the French rule of her congregation—a contract and suitable revenue fixed in advance—could not at this time be carried out. Instead, her sisters would share the hardships of their pioneer neighbors.

In February she wrote the young pastor, "We shall send you three sisters in March, but I want very much to wait until the feast of St. Joseph, in order to have the installation ceremony on that day. I want to place our first branch establishment under his protection." To this the pastor was happy to agree, because he himself had St. Joseph as his patron saint.

Sister Vincent was to be superior at the new mission; Sister Marie Joseph was chosen because she was the one sister who could speak German; Sister Gabriella was to teach the English classes. Mother Theodore planned to go with them and see them established, for this, their first move from the home convent, was an important event.

It was not a long a trip but a difficult one, as was all travel in Indiana. The spring rains had turned the roads to a sea of mud; the Wabash River was unusually high. As yet there were no trains, no bridges over the river. Only an occasional ferryboat made the crossings; only stagecoaches went over the rough roads and only packet boats navigated the rivers.

From Saint Mary's they traveled in what was called a carriage but which Mother Theodore forthrightly called a wagon—on occasion she had even referred to it as "our tumbril." Sometimes the driver, who was armed with an axe, had to get down and chop away small growth and saplings from the road. When they reached the Wabash, they found it was so high that they had to cross in a little Indian canoe and then plow through the mud to reach the packet boat that was to take them to Vincennes. In the stagecoach they took after leaving the packet, they found a group of women who gave the religious dark looks at first—"but by the time we reached Washington we were friends," wrote Mother Theodore.

At Washington, not far from Jasper, they found waiting for them not only a carriage sent by Father Kundek but also the bishop himself, who announced he was going with them. The bishop rode horseback, sometimes beside them, sometimes ahead of them. Unfortunately at one point he rode so far ahead that he vanished from sight, whereupon the driver took a wrong turn through the forest! Their journey began to take on some of the aspects of the first arrival at Saint Mary's—dense woods, water covering the road, little streams, waterfalls. The only cabins they came to were deserted, and it was little wonder, for they were half sunk in the water. Then, as the women were praying with all their might that God and the Blessed Virgin and the angels would get them out of the place alive, they heard the sound of hammering and came on men constructing a flat boat. One of them went on horseback to guide them back on the road to Jasper, where they found the distraught bishop.

"Together we thanked God for the assistance He had given us and then went to our supper of which we had great need," said the first letter to Saint Mary's, and it chronicled also their wonderful and heartwarming reception in the town. The church to which they had been escorted was full of people, and the bishop gave Benediction. Then the newcomers were taken to their own house, the bishop at their head, carrying the Blessed Sacrament. They walked down a street arched with great trees in which the birds were singing as if in their honor. Back of them walked in a procession all the people who had been in the church. The radiant spring sunshine seemed a happy omen for the future.

Mother Theodore was delighted to see that Jasper was evidently a busy and growing settlement, and Father Kundek, who was very proud of it, was only too glad to tell her its history. Built only a few miles from the old Buffalo Trace, on a little river that flowed into the Wabash, it was located within the confines of the old Vincennes Grant—the first and oldest of the concessions from the Indians to the French in Indiana. Its first settlers had been chiefly Protestants who had come from Kentucky; they came to a rich country where they cleared forests and planted fields of corn and wheat. The settlement had been named Jasper by one of the pioneer wives, because it looked as lovely when she first saw it as the heavenly Jerusalem described by St. John in the Apocalypse.

Later settlers were Catholics, immigrants coming from many parts of Germany and Switzerland. They had suffered great hardships on the sea crossings and were happy in Jasper, even though their lives were hard. Bishop Bruté had stopped at this small settlement and had wept because he knew no German and so could not preach or hear confessions. Young Father de Saint-Palais, who knew something of the language, came occasionally, a long trip on horseback, to say Mass in a private home for the Catholics in the settlement.

Now they had a church and a resident priest, and when Mother Theodore met the blue-eyed, bearded young cleric, she thought that the definition of him by Bishop de la Hailandière was very good. "He is all energy and zeal," the bishop had said.

A comfortable house with a bit of garden was waiting for the sisters. The school was ready, too, and sixty pupils were already promised. Despite all these good prospects, Mother Theodore warned her daughters that they must not expect the future to be all sunshine and singing birds. Her keen eyes had noted that some people who watched the procession go down the street had stared in a very unfriendly way. However, she thought that Father Kundek looked well able to defend those whom she was entrusting to his care.

She stayed with the sisters until May. The trip back was much easier, with pleasant skies and gentle winds. All the way she marveled at the beauty of late spring in Indiana—the tall magnolias and catalpas a riot of white blossoms, flowering vines festooning the oaks and maples. Hummingbirds darted across the path. Sometimes deer stood by the road staring unafraid at the carriage and its occupants. "Our eldest daughter," as she called her first mission, was indeed settled in a lovely place. And she thought again with what truth this fair land was called the New World.

She had been so busy and interested that not until she came home did she realize she was ill. Her sisters did, and they insisted that she rest; she was so tired that she agreed. It was not a serious illness this time, but one of those periods where she was, as she had once expressed it, "not quite so sick as usual." Her strong spirit won as usual over the weak body, and by the end of May Mother Theodore was again at work.

Mother Theodore had been right in her fears about Jasper. Despite the Catholic procession and the happy singing that welcomed them, the sisters found great intolerance in the town, and also indifference among the Catholics themselves. Father Kundek was often away, and then there was no Mass. It was not his fault, for he had two congregations to serve and other settlements to visit occasionally, but it was hard on the sisters to be deprived spiritually of what they needed most.

Then, too, there was a great amount of physical labor, for the sisters did much of the work at the rectory and in the church, as well as caring for the students. The three not only taught classes but also had in their charge the church linen, the priest's laundry, and his meals to cook. They had a cow to milk; they did all their own housework and that of the school. Since Sister Vincent did little teaching, this housework fell chiefly to her, so that after a while she was taken ill from overwork. The alarmed Father Kundek, expressing great remorse for his thoughtlessness, found a young girl to help her. "He neglected nothing to restore me to health," Sister Vincent wrote home gratefully.

Bishop de la Hailandière took great interest in the mission at Jasper, so great, in fact, that he began to interfere with the jurisdiction of the motherhouse regarding it. When Mother Theodore gave orders that conflicted with his, he explained that his were the ones to be obeyed. His reasons were evidently sound to him: once the sisters were sent to a new mission, he wished the jurisdiction of the motherhouse considered at an end and the parish priest to be superior of the new group. This, of course, did not conform to the Providence rule, but Mother Theodore gave in to the bishop as much as possible, even to the extent of not visiting the Jasper house on one occasion when the bishop did not wish her to do so. She did not want to antagonize him and so agreed for that one particular time, but she intended on other occasions to abide by the Providence rule.

Father Kundek did not wish such powers put in his hands. The sisters were a joy to him and made his own lot much easier. He wanted nothing to interfere with their remaining in Jasper. Father Kundek seldom complained of his days and nights of hard work, his long journeys on horseback to serve some distant group of Catholics, but once he said wistfully, when he heard that a friend of his had become a Jesuit, "How happy I would be if I could follow him." Then he looked at Sister Vincent, and there was decision as well as regret in his voice, "But God wanted me here, and here I stay."

The sisters never once complained about their own hard work either. They loved their mission, and it was Father Kundek who made them happy there. He was so good and loved God so much that it was a delight to have him come to talk to them in the evenings when he was at home. When he rode out on a sick call with the Blessed Sacrament, he carried a little bell that he rang when he saw some of his flock in the fields or passed a house where one of his families lived. They knelt as he blessed them and rode on. His people were very proud of him, so proud, in fact, that they wanted to place his name as a candidate for the state legislature, an offer he laughed at and refused.

When he learned that the sisters were planning to go to Saint Mary's for their annual retreat, he was greatly alarmed, for it had not been easy to procure religious for his small parish.

"I am afraid you may not come back," he said unhappily, and he was so distressed that they all but decided not to go. But Mother Theodore, who knew how important this time of retreat was for her sisters, who needed a physical rest and also spiritual aid, succeeded in persuading the priest to let them go by giving her solemn promise that they would return as soon as the retreat was over.

In the autumn of that year, another mission was opened, at Saint Francisville, a very different place from Jasper. It was a small French-Canadian settlement about twelve miles from Vincennes. Years before, Bishop Bruté had stopped there more than once, and he had written of the widow's log cabin where he said Mass—"the loom on one side of me, the cask and pot of soap on the other." Young Father Corbe had been in charge there for a time, but now he was president of the seminary at Vincennes and Father Ducoudray, one of the priests whom Mother Theodore had known at Rennes, and the bishop's cousin, was pastor. He had asked for two sisters for his school and Mother Theodore agreed to send them.

She had chosen Sister Liguori and Sister Augustine, who spoke English, to go there. She was afraid this might prove a lonely enterprise and so went with them when they set out, just as she had gone to Jasper. This time it was in the vivid sun of an October day, over the ancient trail on which George Rogers Clark had gone sixty years before, in that advance on Vincennes that had won the Northwest Territory for the United States.

Father Ducoudray had a church at Saint Francisville, a small house for the sisters, and forty pupils waiting. Since there was no one else to do it, they were to prepare the boys also for First Communion.

On her way back to Saint Mary's, Mother Theodore met Father Sorin, who journeyed with her and her companion as far as Terre Haute. He told her that the Holy Cross brothers had remained at Saint Peter's for only a year. They were even now being settled at South Bend, and they were glad to leave the poor little house that had been theirs. Bishop de la Hailandière said he was very happy to see the brothers getting along so well; they and the sisters were his only joy in life, he had told Father Sorin.

Mother Theodore, even though she found the bishop hard to understand sometimes, knew he had little to make him happy just then. His debts and his responsibilities were huge; some of his churches were in actual danger of being sold to Protestant sects, and he sometimes had to beg money to keep his priests alive. But it was already sadly apparent to those who worked with him that he used his own unhappiness to make others unhappy. He was unpredictable, too, and one never knew what his reactions would be. He had for some reason been very cold to Sister Francis when she first came to America, yet it was he who had been most anxious to have her come. He was increasingly severe to Mother Theodore and began treating her shabbily, even in front of the postulants, when he came to Saint Mary's.

When, after one such occasion, he returned to Vincennes, he wrote her a very sad letter, the gist of which was, "Don't blame the bishop of Vincennes." To Father Buteux he wrote: "It is to our interest to keep these dear Sisters of Providence," and he wrote to Mother Theodore how much he owed her: "That is why I am overwhelmed with a depression that nothing can relieve, not even the remarkable successes God has given you." To Bishop Bouvier he wrote late in 1841, "God has preserved her for us," immediately after one of her severe illnesses. "I am well satisfied with her."

Mother Theodore, to whom all this had been relayed at different times, decided that the bishop's irritation stemmed from conditions and not from the actions of her sisters or herself, and she bore in patience his occasional rudeness and interference.

At first they had not been able to open the free school at Saint Mary's, which they were obligated to open as soon as possible. There had been few children living in the area when the sisters first came there, but even by their second year the Catholic population had increased. In the spring of 1842, the school had been opened in the little frame building once used by Father Buteux as a church. The school had been intended for girls only, but the mothers begged Mother Theodore to take their boys as well and she agreed. It was planned that later classes were to be opened in the basement of the academy building.

Sister Liguori, who now spoke English well, had been in charge before she went to Saint Francisville. When the first children came to the free school at Saint Mary-of-the-Woods, she was to make sad discoveries: she found children who came from Catholic homes who had never heard the name of God, and boys of fifteen who had not yet made their First Communion.

Later Sister Francis took over the teaching, a task she loved. Her stories about her pupils were the delight of the motherhouse. One six-year-old, always anxious to answer, when asked the difference between men and animals and after examining carefully a picture in Sister's Bible, said "One has two legs and the other four." Some of these children knew nothing of genuflecting or joining their hands in prayer; one small lad, after being taught the act of contrition, complained, "I can't think of what I have to say and at the same time remember to make my bow."

This school had required hard work, but it was worth it, the sisters thought, when they had ready their first First Communion class of nine boys and six girls. Each child held a candle and each little girl wore a veil that belonged to one of the novices. With full hearts, the community offered to God these first fruits of their mission at Saint Mary-of-the-Woods.

After its first year, when the village school carried out its closing exercises, Sister Francis arranged prizes for the occasion. They were so simple, however, that Mother Theodore, who had been invited to speak to the children, looked at the display with disfavor. Sister Francis decided that next year she would write to friends in France for little flutes and spinning tops for distribution. However, she herself had been quite proud of the little carved peach stone that was the first prize.

This day school, which had been named Nazareth, led a wandering sort of life, now in the old log cabin church, now in one of the other huts on the grounds, but the pupils were very happy in their school, no matter where it was held. "To teach children, two virtues are essential—justice and kindness," Mother Theodore told her sisters, and it had been proved true success with these neglected untaught children.

By their second winter in Indiana, the sisters had grown accustomed to the cold winters and the limitations of their resources in coping with them. There was no house for the chickens; they roosted in the apple trees and frequently their combs froze. The sisters' watch—their one timepiece—often stopped because of the bitter cold. Sometimes the wine froze in the chalice at Mass. To their surprise an old man in the settlement told them that their first winter at Saint Mary-of-the-Woods had been one of the mildest he had ever known; it had seemed bitter to the French sisters.

The winter evenings, however, were pleasant, with a warm fire of their own logs on the big hearth: Mother Theodore at her desk, writing letters on the pale blue paper she had brought from France; Sister Olympiade, mending; Sister Agnes, having put away the pots and pans, coming in from the kitchen to get warm; the novices preparing work for tomorrow's classes; and in a corner Sister Francis teaching the postulants in her still accented English.

At the beginning, poverty had been their one great difficulty at the motherhouse; no exterior troubles had entered the peaceful convent. Poverty could be borne, and Mother Theodore could bear her frequent illnesses with equanimity. It was when such difficulties as those with Sister Aloysia happened that life became really hard. Even now, difficulties caused by Sister Aloysia were still troubling the community. Many of their former boarders were at her school in Terre Haute, as well as some new students who had originally promised to come to Saint Mary's. There was nothing to be done about it for the time being, save to go on with their own excellent teaching and wait for future vindication.

The bishop made life difficult at times, too, by his insistence on doing things that Mother Theodore could easily have carried out herself. He wanted to go about everything with great speed; every plan must be carried out immediately.

"In this country everything is done fast," he told her. "Nothing comes slowly," he would say impatiently when she drew back from some idea he had presented, like the reception of certain new members or their too speedy admission to the habit and the vows. Her long and careful French training and her obligation to the rule made Mother Theodore want to go slowly and carefully, but the bishop was caught up in the tempo of the New World and as eager to make haste as any American.

On the other hand, Mother Theodore would tell herself, the bishop was good to her community. He gave them money from his own inadequate resources, but it was also true that he demanded much in return. That year he had had a little church built to replace the one that had burned before they came. It was of course a diocesan charge, but sometimes the sisters' fund was called on to help with the decorating, and the sisters were expected to take care of it.

This tiny church had taken a good deal of money, but there was little doubt that the bishop really enjoyed ordering a new building, whether a cathedral or a small mission church. When he began to suggest additions to the motherhouse, Mother Theodore wrote to Mother Mary: "All this is very nice, but it must be paid for, and I would a thousand times rather have our little log cabin than owe debts on a new one."

Her sisters were beginning to be greatly distressed about the attitude of the bishop towards Mother Theodore's illnesses. The year before, he had insisted on a doctor from Vincennes and good care for her; now he seemed indifferent about her condition and the community had recourse only to the local doctors, whose methods were not those of the skillful Dr. Baty.

Then, evidently not content with the unfortunate affair of Sister Aloysia, the bishop during 1842 produced another prospective member for the community—"thirty-one, condition good, *fortune belle*" [sic], he described her. Mlle. Bernard had had some two years before been rejected at Ruillé, but she had now come to the United States and made her way to Vincennes. It was considered all but certain that she had been encouraged in coming by the bishop.

His request that she be received into the community alarmed Mother Theodore, who had already had a communication about her from Mother Mary. The latter had counseled against receiving her if she came. Mother Theodore had not talked with the newcomer for five minutes before she was certain that she had not the shadow of a vocation. Reluctantly, and chiefly in deference to the wishes of the other professed sisters, Mother Theodore took the young woman into the house, still opposed to her as a prospective member. Mother Theodore was also worried by the fact that if the bishop continued to act as if he could admit anyone this sort of thing could happen again and again. Surely if she was permitted nothing else, she should have the power to make her own selections regarding new members of the community.

During her first weeks in the community, the newcomer was humble and quiet and did exactly what was asked of her. Mother Theodore breathed more easily and thought perhaps she had been wrong in her first judgments. A few weeks later, however, Sister Francis came to her in great dismay. As assistant in the novitiate, she had been in close contact with the new postulant and was evidently alarmed about her.

"Never have I met a mind like hers, Mother," she said. "She is enough to cure one forever of having the smallest delusions. She tells me I told her things I never dreamed or thought, much less said. She takes dreams for realities—and what dreams!"

The honest bewilderment on Sister Francis's face would have been amusing had she not been so serious. "Just now she said to me mysteriously, 'Have no uneasiness, Sister. I have seen all but I will tell nothing.' I thought it time to see you, Mother."

It took the community some months to get the new recruit out of the house, even after she had been asked gently but firmly to leave. This time the bishop did not, as he had in the case of Sister Aloysia, support Mother Theodore in the matter. Mlle. Bernard was finally sent away, but it was over the bishop's openly expressed objections. Evidently she had shared her "visions" with the community and had not done so with the bishop.

It irked him greatly that she was gone, when he had wanted her to stay. One other thing increased his unhappiness regarding the dismissal of Mlle. Bernard: the *"fortune belle"* which she had brought with her as postulant's dowry—the fine sum of eleven hundred dollars—had to be returned to her.

CHAPTER TEN

No Hidden Thorn

ℰ

From the time Mother Theodore left her motherhouse at Ruillé to establish the Sisters of Providence in America, she had never ceased to think with deep affection of her old home. She still considered the mother general there as her beloved mother, and many affectionate letters made that fact plain.

Yet very few letters and few parcels came from her superior. Perhaps to Mother Theodore this was the hardest to bear of all her crosses, heavier than poverty or the bishop's varying attitudes or the loss of pupils and the reputation of her school.

"O my dear Mother, do you at least pray for us and for me in particular?" she wrote. "I do not know which way to turn." But no answer came from Ruillé. There were never any reproaches in Mother Theodore's letters, but once with gentle dignity she wrote, "My heart no longer is sensitive, and all it has suffered seems to have sheathed it in a cuirass which renders it insensible to every shaft." But that was not quite true, for unkindness always hurt this woman who had never really hurt anyone.

Mother Theodore always wanted to keep a connection with the motherhouse in the Old World. If anything, she felt more attached than ever to Ruillé, as did the French sisters; and this affection was in some measure shared by the American sisters, who had never seen the motherhouse in France but who had heard so much about it that they regarded it as the living source of their own community.

To the bishop of Le Mans she wrote too—for he was the friend to whom she could open her heart, to whom she could confide her fears. Even now her community was not well established financially and they were still in an inaccessible forest, she wrote; there were times when she actually did not have bread for her sisters, for the pupils must always be fed before the sisters thought of their own needs. But she added that it was also true that help always came. They were the children of Providence, and Providence was looking out for them.

Other fears filled Mother Theodore's heart, intangible ones sometimes, fears of what might happen to her community, such as her constant terror that those who hated the Church might burn down their house. Convents in the East had been burned, and so the fear had a certain basis of reality. "How often this winter have I not started out of my sleep thinking I heard the flames and saw their terrible light," she wrote the bishop. "When I watch my dear sisters leave the chapel, how often after night prayers have I not said to myself that it is perhaps the last time we shall meet together at the feet of Our Lady."

The letters were also full of thanks to the bishop for the help he sent them from time to time; the money was like a gift from heaven and one more proof that God was watching over them. Once a sum came at a time when Mother Theodore had exactly a dollar in the house, and that had been lent to her; she did not know where to turn for more—and then his gift arrived. "Now we have bread again and some necessary clothing, thanks to your generosity. Shall we not in all truth call you our father?"

She wrote too of her increasing perplexity regarding Bishop de la Hailandiére, who was so good to them in some ways and so difficult in others: "One would require a talent of never seeming to oppose the will or even the desire of our bishop, instead of bringing him always, and by good reasons, to will of his own accord what we desire, and let him think it done as he wished." And that, she admitted, grew very wearing.

By August of 1842, they had at Saint Mary's six professed sisters, nine novices, and a group of postulants. During all that anxious year, the community had grown steadily. With the few troublemakers gone, the spirit of the house was wonderful. The English of the French sisters was improving; the Americans were becoming proficient in French. The first mission was already doing well; the second was ready to function. There was a sense of charity and a deep affection among the sisters and a unity that made up for other things not so pleasant.

In areas outside their own, anti-Catholic agitation was rising, due in part to the growing immigration from the eastern part of the country. This had brought to the midwest area many bitter opponents of the Church, and they sowed seeds of discord among the people already living there. There was also an increasing amount of anti-convent literature—booklets and leaflets and vitriolic newspapers.

In one very painful way this anti-Catholic publicity affected the sisters. The phrase "cash only" came to their ears more and more often, and it grew hard to obtain credit, though they paid their bills as best they could. It had not been Mother Theodore's wish to run bills at all; she was French and accustomed to keep her accounts carefully paid. But the bishop said impatiently, "Do as everyone else does. Pay cash only for small amounts. No one expects ready money." It went against Mother Theodore's deeply ingrained principles to do that.

Bishop de la Hailandière was still paying many of their bills, as he was supposed to do. The money he thus spent had been given to be used expressly for the sisters' needs; it came to him rather than directly to the community only in deference to his position.

The bishop was a man of great generosity, when he had the money and he paid it out freely—often in too much new construction. When he became impoverished, it was the sisters who suffered. Again, tuition was not always paid promptly by the academy pupils; sometimes it was never paid. There were children who were admitted without tuition. However, with all their problems, the community had been able to keep its credit in good standing.

Now, and suddenly, the matter of credit grew very bad. In September the boy who was employed on the farm returned without the provisions he had been sent to get at Terre Haute, with a note from Samuel Crawford, owner of the general store there. Instead of the flour and coffee and sugar that Mother Theodore had ordered came a peremptory demand that she settle her account before he could send them anything further.

For a moment even her brave heart failed her. She had no money on hand. The children must eat, so must the men who worked on their land, and so must the sisters. She suddenly remembered their harvest, which was a good asset for credit. There were at least a hundred and fifty bushels of wheat and the same amount of oats stored in their new barn; there was plenty of corn and hay, of bacon and lard from their pigs, and corn shucks to fill their mattresses. Surely all this would bring them credit at the stores, since it was evidence of their stability.

Even so, she was seriously disturbed by the Crawford demand, for credit once refused might not be easily restored. In fact, others began to ask for their money soon after Crawford, and she wrote to Mother Mary that she was so hounded with demands to pay their outstanding bills that "this money famine may cause our destruction in this country where we thought our congregation was called to do so much good."

She was right to be alarmed, for one day a creditor actually walked into her room with his demand for payment. They owed him very little, only about twenty dollars, and had paid him money on account only the month before. But, as so often happened, a sum of money came unexpectedly, this time from friends in New York, and again the community was saved, even if only temporarily.

During this very difficult time, little help had come from the bishop, who said he was hard up too. Nothing came from the superior general in France. Mother Theodore knew, of course, that Ruillé badly needed its own money for the construction of a new addition to its motherhouse; she knew that every sou of its cost had to be on hand before the ground was broken. She expected little financial aid from that source, but she did need loving words, and none came from Mother Mary. The coldness, the indifference of the superior general towards her daughter in the New World was a thing very difficult to understand.

One bright fact stood out for Mother Theodore: all her sisters stood loyally by her and gave her courage. She thought with special gratitude of Sister Olympiade, for whom no labor, no matter how menial, was too much, who took care of the academy laundry and the mending as well, who was baker for some forty people, who cared for the stock, acted as infirmarian and who, best of all, was always as cheerful as she was efficient.

It was Sister Francis who was perhaps Mother Theodore's greatest comfort and joy. The very opposite of Sister Olympiade, Sister Francis was never able to do any hard work, but her humility and her love of God were a constant inspiration to her superior as well as to the novices whom she trained. At Ruillé, Mother Mary had said Sister Francis was "good only to love God," but it was this love which gave her value to her congregation. As time went on she lost much of her early timidity—no doubt because of her constant work among novices and postulants. Her English was still faulty, but even so she made an excellent teacher, one who taught by example as well as by words. More and more she was put in charge of the convent when Mother Theodore was ill or away on a trip. Of herself she wrote to one of the sisters at Ruillé, "I am a little less disorderly in my affairs, a little more proper in my appearance—but my cap is still always a little crooked."

Sister Basilide was at the academy, Sister Vincent at Jasper, Sister Liguori at Saint Francisville, and so Sister Francis was the only one of the professed sisters at the motherhouse. That was why authority came often to her, a thing which she had never desired. Once when she was temporary head, she said ruefully: "I think the good God placed me here like the straw figures in the cherry tree—to prevent birds from eating the fruit."

Mother Theodore called her the saint in the house, the angel of virtue whose example animated her, "I am in the chapel near her, distracted with temporalities and business, and see her there, lost in God," she said, "and I come away strong again to meet life."

By late summer of 1842, Mother Theodore had had to meet one more of these difficulties of temporalities. The bishop of Vincennes was again demanding rights that the rule did not grant him. On the other hand, Mother Theodore found it all but impossible to refuse him. More than once Father Perché had counseled her to insist on a proper sum of money from the pastor or the church trustees of the missions she was expected to open or operate. He felt, and so did she, that from France should come chiefly advice and aid in interpreting the rule, if that became necessary. But Bishop de la Hailandière was making very clear what he regarded as proper canonical relations: it was not the rule which he wanted to see followed but his own will. It grew increasingly clear, as the matter of more missions came up, that he intended to rule each new mission through its pastor, instead of leaving this to the motherhouse at Saint Mary's. For instance, he did not want Mother Theodore to send an additional sister to help out at Saint Francisville; he did not want her to visit her sisters at Jasper. Each new establishment was to depend completely on the priest in charge, the bishop insisted, and in case of trouble it was the authority of the bishop that was to be invoked. Mother Theodore's authority, according to him, was to end when once she had sent sisters to a new mission.

It was, of course, easy to feel sorry for the bishop, even while one was annoyed with him. He might at that time have welcomed advice, but he had no one to consult. He felt he needed a coadjutor, he had said some months before, one who knew English well, for the bishop's difficulty with that language still made trouble for him. There were money difficulties too. "My situation is insupportable," he wrote to Father Martin. "The Propagation of the Faith is sending less than half what was allocated to me last year…. The future of the diocese is very sad."

Despite his complaints, however, one trouble was that his expenditures were always larger than his very considerable allowances from Europe. But Father Martin offered to come from Logansport to help him, and the bishop accepted thankfully, making him vicar general at Vincennes in the summer of 1842.

However, it soon grew clear to Father Martin, as it had to others before him, that the bishop did not really want advice; he wanted to be agreed with, as Mother Theodore understood well by that time. "He possesses a disposition," she wrote to Bishop Bouvier, "calculated to make a martyr out of its possessor, but still more out of those who must bear with him." She added that he was also pious and zealous and so might be forgiven this other trait—"but it is true that he is jealous of his authority and wants to do everything himself, with no delegation of anything."

The bishop of Le Mans wrote encouragingly, and his letters gave her reassurance when it was most needed. When matters with the bishop of Vincennes became too difficult, it was the bishop of Le Mans who spoke the authoritative word that eased them. When she wrote him of her doubts that she would ever make her group into a fine community, he reassured her. When she was cast down by responsibilities, he heartened her. Perhaps, Mother Theodore sometimes felt, without him the congregation would never have weathered the darker days of its first years.

Poverty, adaptation to a new environment, a temperamental bishop—all these could be borne. Now came a much worse thing.

October 2 was a beautiful day. All summer there had been excellent growing weather. Only the day before, the last of their harvest had been stored in the granary. Work was almost over for the season, and farming implements were stored away in their fine new barn. The harvest had exceeded even the best hopes of Mother Theodore, and the provisions in the barn gave promise of a far better winter than the one before. The day was Holy Rosary Sunday, and also Mother Theodore's birthday; she was forty-four years old.

She was sitting in her room talking with one of the novices and looking from her window at the lovely vista of farm and forest, hazy in the warm midwest autumn. Suddenly they heard voices shouting and saw to their horror that one of the small houses on the premises was burning and that sparks had already set fire to the roof of the barn. There had been no rain for several weeks, and what had been ideal weather for the harvesting now proved calamitous. The flames spread rapidly and it was soon clear there would be little chance of extinguishing the blaze. There was no water except the little stream in the ravine that supplied their daily needs.

The house and the barn were all but gone before farmers in the area could get there. By that time trees had caught fire, and neighbors who brought axes to help the workmen at Saint Mary's cut them down in order to stop the danger of a forest fire and the burning of other houses. Sparks were falling on everyone, on clothing and hair. There were slight burns, but no one was badly hurt.

The sisters and the children helped to fight the fire as best they could, but it was soon evident that nothing would save their barn or the precious stores it held. Mother Theodore, who had helped too, finally stopped.

By four o'clock the fire was out, but the two buildings were a mass of ashes and burned timbers. Mother Theodore gave it all one last look, and then turned to the others. "The Lord has given and the Lord has taken away," she said quietly, and, even as she spoke, several of the big beams collapsed, making the ruin complete. She went into the convent and came back with the wine they had brought from Soulaines that had been carefully saved to use at Mass. Mixed with sugar and water, the wine was offered to the neighbors and farm hands who had worked so hard to help them.

During the evening, men kept watch lest another blaze start, but the little fires that sprang up were easily extinguished. No more buildings burned, but their barn was gone—"and our dear wheat all threshed," wrote Mother Theodore to Mother Mary.

The cause of the fire was never learned. It might well have been incendiary in origin, and thus justified Mother Theodore's constant fear. A fence was broken down on one side of the woods, and some theorized that the fire might have been set while all were at Mass in the chapel and then covered so that it would break out a few hours later.

Perhaps it had been merely an accident due to a workman smoking too close to the barn and scattering a few still burning ashes on the parched grass. What mattered was not the reason so much as the fact: a loss of some four thousand dollars in building and equipment and food, a community destitute just as winter was coming.

The effect of the calamity on friends and neighbors was immediate and heart-warming. Mr. Crawford, who had cut off their credit, came to tell them that he would give them all they needed from his own supplies and they could pay him at their convenience. Bishop de la Hailandière promptly sent barrels of sugar and coffee and a sum of money. Their old New York friends responded; Mr. Byerley sent a hundred dollars and Madame Parmentier sixty dollars. As soon as word reached Ruillé, Mother Mary sent a letter of consolation and a thousand francs. Bishop Bouvier sent his prayers and five hundred francs: "I wish I could give you a great deal more. Let us hope God grants you sums from other quarters." Next month came three thousand more francs through him; M. de la Bertaudière had just heard of their loss and wanted them to have this sum.

By the time that Mother Theodore had written her grateful thanks to the bishop of Vincennes, he was again ready to find fault, this time with the wording of her letter. There was too much sadness and lamenting in it, he thought, and added, "Be calm, and for my consolation do not write such things to me." There was far too much complaining about the fire in her letter, he told her. The increasing irritability that everyone was noting in him came out strongly in this letter: "Have a little confidence in God—I mean practically—why not ask for things without always waiting for an order from me?"

Unfortunately some of the money sent by her friends did not reach the convent until winter was well on them, and it was to be a very hard and cold winter. Forest and field were buried deep in snow for months. The community at Saint Mary's went on with life as best they could. They gathered their apples and potatoes, a great deal of this done by the sisters themselves, for they had to send away their helpers since they could no longer pay them. They kept only one man. The old Thralls gristmill was sold for a thousand pounds of wheat flour; three calves were exchanged for corn. Tuition came to help, but slowly. Children who paid no tuition were still in the majority.

However, this was their one bright spot—their school. By the year's end they had the promise of more students. The teaching was improving all the time; the teachers were better able to carry out their work as their experience increased and the French sisters began to speak better English. They were much reassured by the promise of the return of some of their former pupils as well as by letters with word that others would come for the next term. In this, their school, the sisters knew they must place their hopes for the future.

Late that autumn one of their prayers was granted: they received a permanent chaplain. Some time before, the bishop had removed Father Buteux entirely from the motherhouse and from the parish; the community was given a temporary chaplain, Father Antoine Parret. Now word came that Father Corbe, director at the Vincennes seminary, would take the post.

Bishop de la Hailandière had been slow about making this appointment, feeling that Father Corbe was badly needed where he was. He was still young, only thirty-six, a scholarly retiring man of artistic tastes. He had come to the United States in Bishop Bruté's group, and the latter had placed the young Breton at Saint Francisville. The bishop had been devoted to the young priest and Father Corbe had been at his bedside when he died.

"Notre Père," as Father Corbe came to be known at Saint Mary-of-the-Woods, was indeed to prove a father in every way. He was a tall, dark man who looked like a throwback to one of the early Celts of the land from which he came. He had taught a class in drawing at the seminary, and he was also an ardent botanist. In search of specimens he had more than once come to Saint Mary's and stopped to visit, often discoursing to the sisters on another enthusiasm of his, the photographic experiments of Daguerre.

Several of the sisters had known him in France when he was a young priest. To see him, formerly the decorous and well clad abbé, tutor of noblemen's children at Rennes, here in Indiana clad in the butternut brown of the Hoosier frontiersman, was at first startling, and especially, as the dismayed Mother Theodore noted it was, "not very clean homespun, either." But they would take good care of him now, just as he promised to take good care of them. They were as happy in having him as he was happy to come.

He arrived at Saint Mary-of-the-Woods in late November, and with him came peace to a sorely tried community for whom this had been a very hard year. Christmas was a sweet and peaceful day. The new chaplain sang High Mass, the first to be celebrated in their forest. All the pupils were there, for no one traveled more than was necessary in the winter. There was a Mass for the people of the area later in the morning, with the sisters singing the plain chant of the service.

On Holy Innocents' Day, which was also the feast of St. Theodore and the feast day of Mother Theodore, the sisters arranged a party for the children, with as good a dinner as could be assembled.

There were all the usual toasts, and one of the pupils, Martha Richardson, recited a poem in the superior's honor. Winter did not permit the making of a flower wreath, so ran the poem, and instead they had made for her a spiritual wreath, culled from the love of their hearts:

> "No hidden thorn in it you'll find
> To pain the brow 'tis meant to bind."

Sister Francis, looking at her beloved superior enjoying with such delight this unexpected tribute, prayed that this poem might prove true for her dear Mother Theodore all the years of her life.

CHAPTER ELEVEN

The Queen and the Mother

℩

At last the winter was over, a winter so cold that hands stuck tight to icy doorknobs and deaths from freezing were listed in every town. Once Sister Olympiade, going to the shed to milk the cow, found the animal completely encased in a thin coating of ice.

When in April the ice on the rivers melted, the winterlocked settlements greeted with joy the steamboat's first whistle on the Wabash River. There would still be cold days and there would be roads full of water from melting ice, but the worst was over.

The community of Saint Mary's had managed to get through the winter even with diminished provisions; the sisters lived chiefly on corn pone and gave the children what wheaten bread they baked; vegetables and fruit carried them through.

On the first day of Lent there was inaugurated at Saint Mary-of-the-Woods the Forty Hours Devotion, its first private observance in the United States. The sisters did not know it, however, nor were they planning any new devotion. They had long been accustomed to observing it in their own French convents, for in Europe this was already an old custom, having begun as early as the first half of the sixteenth century, when at Milan it was first held to beg divine protection against the Turks.

For three days the Blessed Sacrament was exposed in the little convent chapel. Benediction was given each afternoon by Father Corbe, and people came from all around to attend.

Mother Theodore, always grateful when Mother Mary treated her as if she were actually her daughter, had written happy thanks in answer to the superior's letters about their troubles of the year before. She had thanked her for her generosity, for she knew how little money Mother Mary herself had and how heavy were the expenses at Ruillé, but she added, "a hundred times more do I love your good letters than the money. That is Theodore again, you will say, always running after affection—yes, Mother, after yours."

Yet such warm expressions, all but begging for an affectionate response, rarely brought an answer. Long months would elapse before a letter would come to her from Ruillé. Mother Mary's attitude towards her daughter in America and the American mission remained always detached, formal, almost cold.

For some time Mother Theodore had been considering, though not for sentimental reasons, a voyage to Europe. For one thing, there was a real need of discussing with Mother Mary and the council the final status of the American community, matters of finance, of building, of opening more missions, for which requests came in continually. Older and wiser heads at the motherhouse could counsel her. Another reason, equally if not more important, was that of securing financial aid for her congregation so that it could survive and expand. France was known to be generous with its gifts for the missions.

Bishop de la Hailandière, who had pleaded his own poverty as the reason for giving them very little aid in recent months, thought it an excellent idea. "France is so charitable," he said, "so zealous for missionaries that I am sure you will find help there. Tell them that despite all I have been able to do for you you are yet not securely founded. Tell them of your heavy debts and that I have exhausted my resources for you. Tell them about your log homes and your fire losses. Tell them how poor the country is and how many children you must teach *gratis*. Every word will be the simple truth."

He wrote a letter of introduction for her to use, especially among former colleagues who would remember him. At the same time he gave her a letter for Bishop Bouvier, in which he explained that he could no longer help the Sisters of Providence as he had been doing. His other needs were increasing—a home for the seminary, the great need of orphanages, care of the brothers under Father Sorin, the priests of his diocese who were so poor they could not support themselves. All this meant that he must limit his aid to the sisters.

He gave Mother Theodore a list of people in France who might be interested in her work. He hoped she would go to Paris, where he was certain she could collect a great deal. He promised her that if she returned with ten thousand francs to enlarge her academy, he would give her congregation the deeds for Saint Mary-of-the-Woods, which he still held as the property of the diocese.

To this offer Mother Theodore said nothing, for she was aware that the Picquet family had paid thirty thousand francs for its purchase with the proviso that it was to belong to the Sisters of Providence. However, this was not the time to speak of it.

In a few weeks the plans were all but completed. Then the bishop grew uneasy about having Mother Theodore replaced for even a few months. He worried about the long hard voyage; even after he had again decided she ought to go, he hesitated. Like the lawyer he had once been, he examined both sides of the argument. When Mother Theodore finally said that her sisters approved, he agreed that she should go. In fact, he soon began making all the arrangements himself.

For Mother Theodore, too, it had been a difficult decision to make; it meant leaving her community in administrative and financial straits, leaving them uncertain as to how soon she would be able to return and what the bishop might plan to do while she was away. She was leaving them very poor; they might even have to borrow food at times—and the people they borrowed from were poor themselves. But how good her neighbors were, she thought gratefully, remembering the day a neighbor had come to say she still had six hills of potatoes in her garden. "I'll keep two for my family and you can have the rest," she told Mother.

She had wanted to put Sister Vincent in charge of the motherhouse, but Father Kundek refused to let her leave Jasper, and so Sister Francis was made local superior and Sister Basilide was left in charge of the academy. Sister Francis was still under thirty years of age, but she would be intelligent in meeting problems that might come up. Then, too, she would have the wise counsels of Father Corbe who, after only a few months with them at Saint Mary's, had already proved his great value to the community.

As companion Mother Theodore was taking with her Sister Mary Cecilia, who had been Eleanor Bailly, and who spoke excellent French. Mother Theodore wanted her to spend some time in the novitiate at Ruillé and also study advanced music.

On April 26, 1843, Mother Theodore and Sister Mary Cecilia left Saint Mary's. The superior looked so tired and was so thin that she was no sooner gone than her sisters began regretting her leaving at all. In fact, some wondered if they would ever see her again. At Saint Mary's she could secure loving care and the attention of a good doctor in her many and very serious illnesses. Would she find the same good care, the same affection in the places where she was going? All they could do was pray for her, and this they did, often and fervently.

When the two religious reached New York and were crossing the ferry to go to Madame Parmentier's home in Brooklyn, Mother Theodore spoke of the time she had last crossed there and had been happy to see a French flag on a ship in the river. Now, she said with a smile, perhaps an American flag on a ship at Le Havre would make her homesick for Saint Mary's.

At the Parmentier home they were received with delight, and also with the news that Mr. Byerley and all his family had been received into the Church. A letter from Baltimore was waiting for them. It was from Bishop de la Hailandière, who had gone to the Fifth Provincial Council there and had written very excitedly of the increasing Catholic life in the land—"six new sees have been erected, which brings the total to twenty-three. Oh, what a future for us! And a large portion is reserved for you in this future." It was a very pleasant letter, with not a single unkind or questioning phrase in it, and she prayed that this mood would continue during her absence.

Madame Parmentier had collected a sum of money for the sisters to help defray their expenses; she went with them to their ship, the *Sylvia*, a sailing vessel that the sisters were taking because it was so much cheaper than the newer and faster steamships.

The voyage was a long one—thirty days—but the sea was calm and quiet all the way. The two religious spent their days in prayer and reading and meditation. Also, Mother Theodore instructed Sister Mary Cecilia in some of the customs of the French community, thankful that she had brought with her a member so mature and thoughtful.

She gave thought to her present position with the bishop of Vincennes and planned to talk freely about him to Bishop Bouvier. She knew that disaffection was increasing in the diocese, that some of the best of the clergy there were leaving or planning to go. She knew that he was turning more and more to her community, for they were the only ones who never acted contrary to his orders. However, considering his impetuous ways, she was glad she had left trustworthy sisters in charge at Saint Mary's.

They reached Le Havre in early June and took the diligence, just as Sister Theodore had done three years before when she left Ruillé. They drove through Normandy from Honfleur, past orchards and fields and over ancient cobbled streets, past cathedrals and castles, to the old town of Le Mans, which was their first stop, so that Mother Theodore could call on the bishop, tell him their plans, and show him Bishop de la Hailandière's credentials for her.

The bishop was happy to see his daughter again. He thought her much too thin but otherwise that she looked well. After he read the letter of the bishop of Vincennes, he added as postscript words of his own: "We are compassionate in their great need to these sisters whom we have given to this bishop and whom he recommends to the liberality of charitable souls."

To see Bishop Bouvier again was worth the whole long voyage, thought Mother Theodore. He looked very weary, but he was as kindly and as understanding as ever. It was good to talk with him, for he knew her story perhaps better than anyone; he had been associated with the Ruillé community for years; he had written their second rule, was still their ecclesiastical superior and had followed closely the course of the American mission. Best of all, his advice had authority behind it, for he was one of the foremost authorities in Europe on canon law and theology.

When they left him, they went directly to Ruillé, and with joy Mother Theodore saw again the beloved first home of her religious life, knelt in the chapel where she had pronounced her vows, walked in the little woods where she had cheered old Abbé Dujarié with a bowl of soup. The grounds were more extensive now, and the large new wing on the convent had been completed.

Mother Mary seemed glad to see her and gave her a generous welcome. When Mother Theodore said, "I hope you don't think my coming was a rash undertaking, Mother." Mother Mary said, "No, not if it would help your community." She scrutinized her daughter closely. "You are thin, my Theodore," she said. "Have you been well in the new land?"

Mother Theodore nodded and smiled, not wanting to dwell upon the many and hard illnesses she had endured there. "It is America, Mother. Everyone goes so fast that one has no time to put on flesh."

The sisters who had known her found their Sister Theodore changed and quieter, but with a new air of authority about her. They soon realized from her conversation that though she still loved France dearly she spoke with an even deeper affection of her *Sainte Marie-des-Bois*.

The real surprise to the community, however, was her companion who, they had learned from letters, was a *demi-Indienne*, and who they had no doubt expected would be something of a savage. Instead they met a well-educated young religious with graceful manners, who spoke an excellent and fluent French. Was this an example of the *sauvage* they had read of in missionary appeals, they asked one another in surprise.

After a few days of rest and talks with Mother Mary and the novice mistress, Mother Theodore was to set out on her collecting tour. She planned first to pay a few visits to relatives and friends and began with a visit to the Le Fer de la Motte family. There to her joy she learned that two more members of the family, Eugénie and Cécile, Irma's sisters, were eager to become Sisters of Providence and come to America.

When she went to see her sister Marie at Étables, she found her happy and contented. Mother Theodore knelt in the church where she had made her First Holy Communion and walked with her young nieces to the beach where she had spent so much of her time as a child. The girls listened with rapt attention as their aunt told them fascinating stories of the convent in the woods and of life in Indiana. The elder, Marie-Thérèse, who was sixteen, confided to her aunt that some day she was coming to America to be a Sister of Providence too.

From Soulaines, where she saw the completed church under the guidance of "Monsieur," who showed her every part of it, she went on to Tours. There the bishop took up a collection for *Les Pauvres Soeurs des Bois*. However, as she went through other cities and towns, she began to realize sadly that this was not a good time of the year to have come to collect funds. Harvests had been sparse that year, and money was scarce in the farming communities. This had affected the cities too, and many who would have helped her had nothing to give.

In early September, Mother Theodore and Sister Mary Cecilia returned to Ruillé for the annual retreat. She felt that a definite decision would have to be made regarding the status of the Indiana community, and that she must have guidance regarding her own work and powers. In 1839, Bishop de la Hailandière had agreed to any conditions that were laid down for the sisters, but he asked that Mother Theodore be allowed to come and see for herself before any decision was arrived at. Mother Mary and Bishop Bouvier did not view the situation the same way. Mother Mary issued a letter of obedience to Mother Theodore, stating the position of the latter as superior general of the community, the separation of Saint Mary-of-the-Woods from

Ruillé, and only the mutual interdependence of the two institutes through the ties of love and prayer.

Many of the crosses of Mother Theodore's first year were caused by the failure of Bishop de la Hailandière to come to a decision regarding his wishes, so that if his plans could not be accepted by Mother Theodore and her sisters the little community would be free to return to France or to settle elsewhere. No decision could be made, however, since the sisters could obtain no hint of the bishop's intentions, except such as were to cause them worry and alarm.

In the peace and quiet of the long voyage to France, Mother Theodore had time to reflect quietly on their situation, and it may have been then that she formulated the eleven questions covering every aspect of their status and life: their independence of Ruillé, her own powers as superior general and foundress, her right to admit or refuse women to the novitiate or to vows after informing the bishop of her reasons, her jurisdiction over the houses formed, the rights of the bishop over the community, and many other points.

These questions were discussed during the retreat by Bishop Bouvier and Mother Mary, and definite answers given, clearing away forever the uncertainty that had been a great source of suffering to Mother Theodore. The original plan to separate the new institute in Indiana completely from Ruillé was reaffirmed and was to be made irrevocable as soon as possible.

Mother Theodore regretted the separation from Ruillé, but she knew that no other course was practical. The French sisters did not lose the right of return to Ruillé with the consent of the bishop of Vincennes, but the American sisters were to be Mother Theodore's sole responsibility. One thing that distressed the harassed foundress was that she could no longer expect that sisters trained at Ruillé would be sent to Indiana. From that time forward she was to depend on the providence of God, America, and her own resources.

Mother Theodore and Sister Mary Cecilia departed for Paris, there to resume her quest for funds. When they reached the metropolis, Mother

Theodore took her companion first to the Lady chapel of the Church of Notre Dame des Victoires. There they committed their little community to the great confraternity and then walked about the chapel looking at its walls lined with ex-votos, all bearing the words *Merci à Marie*. Kneeling among the many people there, priest and lay, poorly and fashionably dressed, Mother Theodore prayed for her little congregation, whose convent bore Our Lady's name, and asked Mary's help in her search for funds to help it grow and flourish and benefit America.

Then she and Sister Mary Cecilia went to the Visitandine Convent, where they were given hospitality and where the religious made the visiting sisters a part of their community, admitting them to refectory, choir and recreation. They took a deep interest in the work of the Providence Sisters in America and promised to collect for them after they had gone home.

When Mother Theodore went to the officials of the Society for the Propagation of the Faith, they were very kind to her. They told her that a rule of the organization was that no separate allocation of funds be made to congregations of women, and that was why they had given funds for the sisters to their bishop. In her necessity, however, they would waive the rule, since Bishop Bouvier had written to them about Mother Theodore. They promised her a sum to take back to America with her.

Mother Theodore decided they would go home soon. "We have done what we can here," she said a little sadly, for it was true that the collections had not been as large as she had hoped. She planned to stay a longer time in Paris, feeling that she might find friends there, the very ones she needed. She was right, for she made some very good friends, and chief among them were a journalist, a bishop, and a queen.

The journalist was young Leon d'Aubineau, editor of *L'Univers*, the Catholic Party organ, whom she had met some time before. He promised to write two articles about her work in his paper; later he would have them printed in a pamphlet to be distributed among interested people. Also he would recommend her work to the Conferences of St. Vincent de Paul, from which some fine contributions were to come to her later.

The bishop was Monseigneur Forbin-Janson, primate of Lorraine, who made the two women religious very welcome in his home and at his table and placed his carriage at their disposal for their endless journeys through the city. When a priest expressed some surprise at seeing the religious at his table, a very unusual favor, the bishop said laughing, "My dear man, the Sisters of *Sainte Marie-des-Bois* are not women. They are angels, and that is why they are here." He preached a charity sermon for them and brought in additional money.

The third friend came to them unexpectedly. Mother Theodore had gone through her list of names, only to find that a great many people were still away from the city and so out of reach; they were in their summer homes. Finally she had only one name left on her list, a Mlle. Labrouche, who turned out to be the governess of the children of M. du Nord, Minister of Justice. This woman proved very sympathetic, and at her request the sisters were given an interview with the minister, who suggested that Mother Theodore write a letter to the queen, a woman known for her charity. He would himself deliver it to her. "Ask for an audience—nothing more," he said, and Mother Theodore wrote as he suggested.

Some days later came a letter: Queen Marie-Amélie would receive her at the Tuileries that very afternoon. Meantime Mother Theodore had told Sister Mary Cecilia something about this queen, the niece of Marie Antoinette and wife of Louis-Philippe. When the revolution of 1830 had put her husband on the French throne, Marie-Amélie had been very reluctant to accept the high position, perhaps fearing the fate of kings and queens in those troubled times in France.

In 1843, however, the royal couple were still very popular; they were also said to have the most splendid court in all Europe, and the king had acquired a reputation as a tactful statesman. The queen was a very devout woman who, in the midst of splendor, lived very simply, heard Mass daily, and spent much of her time reading the many petitions for help she received, and even more in acting upon them.

The two sisters found the queen a very gracious lady, deeply interested in their congregation and in the people of the New World. When she learned that Sister Mary Cecilia was an American, she spoke to her in excellent English; she was even more interested when she learned that this charming, well-bred religious was part Indian.

When the queen asked Mother Theodore how she could be of help to her, Mother Theodore told her very simply of the special assistance she needed: money for the steamer passage back to America—for herself, Sister Mary Cecilia, and the postulants they were taking back with them.

When the queen learned the amount she paid, "Oh, that will not be enough. You will need something for small expenses and for your arrival. I shall speak to the king and to my children, too."

As they said goodbye to the queen, she leaned over to look intently at Mother Theodore and took her hands in her own. "Oh, Sister, let us save souls," she said urgently, and there was such deep longing in her eyes and her voice that Mother Theodore was to remember it for a long time afterwards; sometimes in moments of discouragement she would repeat to herself the words of the queen: "Sister, let us save souls!"

At one point in the conversation, Mother Theodore made an odd mistake and called the queen, "Mother." Immediately she apologized for the slip. The queen smiled. "Oh, call me that," she said, "call me your mother. It is a title very dear to me—much dearer than Your Majesty."

When the audience was nearly over, Madame Adelaide, the king's sister, came in, and learning who the visitors were and why they were there, listened to the rest of the conversation. "I think five hundred francs would be a good sum to give Sister Theodore," she said, evidently fearing her sister-in-law's liberality. But Queen Marie-Amélie said quickly, "No, no, sister. I promised to pay their passage, and I intend to do that."

Madame Adelaide said a bit tartly that Her Majesty had a very large heart but she had so many good works to give to that one had sometimes to restrain her generosity. The queen only smiled and assured Mother Theodore that she was to have the promised amount. Mother Theodore, who during the past weeks had gone up and down many stairs and into many offices, sometimes receiving only a few *sous*—and not always with such kindness as this—said goodbye and promised to keep the queen always in her prayers.

When the sisters returned to Ruillé, Mother Theodore found that the queen had kept her word: the money to defray their steamer expenses was already waiting for her.

Later, when they reached their ship at Le Havre, they were to find additional gifts from the queen. One was a large basket of fine food—"chosen from her own table by Her Majesty," said the accompanying card. The other was an oil painting of Marie-Amélie, a very good likeness.

"I shall place it in the convent parlor as soon as we reach Saint Mary's," promised Mother Theodore.

CHAPTER TWELVE

"Mend the Broken Platters" (1844)

C

For some days Mother Theodore had been well aware that it was time to return home. Her community needed her. Trouble with Bishop de la Hailandière had arisen at Saint Mary's, just as she had been afraid it might. Her friends urged her to remain longer; it seemed a pity that she should leave France just then, they said; the next months would be far better for collecting funds than the previous ones had been.

It was the letters from home that made her feel she must go soon, despite the advantages in staying longer. Things had grown difficult for those left in charge at the motherhouse due to the insistent demands of the bishop, so letters told her. When Bishop Bouvier had read these letters, he agreed that she ought to go. So did Mother Mary. "If your visit to France has been useful, your presence at home is more necessary now," she said succinctly. And Mother Theodore knew she was right.

She had known for some time that all was not well at home in America. Letters detailing trouble had begun to come across the ocean from Indiana a month after the sisters left Saint Mary's, and not only to her but to Bishop Bouvier. Filled though they were with details and requests for advice, the story of what was going on both at Vincennes and at Saint Mary's was difficult to understand.

The first disturbing news had come to Mother Theodore from the bishop of Vincennes. He wrote to her mysteriously of "events that have taken place at Saint Mary's" and that "bear heavily on my mind and heart, coming as they do from those to whom I have shown much friendliness." He added that there had been an election in the community; Mother Theodore had been elected superior general for three years. He had himself appointed Sister Basilide to take Mother Theodore's place until her return.

This last statement was completely incomprehensible, for everything about it was wrong. There was to be an election for superior general eventually, but as yet there were not the twenty electors necessary, nor was there any sister qualified to fill that position. The bishop of Le Mans had granted to the congregation a dispensation that appointed Mother Theodore foundress and superior general "for as long as the interests of the new community require, and until both the bishops of Le Mans and Vincennes should formally decide otherwise."

It would therefore seem that the bishop of Vincennes ought to have conferred with his colleague before acting, and Bishop Bouvier expressed an understandable surprise when he heard of this step.

"I know that he is a good man and means well and is prompted by the best of motives," he said, but it was clear that he was puzzled.

"St. Teresa said her greatest suffering was to be persecuted by good people," said Mother Theodore. "I have sometimes felt like that about the bishop," and she showed him an earlier letter from that prelate in which he had written, "The longer your letters are the more I am pleased with them. I could not express all I feel for you; you will know it only when the good God allows you to see the most intimate feelings of my heart."

Bishop Bouvier knew more about the actions of the bishop of Vincennes than Mother Theodore realized, for clerics and others had brought him word from time to time. The bishop, they were all agreed, was a pleasant man when pleased, but otherwise he was very difficult; when something went wrong, he was apt to make those about him quail. He was an affable and generous man until things went badly. He was sometimes too severe, and sometimes too indulgent. He found it difficult to deputize any of his work. He had a vicar general, a director of the seminary, a chaplain for Saint Mary's, a rector for his cathedral, all able men—and not one had the power to do a thing without his permission. "All over the diocese he stretches his hand," said one priest, "and in consequence there is unrest and uneasiness, and it is growing."

Bishop Bouvier could in some ways sympathize with his colleague. The Vincennes diocese included all of Indiana and the eastern third of Illinois. Bishop de la Hailandière had inherited many of Bishop Bruté's difficulties. Then, too, the city of Vincennes had remained a small settlement; it was not growing as had been expected and many were beginning to think that it had been a poor choice for an episcopal see.

Letters from her sisters went into particulars as the bishop's did not, and it was clear that he had not waited long after Mother Theodore's departure to meddle in convent affairs.

When he paid his first visit to Saint Mary-of-the-Woods, he had asked when they planned to hold their retreat. The sisters replied that they were going to wait until Mother Theodore's return. They were afraid, though they did not say so aloud, that if they held it sooner the bishop might request a clothing and a profession of members not yet sufficiently prepared. This decision had apparently annoyed the bishop, who began to talk about Mother Theodore's "despotism" and then of what he called her "horrible fault," which was her insistence on preserving the rule. He spent several hours trying to win Sister Francis to his point of view.

"To oppose me is to oppose God," he told her firmly. "I alone have any authority over you, and the least priest in the diocese has more power over your community than has Mother Theodore."

A week later he returned to ask if they would accept a new house at Vincennes, and added, "Say yes or no, and do not make the absence of your Mother or any similar nonsense an excuse."

Sister Francis said quietly that the Emmitsburg Sisters of Charity, who were still there, were doing an excellent work; she would not wish to interfere with their little mission. The following day, the bishop sent a letter to the sisters through Father Corbe, and their chaplain brought it to them in pained silence; it defined the bishop's rights, and among them was the power to place and replace sisters and to change their rule if he wished. He insisted that the retreat be held soon, and he saw to it that it was. At its close he came and did exactly what they had feared he would do: he received the vows of two sisters who were far from ready and on whose fitness for vows the other professed members had not even been asked to pass.

On the feast of the Assumption, the bishop came to the convent again, and this time he called to him the four older professed sisters, Sister Francis, Sister Basilide, Sister Liguori, Sister Olympiade, and the two newly-professed, Sister Mary Xavier and Sister Agnes. He announced that they were to elect a superior general; he had deposed Mother Theodore, whose term, he said, had expired.

The amazed sisters decided it would be best to follow his orders and did so. When the votes were counted, they were all for Mother Theodore, and the bishop then invested Sister Basilide with full orders until Mother Theodore's return. Poor Sister Basilide, informed of the honor awarded her, was overwhelmed with embarrassment, but she knew if she refused it would only make matters worse. The best thing was to say nothing, continue managing the house, and pray that her superior would not stay away too long.

It was such startling information as this that made Mother Theodore decide not to linger in France. Mother Mary expressed her own feelings when she said, "All the gold you may collect by staying longer will not repay you for the injury that your absence might cause to the spiritual health of your community." When Mother Mary heard about the surprising election and the appointment, she said, "Make haste, my daughter, to fly to Vincennes to mend the broken platters. You must be there to watch over your flock and prevent the enemy from sowing cockle among the good seed." Mother Theodore smiled a little sadly to see that for once her superior was wholly on her side.

Sister Basilide had written too, much troubled at being put in such a position by the bishop and hoping her superior would understand why she had accepted the office. She also had a personal problem: "When we came to

America I had specially asked whether we were separated from Ruillé, and I was told no. Now if things are to be changed, this would seem like another community, and I would want to go back to Ruillé."

In a less agitated letter, Sister Francis wrote to say she thought there was no great need for Mother Theodore to hurry back, since all the harm which could be done had been done, and besides, much of it was only threats. They had several new boarders, and Mother Theodore would be interested to learn that two of them were the daughters of Mrs. Williams of Terre Haute, who had set up the school with Sister Aloysia and who now thoroughly regretted it. The school there had failed. When Mrs. Williams abandoned it, that was its end. Father Corbe thought the girls should be accepted as students. There was a new postulant too. Finally, the premiums for the academy prizes had been very pretty and Mother would have liked them. Evidently Sister Francis was still a little bothered about the reception the peach stone prize of a few years ago had received.

Mother Theodore relaxed a little, until another letter brought more disquieting news. The bishop wanted Sister Marie Joseph, who was still a novice, to be superior at Jasper. He wanted the two sisters at Saint Francisville sent to Saint Peter's. The real reason behind this suggestion was that Saint Francisville was to be included in the new diocese of Chicago and would no longer be under his jurisdiction, but he had not mentioned that. Nor did he say that he had announced the coming of the sisters at Saint Peter's before he told the sisters of Saint Mary's that they were to go there.

On the heels of this move, the bishop had come to Saint Mary's to say that two Sisters of Charity at Vincennes were leaving and he intended to replace them with several Sisters of Providence. They told him they had no American subjects to give him. He asked for Sister Stanislaus, who did not intend to remain in the congregation and who planned to return to the world as soon as Mother Theodore would come home. They finally sent Sister Vincent, but even so the bishop insisted that Sister Stanislaus come to the house at Vincennes.

Before he left, after this last order, the bishop called the community together for what he termed a "religious instruction." "Suppose your superior and I were of different opinions, whom ought you to obey?" he asked, and without waiting for an answer he gave his own. "I am the one you should obey." Before he left, he made one more stipulation: he wanted the novices to go to the academy parlor to entertain visitors on visiting days and one novice to keep house for the workmen at their quarters. This Father Corbe strongly opposed and said he would refuse to hear the confessions if the sisters lived at the farmhouse with the workmen. Nothing more was heard of this odd proposition.

Bishop Bouvier decided the time had come for him to enter this interesting affair. He wrote a letter to the bishop of Vincennes, mentioning among other things the large sum set aside by the Society for the Propagation of the Faith on Mother Theodore's recent visit to that organization. He had seen to it that this amount was given directly to Mother Theodore instead of having it come to her indirectly. This direct aid would, he felt certain, enable her to extricate herself from her financial difficulties and would give her a good start on future expenses.

He wrote also to his brother bishop of another matter which gave him grave concern. Mother Theodore was very uneasy about developments in the congregation during her absence. Bishop de la Hailandière, for one thing, was supervising much of the work at the motherhouse. In a restricted sense this was his right, but it was also true that the congregation must have free action and not be arbitrarily ordered to do anything that would be contrary to its rule. The bishop had the right, for instance, to forbid the entrance of an applicant if he considered her dangerous, but he could not order the admission of anyone for vesture or profession without the consent of the sisters. He could not handle the community's temporal interests either. He was their guardian and their protector; he was not their manager.

The last paragraph of the letter was direct and uncompromising: "I cannot understand, My Lord, how you have deposed Sister Theodore and caused an election to be held in her absence, an absence undertaken in her capacity of superior and with your fullest consent given in writing. Happily this fact is not known here, for I assure you it would have produced a very bad effect."

When Mother Theodore came to Bishop Bouvier to tell him she was going home, he approved and showed her a second letter he had ready to send to the bishop of Vincennes; it stated that the rule of the Sisters of Providence of Ruillé had been carefully examined in Rome and the Holy Father had praised it highly in a special decree, a copy of which Bishop Bouvier was sending with his letter.

Bishop Forbin-Janson, passing through Ruillé, had learned that Mother Theodore was leaving almost immediately, and he came to her to remonstrate. "Tell me, my dear daughter, what has interfered with our conspiracy against your immediate and precipitate departure?" he asked. "I thought we had decided that two or three months of journeyings over France at a propitious time would net you a plentiful harvest."

Mother Theodore looked very sad. "I want so much to stay, but I must return," she said. She knew as well as he that she ought to stay. Since she had come so far, it would be better to collect funds at a time when people were returning to the cities for the winter, especially since many were so interested in what they had heard about the "convent in the woods."

"Well, I have done little for you so far," said the bishop, "but even if you must return home we will finish your work for you. I promise to do my very best to collect further funds," and he blessed her.

Mother Theodore knew the bishop would keep his promise, just as she knew she would have help from others after she had gone. Even though it had been an unpropitious season, many had helped. Abbé Pelletier, well known as a successful "charity preacher," and the Jesuit Père Loriquet had both preached for her, and in Paris several others had talked of her work. They all promised to continue their collecting after she had gone. Canon Lottin of Le Mans, who had offered to act as treasurer for all funds collected, brought her a relic of the True Cross as safeguard for the journey home.

She was not returning without considerable success either. In addition to the collections, she had six thousand francs from the Society for the Propagation of the Faith, and also she had saved a good deal of the money Queen Marie-Amèlie had given her: the little group was traveling by sailing vessel, as the sisters had come. In addition to the superior and Sister Mary Cecilia, there would be three postulants and a gardener.

When Mother Theodore took leave of her beloved Ruillé, it was with the feeling that this would be the last time she was to see it, the last time she would come to France. With her went the prayers of those who knew she would face great difficulties when she reached Saint Mary's.

They sailed from Le Havre on the *Nashville* on November 27. The ship looked very old and, to Sister Mary Cecilia's distrustful eyes, very unseaworthy. She looked forward without pleasure to a disagreeable voyage and in this she was not disappointed. Then, too, she worried about Mother Theodore who, though she had had no serious illness on the trip, had not been well either, and was a very poor sailor.

The voyage began badly. For some reason they had not been informed of the hour of sailing; the boat had left the wharf when they arrived, and they had to hire a skiff to row them to it, only to find their haste had not been necessary; a calm held them for flve days in the channel.

When the ship finally sailed, the weather was very fine and continued fair for some weeks. Then, just before Christmas, the wind changed and a terrible storm blew up, the huge waves breaking against the ship with the noise of cannon balls. Shut in their tiny six-by-four cabin, the women waited and prayed while the waters roared over their heads. No one slept; death seemed too near.

Suddenly one wave rushed through a broken porthole and water inundated their cabin. The captain and one of the sailors plugged the hole by nailing boards over it. The passengers amidships, completely drenched, were weeping, but the captain said the danger was over—"for the present," he added cautiously.

Next day the storm renewed its force. Animals below deck were swept overboard; crates of chickens went, and even the lifeboats. Early in the afternoon, the sky was as dark as a moonless night and the ship shook continuously. The sisters, back in their cabin, made the Way of the Cross and offered their lives. A family of Creoles bound for New Orleans came to ask the sisters whether they might say the Rosary with them.

Early next morning, wails came from a nearby cabin; a child had died during the night, some said of fear. When a bell rang, most of the passengers assembled on deck; it was still dark and a pale sun was trying to shine through the murk. The child's body, wrapped in a sheet, was placed on a plank and a stone attached to the feet. The captain said a prayer, to which Mother Theodore added her own. Then the plank was lifted; with its burden it was pushed over the rail and disappeared in the tossing gray waves.

That morning Mother Theodore made a vow: if they were spared, she promised, in the name of herself and those with her, to build a memorial chapel to St. Anne d'Auray to show their gratitude.

In the afternoon, after a comparative quiet of some hours, there suddenly came a deep dead silence and then a crash, as if the vessel had come apart. Only later did they learn the cause. The ship had actually capsized; it had been thrown off its beam by a sudden large wave and was in great part under water, the keel above, the sails below. Water rushed in from all sides and everywhere were cries and shouts and confusion. The sisters had been thrown to the floor by the shock and could only lie there and call on St. Anne.

Suddenly the wind veered and lifted the ship upright again. The tempest raged for a time longer, but that night it died away and the sea grew calm. They were now so delayed that on New Year's Day they still had a thousand miles to go. The captain was afraid to take the Bahamas route, and so they sailed with a fair wind for the Antilles. Provisions were low, but a passing ship sold them flour, salt fish, and bread.

On January 14 they came in sight of land—the island of Santo Domingo, and a few days later they skirted Cuba. The winds were fair and the passengers were happy. The cabin passengers, who had up to this time mingled with no one else, now came up to talk with the sisters. They were an odd lot—an atheist, very proud of it; a skeptic who wanted to argue about what he did not believe; a young man who boasted proudly of his lack of faith; a pretty young woman who said she was a freethinker. The sisters soon discovered that all these people wanted to do was air their own views; they were totally uninterested in any of the sisters' arguments.

After forty days on shipboard, they entered the Gulf of Mexico in a thick fog. A ship guided them into the Mississippi River and, when the fog lifted suddenly, Mother Theodore read with amazement the name of one of the ships near theirs. It was the *Cincinnati*, the vessel which had first brought her to the New World!

The land they now saw, thought Mother Theodore, was not so much land as a swamp full of dead reeds and dead trees. "This is how things must have looked to Noah when he left the Ark," she said to Sister Mary Cecilia.

Farther on, the banks showed the luxury of lemon and orange trees, of rose and laurel. They saw deer on the shore and swans in the river. When really solid land appeared, there were fine houses, the homes of rich planters, with splendid gardens; but not so pleasant were the cluster of little cabins beside each great house, the cabins of the slaves looking, thought Mother Theodore, like the cells of convicts. The ship passed a cemetery with many crosses, and she said a prayer for her countrymen, the French of Louisiana, who were buried there.

The ship sailed past fields of rice and finally reached New Orleans, where the women were met by the vicar general, whom Bishop Blanc had sent to meet them. They said goodbye to the passengers and crew and had an especially warm farewell from the captain, with his heartfelt thanks. During the voyage he had injured himself by trying to hold down a drunken sailor; he himself had been thrown to the deck and lay there unconscious, his flushed face indicating a stroke. Mother Theodore had come forward with an offer of help; she produced a lancet from her medical supply and bled the sick man. He soon opened his eyes and gazed with surprise at his physician. Within a few hours he was back on deck again, commanding his ship.

The group from Ruillé was very glad to leave at last the battered *Nashville* and go to the Ursuline convent, where the bishop had arranged hospitality for them. It was a very large and fine house and well appointed, but Mother Theodore loved most of all the kindness with which the weary travelers were welcomed.

First of all, they were taken to the chapel where they knelt to thank God for their safe arrival after the terror of the deep that they had so long endured. It was a Saturday, Mary's day, the same day of the week on which Mother Theodore had come to New York four years before.

Letters were waiting for her from Saint Mary-of-the-Woods; all were well and they hoped to see her soon. Many of the letters gave her further light on the situation at home. It proved to be very complicated, even when it was carefully explained by three people—Father Corbe, Sister Basilide, and Sister Francis. There was no letter from the bishop.

Only now did she learn that he had opened both new houses. "We did not want to leave," wrote the superior sadly from Saint Francisville. "We had almost forty children and nineteen had made their First Holy Communion while we were there—and now we have to leave them. God knows what is best, but we found it hard to go."

For the first time, Mother Theodore learned about the letter that the bishop of Le Mans had written the bishop of Vincennes and its effect on that resentful prelate. Sister Francis wrote that he had come directly to her after receiving it.

"This is all your fault," he stormed. "Why did you write all this to France? I tell you very plainly that it will not change my intentions at all, except perhaps to strengthen them." He added his terrible intention: he could not allow Mother Theodore to come back to Saint Mary's at all; since Sister Basilide had done very well in the position, he would appoint her in place of "your former superior."

He had also withdrawn sisters to staff the two new houses, had given the habit to two postulants, had admitted two sisters to their vows, and had received three members of another congregation at the motherhouse—and all of it without the advice or consent of the sisters at Saint Mary's.

Father Corbe wrote that the bishop had explained to him what he wanted done. Evidently the bishop had thought it would be all accepted peacefully, something which Father Corbe said had not come about, to judge from the reactions of the sisters. The bishop had also said he hoped that Mother Theodore would not in the future listen to the advisers she had followed in the past and in whom she ought to have no confidence. "It is difficult, I know," he had said to Father Corbe, "but the peace, the very existence of the community, depend on such sacrifice."

These letters really told Mother Theodore very little, nor did the one from Sister Basilide, for she wrote to warn rather than to give news. She hoped that Mother Theodore would act with the greatest prudence when she saw the bishop for the first time and would not express herself too freely about any proposition he might make. To Sister Basilide, the bishop had said, "All depends on your Mother. Either confidence and simplicity must be restored here, or separation will be necessary." Sister Basilide wrote that she had not dared ask what he meant, but she did want to say that she now understood better Mother Theodore's difficulties with him in the past.

Other things, the letter said, were going well. The academy was increasing rapidly and there would soon be need of another wing for the building. "But of all this we can talk when you get home. Soon we shall be reunited and I can assure you that unless you send me away I shall never leave you," she ended fervently.

The letter from Sister Francis was the shortest of them all. She had evidently left the detailing of events to the others; she wrote chiefly of the joy of knowing she would soon see Mother Theodore again. She would wait until she saw her to tell her more: "I would almost say I dare write scarcely anything, for I cannot know if my views are false or not. But this I do say: do not come to any conclusion until you have seen and talked with us."

Perhaps it was the result of the hard voyage, perhaps the worry about matters at home, perhaps only that her frail body was very tired, but Mother Theodore fell very ill, too ill to leave for home immediately. The day after their arrival, she fell faint at Mass and was put to bed. At first the doctor was afraid she had the dreaded yellow fever, but it proved instead to be a wasting and malignant fever common in New Orleans.

Mother Theodore was very sorry to be so much trouble to the Ursulines, yet she could not help being happy at the loving way they cared for her, as if she were a suffering member of their own community and not a stranger. She felt as if she were back in long-ago days at Ruillé, with Mother Mary coming to her bed to see if she had a fever.

When, after ten days, it was clear Mother Theodore could not travel for some time to come, it was decided that Sister Mary Cecilia and one of the postulants would go ahead to Indiana and the other would remain as Mother Theodore's companion.

The illness proved to be a very long one; it was seven weeks before the fever left her and she was ready to start for home. When she was better, the sisters took her for drives about the city and showed her the old French part of New Orleans and also the fine modern areas. The scenery was wonderfully beautiful, and the houses as fine as any she had ever seen; but for her one thing obliterated all the beauty of nature, all the elegant estates and even the delightful people she met—and that was the sight of a slave auction. Was it possible, she thought, that these Americans, so proud of their liberty, would thus make game of the liberty of others? She yearned for great wealth so that she could buy all the black people she saw and set them free and say to them, "Go—bless Providence—you are free."

Later, when she set down an account of her voyage for the newspaper *L'Univers*, she wrote, "Such feelings must be concealed from the Louisianians, as this is a point on which they are very sensitive."

At last, on St. Joseph's day of 1844, Mother Theodore and her companion left the Ursuline convent after a Mass that included an inspiring sermon on the virtues of Joseph's mastery of the interior life. Up the Mississippi went their large ship, gliding between dozens of steamboats of all sizes; the air was dark with their smoke and noisy with their wheels and engines. As the ship went north and farther north, the landscape grew more wintry, something which did not disturb Mother Theodore at all, for it meant she was getting nearer home, nearer the joy of a northern spring.

"Nearer home" was the phrase she used in her own mind, the word she used about Indiana when she spoke of that state. It was now home to her, no longer the land of exile but the portion of her own inheritance, where she hoped to abide all the remaining days of her life. She saluted the guardian angels of Indiana and prayed for them to watch over the souls under her protection.

When they reached Evansville the travelers were again in Indiana, in the diocese of Vincennes. They stopped for the night with the Lincks, the family of one of the novices, and next morning went to Mass in the little brick church where Father Deydier was pastor. Afterwards they talked with him in his cabin, a single room some ten feet square, with an unpainted wooden chest that evidently also did duty as a table; there was a cot, a chair, some books and a little stove, nothing more. It was obvious that Father Deydier was unmindful of the poverty of his surroundings. He looked very happy as he told them that his little parish was increasing and that he had that morning received two converts into the Church.

"One thing we can do for you," said Mother Theodore, "and that is give you some ornamentation for the inside of your church. Thanks to our dear friends in France we are almost rich in devotional articles, and you shall have your share."

Next day they took the stage for Vincennes, going through the same forests where Bishop Bruté had so often gone to visit his flock. Hours later Mother Theodore saw in the bright sun of March the spire of the cathedral at Vincennes, the cross at its top gleaming in the rays of the sunny afternoon.

She went with Julienne, the postulant, to the convent that the bishop had opened during her absence and was greeted with joy by the sisters. As soon as they saw her it was plain that all four were concerned to see how thin and pale their Mother was after her long illness.

To be with Sister Vincent for a few precious hours was wonderful for Mother Theodore, and at first they talked only of Ruillé. Then the talks turned to the community's present situation, and Mother Theodore learned for the first time just what had taken place in the setting up of the new Vincennes house, learned that all over town had gone the gossip that Mother Theodore was to be dismissed from her congregation and driven from the diocese. It sounded fantastic, and were it not for the fact that the people who told her this incredible thing were sensible men and women Sister Vincent said she would never have credited it.

Next morning Mother Theodore went with Sister Vincent to the cathedral for Mass and afterwards to call on the bishop. She was still weak from her long illness and hoped to make it a short call. The two hours over which it extended took most of the strength that remained to her.

At first the bishop said nothing at all after greeting her. He merely sat in heavy silence with no word of welcome and without asking her to sit down. Then he began to speak of his disappointment with Mother Theodore and loaded her with reproaches for having let those in France give her advice. Mother Theodore tried to say a few words but he gave her no chance.

"Sister Basilide is doing a fine job," he said suddenly. "I shall retain her where she is." Then a very angry look came over his face. "But that proud little thing at the convent at Saint Mary's—she must go." It was obvious that he meant Sister Francis, but in his anger he could not even speak her name.

Suddenly he changed the subject. "Now about the money you stole from me in Paris—that you must refund to me immediately."

Mother Theodore explained that the money all had come from private sources except what the Society for the Propagation of the Faith had given her.

"That is the sum I am referring to—that is my money and you must refund it," he said decidedly. Mother Theodore said nothing at all, one reason being that she did not really know what to say.

The bishop, however, did not wait for an answer. He went on to other accusations. Mother Theodore was now waiting for the fatal words that she was not to return to Saint Mary's. Instead he merely continued complaining about her. He complained of the sisters and even about his priests and the brothers. Finally, after two hours of this, Mother Theodore felt she could bear no more.

"I have been ill, Monseigneur," she said. "I am really very tired." On that plea he let her go, but he asked her to come back to him the next day.

She found him in a better mood on her second call. It was due, she learned later, to a letter he had received from Father Corbe, and it had changed his determination to forbid her to return to Saint Mary's. After he had announced that she could return, as if it was a great favor he was granting her, the bishop began a new line of attack.

"I learn you were not ill at all in New Orleans," he said. "I learn that you were staying there merely to work up a plot against me."

She looked at him to see whether he was serious, and from his angry suspicious eyes she saw that he really was. It was impossible to know how to answer him; whatever she said would be the wrong thing, since she could not admit the implication. Finally she felt faint and asked if she might sit down.

"I am still ill, Monseigneur. Surely you can see that," she said pleadingly, and then, for she could not bear this monstrous accusation, she said in a low voice, "I have plotted nothing against you."

Evidently he was a little moved by her appearance, for he spoke more pleasantly. When she saw his more favorable attitude, she decided to make a request. "I want to write a few words to the sisters to tell them of my arrival.

Will you let me add that you are giving them your blessing?"

When, still pleasantly, he agreed, she wrote at his desk that she was returning to Saint Mary's by the first steamboat. This note was being written in the presence of His Lordship, and he sent his blessing to the community. This letter, she ended, would inform all the sisters that she was on her way home.

Then the sisters said goodbye to the bishop and went back to their convent. Mother Theodore had wanted to visit Saint Peter's and Jasper before going home, but those missions were rather hard of access, and besides she felt she must hasten to the motherhouse as soon as possible. The next day they started on the homeward journey, the trip up the river, the crossing of the Wabash by ferry, the rugged drive home.

It was almost dark when the two women descended the steep ravine, crossed the little brook, and climbed the other bank. The sisters had heard the carriage and were at the door, ready to greet them and throw their arms about them.

As was her habit when she came from a journey, Mother Theodore spoke no word until she had gone to the little chapel and there, at the foot of the tabernacle, with her sisters about her, she gave thanks that she was again at home. It was Monday in Holy Week. She knew she would have a peaceful and happy Easter at her Saint Mary-of-the-Woods.

Chapter Thirteen

"At Least, a Lock for the Door!"

℮

For a time after her return from France, Mother Theodore and her daughters forgot everything else in the joy of being again together after the long absence. Relations with the bishop, too, were quiet. In fact, several times he spoke with satisfaction of her work and was now beginning to find fault with poor Sister Basilide for small things that had gone wrong while her superior was away. But the peace was an uneasy one, as Mother Theodore well knew.

When Sister Mary Cecilia, on her way home from New Orleans in advance of Mother Theodore, had stopped to pay her respects to the bishop before going on to Saint Mary's, he asked her what she thought of Mother Theodore, an odd question that she answered frankly.

"I am devoted to her and to our work," she said.

The bishop shrugged his shoulders. "So they taught you at Ruillé to despise your bishop," he said bitterly.

Sister Mary Cecilia said he was mistaken. "No one ever taught me such a thing, Monseigneur," she said earnestly.

He only looked more bitter. "Well, if she will not sign the articles I shall present to her, she will not remain at Saint Mary's," he said flatly.

The threat had not been carried out when Mother Theodore returned, but she knew well that it might happen at any time. She was willing to obey the bishop in anything that concerned the good of her community or make any changes that would better adapt the congregation to the American scene, but she was also determined to follow the rule, especially regarding the visitation of her houses. The bishop had recently informed Father Corbe that he forbade Mother Theodore visiting the "establishments of the Bishop" without his permission or Father Corbe's in the absence of the bishop. This would apply to Vincennes and Saint Peter's, founded in her absence. Yet these were her houses too, for her sisters were in charge of them, and they were not yet self-supporting. She was planning a visitation soon and wondered if she would meet with trouble in carrying it out.

Meantime she fell again into the routine of her days as head of her congregation. She went over the accounts and the work that had been done. She welcomed the new postulants, one of whom was Jane Brown, the first to enter from the academy. She was a girl of eighteen whose ancestors had been early settlers in Maryland, English recusants who had left Saint Mary's County in 1785 when anti-Catholic sentiment developed there; they had gone to Kentucky and later went farther west to the prairies of Illinois. Jane and her sister Matilda had come to Saint Mary-of-the-Woods as two of its first students. Now the elder girl was to become a member of the religious family there.

Mother Theodore distributed the religious articles she had brought home with her, the statues and pictures and vestments. The painting of Queen Marie-Amélie was set in a place of honor in the convent parlor, and Mother Theodore wrote the queen a long letter, telling her of the voyage home and the safe return; she wrote that she and her sisters were praying that God would pour out blessings on the queen in return for her great help to them. A special prayer for her intentions was being said daily in their chapel.

One of the happy results of the French visit was that now Mother Theodore could pay off all the small debts and be concerned only with the present and the future of her finances. Sums of money came steadily from France, sent to the French ambassador who forwarded them to the community in the care of the governor of Indiana. It was with joy that Mother Theodore paid the carpenter, the tinner, Mr. Crawford, and the workmen on the place. Best of all, Canon Lottin was beginning to send her money from France, really substantial sums of from one hundred to three hundred dollars a month. On the strength of all this, the old wagon was reconditioned and a new one ordered.

Mother Theodore also paid Madame Parmentier a sum still due her, thanking her for waiting so long for it. The community was growing fast, she told her friend in New York; nine postulants would receive the habit later in the summer. She described the tiny chapel being erected on their grounds; it was to be dedicated to St. Anne, in fulfillment of the vow Mother Theodore had made if the lives of herself and her sisters were spared during the terrible storm at sea. It was to stand on a little knoll and be built of logs; inside it was to be plastered, and shells were to be set in the wet plaster, some of them brought from France, but most of them picked up by the postulants on the banks of the Wabash. The shells were to be set in designs showing groups of Indians, a map of Indiana, and also the brave ship *Nashville* that St. Anne had saved from shipwreck. The sisters were training a big wild grape vine to cover the roof of the chapel. Mother Theodore wished that Madame Parmentier could come to see it when it was finished.

In May, Mother Theodore decided it was time she went to see her sisters at Jasper and Saint Peter's, the house opened by the bishop in her absence.

She thought the house at Vincennes a very poor place and her four sisters there were obviously poor; they had no glass or napkin to put at her place at table, she had noted, and the bit of corned beef that formed the chief part of the meal was evidently considered luxurious eating.

But when she reached Saint Peter's, she found it to be in much worse condition; the Saint Francisville house that they had left was a good one in comparison with this old cabin. It had been the first motherhouse of the brothers whom Abbé Moreau had sent from France. They had spent their first winter in this cabin, and Mother Theodore remembered that they had written her to say how glad they were to get away from it to better quarters.

Sister Liguori and Sister Augustine welcomed her with delight and, though she was equally happy to see them again, she was not happy about their circumstances. The chairs were made of tree trunks; their food was corn meal and salt pork. The log cabin was open to every breeze. The furniture consisted of two chairs, two cots, two benches, and a few cooking utensils. The tuition of their pupils, when it was paid at all, was paid in food. Mother Theodore knew that if she had seen this place sooner, she would never have allowed her sisters to spend a winter there. She wondered how the hardier brothers had done so.

She was very worried about the two young sisters. Strong though they were, this poor cabin, with cracks between the logs through which wind and snow could come, would sap the strength of anyone. She was anxious to take them back to Saint Mary's with her, but they insisted they wanted to stay. The children needed them. The bishop had just sent them money to buy a cow, and then they would have milk and butter.

"Supposing I bring you home when the school term is over," she suggested, but they begged to be allowed to stay on. She looked at them in admiration. "The brothers must have left their spirit of poverty here for you," she told them. "But, my dear children, to live in this old shed," and she looked about her in dismay.

When it was learned at Saint Peter's that the sisters might be leaving, people came to beg Mother Theodore to let them stay. In the face of all this, she consented, but reluctantly. She insisted that some repairs be made to the cabin, a lock put on the door, and new bedding furnished if the sisters were to remain. It seemed to her that holy poverty was being carried to excess when one had to put a chest against the door at night to keep it closed.

She learned that one reason for this Spartan living was that the pastor was something of an eccentric. He wanted to see carried out in all its rigor the admonition of our Lord that every apostle be without staff or scrip. And evidently the sisters were done the honor of being considered apostles like himself.

Mother Theodore found the children in the little school very gentle and pleasant, and she saw why the sisters loved to work with them. She gave them all a holiday while she took the two sisters with her to Jasper. A ride through the beauty of Indiana in May would give them at least a brief respite.

They all enjoyed the trip. They looked with delight at the tulip trees, the wild chestnuts with their big flowers, white against the delicate green of the spring leaves. Song birds were everywhere, bluebirds, cardinals, a brilliant crowd. Occasionally they saw a deer slipping through the woods.

"It is in every sense a new world," said Mother Theodore, but she added that there was one creature whose confidence she would gladly dispense with, and that was the snake, of which there were far too many in Indiana for comfort. "And the mosquito too," she added. "He is even worse, for one can kill a snake, but the only defense against the other is a thick choking smoke."

She found the community at Jasper getting along very well. With deep emotion she embraced Sister Marie Joseph and Sister Gabriella, whom she had not seen for two long years.

The visitors had come on Ascension Day and were in time to see a whole parish walking in procession, the cross-bearer at their head. During Mass there were two sermons, one in English, the other in German, and by the time it was over, Mother Theodore was very weary, for it was past two o'clock. Then she saw with a feeling of shame that the people were re-forming their procession and that some of them must walk as much as ten miles to their own small settlements. When they were out of sight, the sound of their singing came back, always more faint as they went farther, until it died away.

Mother Theodore went to Vincennes to attend for three days the public sessions of the first diocesan synod there, held at the close of a clergy retreat. Twenty-five missionaries were at Mass in the cathedral, and the sermon was preached by Father Timon of the Lazarists. All received Holy Communion at the hands of the bishop of Vincennes.

Mother Theodore was carried away by the sight of so many clergy gathered there. "So heavenly was their appearance that they scarcely seemed any longer to belong to this world of sorrows," she wrote to Bishop Bouvier, and told him of the beauty of the singing of the *Veni Creator*, the recital of the

Litany of the Saints, the long Profession of Faith.

Only a few years before, said Father Timon, there had been in that area not a single priest—and now they were holding a synod. Vincennes had a bishop, a cathedral, and more than thirty churches in its diocesan area.

On the following day there was a Mass of Requiem for Bishop Bruté, and Father Deydier preached a sermon of eulogy on him whose companion, friend, and confidant he had been. He spoke of the bishop's heroically simple life and pointed out that at the college in Emmitsburg almost every bishop now in office in the United States had once been his pupil. He spoke of the bishop's long days of labor, his nights of continuous writing, of his diocese in the vast midwest with no churches and few priests. Father Deydier dwelt on the voyage to France, where Bishop Bruté's eloquent appeals had brought back with him nineteen priests and brothers to the New World. The bishop, who had wanted only to remain among his beloved books at his college, had not only built up the diocese by his administrative ability, but had, when there was no one else to do it, chopped wood for his fire and rung the bell for Mass.

The priests sitting before Father Deydier were visibly moved, for they had all known this bishop; they were his sons. When the preacher ended by saying, "When he was with us we did not feel our fatigue. We scarcely knew we were poor though we really lacked the very necessities of life, for we had him." Every priest there sat up straighter and looked proud because he had known and worked with the bishop of whom the orator spoke.

After the synod was over, several of the missionary priests came to Mother Theodore to beg her to send them sisters for their work. She told them that would be her dearest desire, but that for the present she could do little. One request, however, she did accept: she promised to open a school very soon at Madison, where Father Delaune was pastor. Other offers she had to refuse since there were not enough sisters nor enough funds as yet.

The community retreat that summer was well attended. The sisters came from Jasper and Saint Peter's and from Vincennes. Father Augustine Martin presided at the profession and reception ceremonies; Father Deydier and Father Corbe assisted.

As Mother Theodore looked at the ranks—they could really be called that now—of her community, she felt she was well repaid for past sufferings, since this result had been achieved. There were now thirteen professed sisters; nine postulants had received the habit; with the novices not yet ready for profession and the postulants, there were now over thirty in the community.

When, at the end of the retreat, the sisters returned to their houses, Mother Theodore went with them. She was to open the new mission at Madison, where Sister Liguori had been appointed superior.

Madison offered better possibilities than many missions. It was a prosperous and growing town, and Father Delaune had rented a very nice house for the sisters. The town was, however, a long way from the motherhouse: located on the Ohio River, it was one hundred and fifty miles from Saint Mary's, and took three days to get there by carriage and ferry.

The location and the prospects too proved excellent. Both boarding and day pupils were already enrolling, Protestants among them. Unfortunately, the church was a mile away, and the sisters would not have a chaplain of their own. This long walk to Mass and back was to prove a small martyrdom for those who traveled it twice a day. It was not the walk, of course, for they were pioneers and accustomed to that. It was that Madison had bitter anti-Catholics among its residents, always on the alert for "machinations from Rome," and in their eyes this school was a nest of Roman spies.

When the sisters walked to church, stones were sometimes thrown at them by undisciplined children; snowballs hit them, and people even spat on their habits. It was a violence that did not, however, last long, for the accusations were too implausible. For example, one minister claimed that he had seen from his own pulpit several of the nuns climb through the window of the public school to steal textbooks, and a much worse accusation was made that the sisters had killed a child they had kidnapped. The child was found; the abductor was caught and punished.

The better elements in the town intervened, especially those who were already sending their daughters to the quiet French nuns. Active persecution by hoodlums became a battle of words among the townspeople, in which the sisters were only an audience.

During their second winter in the town, a series of controversial talks was given by Reverend Martin Spalding of Louisville, a Presbyterian minister. The sisters attended the lectures, since that had been the custom in France. They were held in the evenings and the sisters came home very late, but Sister Liguori felt they ought to hear the debate. "We were like Eve," she wrote to Mother Theodore. "Having looked upon the fruit we wished to touch it and taste it. We assisted at all the lectures."

The fires of intolerance died down gradually, and the sisters walked unmolested on the streets of Madison. They had won. They had not been belligerent, but neither had they ever retreated. It was clear they were now accepted as citizens of the town.

Before returning to Saint Mary's after installing the sisters, Mother Theodore went to Vincennes to call on Bishop de la Hailandière. She had one request to make of him: Would he, as soon as possible, approve their rule? Neither she nor her growing congregation wanted to continue any longer in a diocese where the rule did not have the express approval of the diocesan head.

"If you would write us what you wish altered, the sisters will consider those changes and decide whether we can observe them or not," she said, but she saw in his face a growing opposition. Suddenly she spoke out. "If the sisters do not think they are called on by God to follow a different rule, surely, Monseigneur, you will not find it amiss of them if they go elsewhere; if they withdraw to a diocese where they can follow their own rule in conformity with their vows."

The bishop looked slightly taken aback at this firm statement from the always gracious Mother Theodore. "But there is no one here, Mother, who loves your rule more than I do," he said. "And if you speak of leaving me that would be really wicked, for you know I could find no one like yourself to put at the head of a new community."

Then, and surprisingly, the bishop agreed to discuss portions of the rule with her and said he was completely in agreement with its provisions. And now at last he promised what Mother Theodore had been so long asking, the things necessary to their future security: he said he would turn over to them the property at Saint Mary's by giving them the deeds and a clear title to the property, and he would approve the rule.

Two little girls had come as boarders to the school in Vincennes, and Mother Theodore had them transferred to Saint Mary's because there were as yet no accommodations for boarders at the other convent. It had never once occurred to her, since this was a routine matter, that the bishop would think this an arrangement about which he should be consulted. Had she thought about it she would have asked him about it, since it was too small a matter for argument involving authority.

A letter had come immediately from the bishop, but not to her. It came to Father Corbe, appointing him ecclesiastical superior to the Sisters of Providence. Meantime, Mother Theodore, having learned that the bishop was vexed, deplored her error in tact, even though her sisters sensibly pointed out that it would be all but impossible to avoid offending the prelate's tender sensibilities.

She went to Vincennes to explain why she had done this and to ask the bishop to continue as their spiritual head. Before he answered her request, he took advantage of her apologies to renew his former demands about the missions and his authority over them. Mother Theodore stood firm on that point. She had come for one thing; the other matter would need more thought and advice, since it was directly concerned with the rule itself, she told him.

The bishop looked at her with hostile eyes. "Very well," he said with finality. "I will consent to remain your superior, but on one condition. You are to write a statement that all your sisters and yourself have said about me in France was false. I demand a retraction."

He told her what he wanted retracted. It was a long list, but most of it was only suspicions of what she might have said, inferences she had never made. She listened in silence until he had finished, and then she rose to go.

She asked his blessing and nothing more.

Evidently moved by the request for his blessing, he said with regret in his voice, "I am afraid I have been sometimes cruelly harsh to you—forget all I have said and pray for your poor bishop."

To this she made no reply except to promise him her prayers. As she went back home, she hoped with all her heart that the storm was over now, that they could all work and live in peace for a while. Her hope was vain, for only a few days later came a letter with more recriminations, another demand for a retraction of things she had never said.

It was Father Corbe, noted for his forbearance, who helped her most during those days. He was a singularly prudent man who had a deep affection for Bishop de la Hailandière and was often able to quiet his superior's suspicions. The bishop in turn was devoted to Father Corbe, whom he considered his best friend. But the latter said sadly to Mother Theodore, "Even his best friends cannot hope to escape his displeasure."

Until this time all the building at Saint Mary's had been at the expense of the bishop though, strictly speaking, the funds he used were not diocesan. The money used for Saint Mary's had been given by charitable organizations and friends of the Sisters of Providence in France and the United States, and much of it was sent to him earmarked especially for their use. It was therefore not a disbursement of diocesan funds; they had been put in the bishop's hands as a courtesy to his office. Besides, the sisters had not yet come into possession of their land, a matter about which the bishop remained silent, merely paying the bills as they were presented to him. For the first years there had been no income at all; later boarders brought in funds, but there was still need of other money, and the bishop still paid bills with the money given him for the purpose.

One day in October, Father Corbe (who still considered himself the superior at the motherhouse, since he had been appointed by the bishop and had not heard of any removal from that office) gave permission for a balustrade to be placed around the porch at the academy so that the children playing there would not fall off. He sent the bill to the bishop, and the bishop promptly returned it unpaid.

Mother Theodore decided that the time had come to obtain without delay title to the land that was theirs by right; then in the future they could meet their own expenses. This request, though very politely couched, enraged the bishop anew, and his reply was merely another demand for a "recantation" before anything else would be done. He refused to attend a profession ceremony and inveighed against Father Corbe in strong terms for any part he might have in the matter.

Since there was nothing to retract, the situation remained in *statu quo* until November when the village church, which the bishop had for some time been building at the settlement of Saint Mary-of-the-Woods, was to be blessed and he came to perform the ceremony.

On various occasions when he visited Saint Mary's, the bishop had spoken admiringly of the statue of Our Lady in their chapel. "But it is really much too large for the space it is in," he had remarked after one inspection.

After the blessing of the church, he had asked Mother Theodore to come with him to discuss some improvements he wanted for the grounds. A suspicion suddenly came into her mind, especially since she had seen him speaking to the workmen and had seen them go towards the motherhouse. When she went into the convent chapel after the bishop had gone, it was as she had suspected. The Bertaudière Madonna was gone; the space was empty. She knew well where it had gone: to the niche in the village church, which needed just such a statue.

One of the novices came up to her with something in her apron, and there was amazement in her face. "I found it in the path, Mother," she said, and showed Mother Theodore one of the hands from the statue; it had evidently come unscrewed from the arm while the workmen were carrying the statue and had fallen unnoticed by them.

Mother Theodore put it away carefully. "Mary will come back to us some day and claim her hand," she said.

While the bishop was at Saint Mary's to bless the new church, he came to the convent and demanded a special retraction from Sister Francis. She was known to be a very peace-loving and humble religious, but this time she spoke up spiritedly. "I have nothing to retract, Monseigneur," she said, "and if pardon must be bought with an untruth, that is far too high a price for me to pay."

The bishop explained to her carefully wherein her error lay: she had written to Mother Theodore at Ruillé and to the bishop of Le Mans. "And the bishop of Le Mans has no right to give you advice. The superiors at Ruillé are no longer the superiors of the sisters here," he said firmly.

Mother Theodore felt it was time for her to speak up. "But, Monseigneur, until you have given us approval of our rule or give us another, we must consider ourselves as belonging to the bishop of Le Mans. We have asked you repeatedly to approve or at least advise us of any change you wish made, and we shall be happy to adopt any such changes that do not alter the spirit of our rule."

To this the bishop made no answer at all. He simply walked out. The sisters who had been present at the altercation felt very discouraged, but if Mother Theodore did she did not show it. "Courage—hope and pray," she told them.

The bishop did not come back to say goodbye before he returned to Vincennes, and the following week came word that he had left for his *ad limina* visit to Rome. When he departed on November 18, he left no word whatever for Saint Mary-of-the-Woods.

On the advice of Father Corbe, Mother Theodore began to work to secure their property in a different way. The academy was continually increasing in number and there was great need of enlarging the brick building that housed students and faculty. Yet the community did not wish to do any further building on land not legally theirs—which could, in fact, be taken from them at the whim of the bishop. They therefore applied to the Indiana legislature for an act of incorporation, for they had been told this was the first step towards being allowed to have legal possession of any property. Then, when the bishop returned, they would present him with this development and renew their request.

Early in the year Mother Theodore had suffered from one of her recurring illnesses—"our Mother's illnesses keep us fervent," said her sisters. For some days she had a fever that increased in intensity until they grew alarmed and wrote Dr. Baty for advice. Even before he received the letter, she was so much worse that another letter was sent asking him to come immediately.

By the time the doctor arrived, Mother Theodore was certain her last days had come. On the eve of the Purification, she asked Sister Francis to recite the prayers for the dying, for she was racked with pain and felt her life was hanging by a thread. Dr. Baty stayed at Saint Mary's for a whole week, but Mother Theodore grew no better and Father Corbe wrote to Father Martin that only heaven could save her.

She recovered, however, as she always did. By March, she was sitting up in a chair for a little while each day, but it was a slow convalescence. " 'To suffer and not to die,' seemed," said Sister Francis, "to be their Mother's motto." By April, Mother Theodore was herself again, supervising the spring planting, the digging of a new well, the building of a new bridge over the ravine. Then she left for a visitation of her houses.

In the summer, the sisters came home for the annual retreat. Five sisters were professed and five received the habit.

For the year just past, Mother Theodore was able to give them a fine report. The days of acute poverty were over now. Pupils were paying well, some even in advance. The missions were beginning to contribute a little to the expenses of the motherhouse, and money was still coming as a result of Mother Theodore's trip the year before to France.

At the end of the retreat, Mother Theodore asked the sisters of the council if they were willing to have the rule changed and adopt the kind of government which the bishop of Vincennes seemed to have in mind for them. Since they all knew the various ideas of the bishop and had all in one way or another suffered from them, they said "No" very decidedly and agreed that a letter be written and signed by them all. It would not be given to the bishop unless that proved absolutely necessary. The letter petitioned him to approve their rule; it also stated that, if he refused, they would feel free to go somewhere else. After it had been signed by the six members who made up the Council, all the retreatants departed for their various missions.

In October, Bishop de la Hailandière returned. He had had a profitable trip and a fine visit in Rome, he told Father Corbe. The pope had received him very graciously. The bishop had offered to resign his see, but the Holy Father had refused to accept it. He had gone to see the bishop of Le Mans, and they had a long and useful talk. And Bishop de la Hailandière asked that Mother Theodore come to Vincennes to see him as soon as possible.

When, some days later, she came, she found herself pleasantly received and presented with relics of St. Urban and St. Theodore. Before she left, the bishop said in an offhand way that Bishop Bouvier had agreed with him entirely when he talked with him about the Sisters of Providence. If they insisted on continuing as they were doing, both bishops thought they would be considered insubordinate and rebellious.

Mother Theodore was not unduly alarmed at this statement, for she had received a letter from Bishop Bouvier in which he gave full details of his meeting with the bishop of Vincennes, during the course of which he had made plain to his visitor how he felt about the entire matter. He wrote, but with reserve, of the bishop's accusations against her, and he ended his letter with the significant remark that if they wished he gave them permission to return to France or to establish themselves elsewhere in the United States. He had already discussed this with Mother Mary; she and her council were in agreement with him. However, Mother Theodore knew this was not a propitious time to mention this letter to Bishop de la Hailandière.

She decided, instead, to ask the bishop to give the community the statement he had several times promised them—an approval of the rule, so that their painful condition of uncertainty would be at an end.

"But I love your rule," he said. "Of course I want to see it observed."

"Then give us an approval of it, Monseigneur," she asked, and to her surprise he said he would. But it was only an oral statement and not the written document she had hoped for. The latter she did not receive, and she went home heartsick. She wrote the bishop, saying that his mere statement to her gave no real guarantee that the community would receive the simple elemental rights to which it was entitled. His only answer was the demand, exactly like the earlier one, of a retraction of what various sisters were supposed to have said about him.

When that Christmas her sisters on mission received from Mother Theodore the customary Christmas letter, its note was one of sadness. There was reason for this, for at the motherhouse there was now a real and very apparent danger: the bishop might suddenly decide to send their foundress away from the diocese. One other danger was coming closer: they might have to leave Saint Mary-of-the-Woods entirely and go to one of the various dioceses that would be only too happy to have them and where their rule would be honored. They loved their home in the forest. They did not want to leave it. That was why the Christmas letter had sad overtones.

"When we go in spirit to Bethlehem with Mary and Joseph," wrote Mother Theodore, "in the hard cold manger we will find the Redeemer of the world; we forget our miseries, our trials…. Pray, my dear Sisters, oh, pray, that both within and without we may enjoy peace. We are in great suffering here at home. I need not say more, for your prayers will not be wanting. In prayer alone is our hope."

CHAPTER FOURTEEN

Survival (1846-1847)

❦

The letter that the council of the Sisters of Providence had written during their retreat in the summer of 1845 was not sent to the bishop of Vincennes until late in November. By that time they were realizing that their one hope of building up their community in peace and freedom was either to secure some written word from him or go elsewhere.

The letter had said nothing really new, only that the sisters wanted him to approve their rule so that they might establish their existence as a religious congregation. It was nothing more than Mother Theodore had asked for often before. The six signatures of her council showed the unanimity of the request.

What they needed was the deed to the property of Saint Mary-of-the-Woods, so that they might safely build as the growing enrollment demanded. It would be painful, ran the letter, "to be obliged to leave a diocese that is ours by nature and adoption, but whatever it may cost us, we believe ourselves obliged to leave and that very soon if Your Lordship disregards our position."

It was indeed clear that they must have some definite word from the bishop on this matter. They must build or they could not accept any more pupils at the academy; there were forty now and no room for more, yet applications continued to come. Materials for building had been bought some time before and were deteriorating because they were not being used. Yet until the Congregation owned the land it would be foolish to build further.

Their claim was clear; the bishop had promised the sisters the land even before they left France, and they had already contributed several hundred dollars towards its purchase. The Society for the Propagation of the Faith had allotted money towards it. Joseph Picquet had given the sum that established them and had several times written to ask the reason for the delay in legal transfer to them, so that they would be protected against any future claims. Then, too, when Mother Theodore went to France in 1843, the bishop had promised to give her the deed if she returned with ten thousand francs; she had brought back even more than his stipulation, but no deed had been given her.

This deed and his approval of the rule were minimum necessities for security. Yet the only response to their repeated requests had been accusations of ingratitude and of a rebellious spirit. The bishop's response to this last letter from the council had been vague and general, but with no approval or promise. It was very disheartening.

Then, as Sister Francis wrote in the annals, the community "received a blow more terrible than all the episcopal difficulties." Mother Theodore fell desperately ill. A bad cold turned into the dreaded "winter fever"— pneumonia. Without a doubt, much of her illness could be attributed to the anxiety and distress she had gone through.

By the end of January, she was close to death and had received the Last Sacraments. Dr. Baty was away, and the sisters had to take complete charge of her themselves. The weary days went by with hope low in all hearts. Prayers and sacrifices were increased. "She is more dead than alive," said Sister Olympiade, her devoted nurse, to Father Corbe, who spent nearly all his time in the sickroom lest his services be needed and there be no time left to summon him.

Finally Mother Theodore began to improve. When the fever left her, her sisters came in to look at her and make sure she was really still with them; to each she gave a warm smile. "They are very tenderly attached to me," she whispered to Father Corbe. She grew better very slowly, and it was not until March 8 that she was able to receive Holy Communion in the chapel and a little longer before she was able to take up her work again. Now she had to consider once again the painful subject of whether the community was to remain in Indiana or go elsewhere.

During the spring of 1846, Father Corbe, in the course of a talk with the bishop, came to the conclusion that the bishop would now be willing to give them the site of their motherhouse if they would send him what Father Corbe called an apology but the bishop still referred to as a retraction. The time was close at hand for the Sixth Provincial Council in Baltimore; the bishop planned to attend and wanted to present such a letter. If the sisters agreed, he would deed Saint Mary-of-the-Woods to them immediately.

The sisters decided to do this, since apparently all he wanted was a sort of blanket apology for anything in their conduct in the past that might have offended him. It was a very carefully phrased letter, setting forth first the difficult situation in which they found themselves because they did not have his approval of their rule. The letter ended: "It is with our whole soul, it is even a consolation for our heart, not only to offer our apologies and ask your pardon for anything that in our conduct, in our association, or in our letters may have escaped us contrary to the respect that we owe Your Lordship, for whom we wish to preserve the most profound veneration, but we would all wish to be at your feet to ask pardon most humbly and we would not rise until you said, 'Go, I pardon and bless you.' These are the sentiments of all the Sisters of Providence."

It was a very tactful statement that was later to be criticized by more than one of the clergy although it really said nothing. Before any word came from the bishop about it, however, Father Corbe opened his mail to find that the bishop had removed him from his position at Saint Mary's and was calling him back to Vincennes. This time, though completely puzzled, the priest prepared to depart, leaving behind him a stricken community. He told Mother Theodore he had thought of going to St. Louis to Bishop Kenrick and seek a refuge for them all there. However, he would go first to Vincennes and consult with Father Timon of the Lazarists, who was preaching the clergy retreat there.

Father Timon, after listening carefully to the whole story, gave his opinion that some kind of agreement must be made if the Lord's work was not to suffer; that was the one important thing. His advice was that the sisters stay where they were for the time being and make no immediate plans for the future.

Father Corbe next went to see the bishop. After a lengthy interview, he was able to report to Saint Mary's that the bishop now seemed willing to come to an agreement of some kind. He had greatly modified the condition he had intended to make and was already regretting the withdrawal of Father Corbe, whom he planned to send back to Saint Mary's.

"But does he still feel today as he did yesterday?" wrote Father Corbe sadly to Mother Theodore. "I wonder. I fear not."

Father Corbe said he could not agree with Father Timon. He thought perhaps Mother Theodore ought to write to Bishop Lefevre in Detroit; he was very anxious to have her in his diocese and had recently written that he would be happy to set them up in a motherhouse in his episcopal city. There had been only one proviso: Father Corbe was to remain their chaplain. That had been the first intimation the sisters had that Father Corbe too was actually ready to leave Vincennes.

The devoted chaplain did not wish to offer her any advice just then, however. He knew Mother Theodore would stay or go, as he suggested, but at the moment the bishop seemed ready to grant their request about their property, and their investment of building at Saint Mary's was so considerable that it seemed a pity to leave it all and begin anew somewhere else.

Father Corbe went to Saint Mary's to discuss it all further with Mother Theodore. They both knew the Detroit offer was a very generous one, and it was clear they would have a fine home there. The simple truth was that Father Corbe was well aware that the sisters did not want to go away. They wanted to stay at Saint Mary-of-the-Woods, which was their home and very dear to them all.

"Even after the sorrow of saying goodbye when I last left Ruillé," said

Mother Theodore, "I knew as soon as I came here again that Indiana was no longer a place of exile for me. I told myself that I hoped to live here all the rest of my life." Then her face grew thoughtful and sad. "But of course I know there must be a measure of peace for us if we are to stay here. I know we can go elsewhere and be welcome. Bishop Hughes of New York has invited us to take charge of a hospital in Brooklyn, Bishop Blanc would like us in New Orleans, a bishop in Texas wants us in his see. They are all fine offers, like Bishop Lefevre's from Detroit, and yet...."

He knew what she meant. She and her sisters had grown to love their home in the forest and their neighbors and their children. They were needed at Saint Mary's, and if they were to go away they might be opposing the designs of God for them. On the other hand, it was hard to carry out God's works against these continuous threats from the bishop of Vincennes—of excommunication if they tried to go away, of deprivation of the sacraments if they stayed and insisted on observing the details of their rule.

The time for the Provincial Council at Baltimore was at hand. The bishop planned to do two things while he was there, so he told Father Corbe: to offer his own resignation and to present the retraction, as he called it, of the Sisters of Providence as evidence of his difficulties with them.

From Baltimore, he wrote Father Corbe that the "submission" of the sisters had reached him just in time to be of use. He now wished he had had it a little sooner—"before the pretended Vicar General of the Eudists was obliged to return home covered with shame," and "before the intrigues of Father Martin had been discovered." He again promised to give the property to the Sisters of Providence, but still with a few conditions attached. However, he would approve their rule publicly and in writing if they wished; then they could go ahead and build with no fear for the future.

In general the offer was so satisfactory that the sisters decided to accept it and remain at Saint Mary's. There were a few errors in the bishop's letter, but they did not refer to the Congregation. It was common knowledge that the Eudist provincial had left Vincennes because he was being installed as head of their college in Mobile; Father Martin's "intrigue" was merely his effort to place the difficulties at Vincennes before the Baltimore Council. When the meeting was over, Father Martin was suggested for a bishop's see. Since the Congregation's troubles seemed to be all but over now, it was decided to give out the contracts for enlarging the academy, which would cost about five thousand dollars. Mother Theodore, so often disappointed, was still a little uneasy. "Wait a moment before chanting a *Te Deum*," she wrote to Father Martin. "Never have we been so near extermination. Before I rejoice, I want to make sure this change is real."

As it happened, she was right in her apprehensions. A second demand came from Bishop de la Hailandière: before he would give her the deed he wanted immediate elections at the motherhouse, and he made it clear that he not only did not want Mother Theodore re-elected but that he wanted her to go away entirely—preferably, if she wished, back to France. When Father Martin (who by this time had come to expect any demand from the bishop) heard this one, he was visibly shaken. "If this comes to pass, I do not give the Congregation a year of existence," he wrote to Bishop Bouvier.

In July of 1846 the bishop brought to the motherhouse the deed for part of the land, some eighty acres; the rest he said he was reserving. The contract also had some clauses that the sisters learned a little later made the deed invalid according to Indiana law. One clause said the bishop must give his approval to every improvement made on the land he was giving them; the law made void any deed to which such conditions were attached. However, the sisters, unaware of this at the time, received the deed gratefully.

In August, the examination of the students took place, with Judge Huntington as examiner. Father Corbe was there with Father Lalumière from Terre Haute and Father Hamilton from Chicago, as well as some three hundred other visitors. The bishop presided. It was clear that the public was very interested in the academy, which was growing rapidly and receiving pupils from very distant areas. Everything was going well; everything would continue to go well, if only their bishop would not put new stumbling blocks in the path of their progress.

The community retreat followed. Two days before it closed, Bishop de la Hailandière arrived at the convent. "When are you holding elections?" he asked the councilors.

"But our rule is not yet approved," said Sister Mary Cecilia. He stood for a moment looking at her in silence. When he spoke his voice was angry. "I shall not stay for the closing of the retreat," he said, and walked away.

Father Hamilton, who was their retreat master, advised them to do nothing at all. No elections were held. The vows of five novices were received at the close of the retreat, and the habit was given to three postulants.

For two years Father Benoit, a priest in charge at Fort Wayne, had been trying to persuade Mother Theodore to open a house there, but for many reasons this had been impossible until 1846, when a mission was made there in September.

Warned by her experience at Saint Peter's and at St. Francisville, where her sisters had been poorly housed and almost starved, Mother Theodore decided to make adequate and definite arrangements with Father Benoit before sending anyone. She was delighted to have him offer a good house and two hundred dollars for furnishing it, as well as a garden of about two acres. When she came with three sisters, she saw that he had indeed carried out his promise well. She was very grateful to him and told him so: "We shall offer an Our Father and a Hail Mary daily for your spiritual and material needs."

Fort Wayne was an old settlement that until 1720 had been a military post. La Salle had been there for a time. Bitter battles had been fought there with the Indians, but now strife was only a memory. Native Americans were still around, of course; in fact, the children of some of the chiefs came to the sisters' academy. Some were of mixed blood and had fair hair and blue eyes. They were children who lived on the reservations during the summer and in the autumn returned to their quiet school life. They seemed to like one as well as the other—"my wild birds of the forest," Father Benoit called them.

In late October of 1846 came word that Sister Liguori was ill, and Mother Theodore hurried to Madison. The weather was bitter cold and the stage was freezing; Mother Theodore had not been feeling well and was glad she had brought her warm old cloak with her. She had left Saint Mary's so hurriedly that she had to send further instructions by letter, which was a difficult matter when one was on a stage bumping along over a corduroy road so rough that she wondered, she wrote, if she would ever survive in her "individual being." The sisters were to see that Joe penned up the hogs; the poor animals would find no forage in the fields and would get thin. The sisters were to make sure that Father Corbe's winter clothing was in good condition; if he had any tendency to a fever, he must be sure to take his sweet drops.

She finished her letter that night in the home of the Drakes, three of whose daughters were at Saint Mary's. She was writing with "an iron stick they call a pen," and plunging it into the very depths of the bottle—"but I do not have to get down deep in my heart before finding the tender love that fills it for you all."

She found that Sister Liguori was very ill indeed; to Mother Theodore's experienced eyes it was clear that she would never recover. She wanted to take her back to Saint Mary's, but Sister Liguori, with the optimism of the tubercular, was certain she would soon be well. Perforce, Mother Theodore left her at her mission, though she knew she ought to have better care than she could get at Madison. She sent letters to her during the next month, insisting on frequent bulletins from the invalid and trying to make herself believe from what she read that Sister Liguori was really improving.

In early January, Mother Theodore received word that Sister Liguori was much worse and that one of the religious at Madison was bringing her to Saint Mary's. This would be a hard trip at that time of year, and Mother Theodore went part way to meet them. At Terre Haute, the river was completely frozen over, but as Sister Liguori was too weak to walk across it

Sister Celestia and Father de Saint-Palais, who had brought her, put her in a chair and the workmen carried her across. The invalid was placed in the infirmary, where she received loving care.

It was clear that she would not live long. The hard life of Saint Francisville had taken toll of a body never too strong. Though she seemed for a while to be a little better, Sister Liguori died in late January. The sisters had been grouped about her bed reciting the prayers for the dying, and when they finished Sister Liguori begged Mother Theodore to have them go to the chapel and recite the Miserere for her—"and the Memorare," she added faintly. They were her last words.

Despite frequent illnesses, this was the first death in the community. Mother Theodore sent a circular letter to the houses. "Be other Sister Liguoris to me," it ended. "Dear Sisters, that will be the best way of consoling the broken heart of your Mother Theodore."

Only a month later, she had to write another letter chronicling the death of another member of the community. Sister Seraphine was dead, only twenty years old and still a novice, one of the happiest of them all. When she entered, Sister Seraphine said she had made a great sacrifice to come. She had been told she would never be permitted to laugh after she became a nun, although she had so great a reputation for gaiety that she had been called "Laughing Eliza" at home. Father de Saint-Palais, who sent her to Saint Mary's, had teased her by telling her that no one ever laughed in a convent; she believed him, but she came anyway. At recreation on her first evening there, Sister Serapine heard the happy laughter around her and realized to her relief that she could still laugh, even if she was going to be a religious.

Now she was dead, and her one fear the day she died was that she could not receive Holy Communion, for her throat was so badly swollen that she could not swallow anything. When Father Corbe brought her the Host, however, she was able to take it without difficulty.

"We had a coffin made of cherry wood, lined with white, and we placed a white wreath on her head," wrote Mother Theodore in her letter to the houses.

When Sister Liguori lay dying, she said to the weeping sisters about her, "Oh, don't cry like that. The sisters in France have a home ready for us in heaven. Think how happy those from Ruillé will be when they see one coming from Saint Mary's." Now another had gone to join Sister Liguori.

In December of 1846, Father Corbe had been summoned to Vincennes and did not return until January of 1847. He had been offered the presidency of the seminary but had refused it. If he left Saint Mary's, it would be to leave the diocese, he had told the bishop. Although he remained with the sisters, from that day they worried about losing him.

Just before Easter came a letter from Vincennes: Father Corbe was to leave Saint Mary's in fifteen days. Mother Theodore, just recovering from severe pleurisy, wept at this news. "O my God," she cried, "You wish then to destroy our poor little community! No, there is no more hope!"

Father Corbe knew there was only one thing left to do now: to try to put off any action at all. It was known that the resignation of the bishop of Vincennes had been approved at the Council of the previous year, but it had not yet been accepted at Rome, and the bishop was still in power. Father Corbe was waiting for and hoping for the final word from Rome. In the meantime, the bishop still had full authority to act; he would, in fact, be in charge of the diocese until a new bishop was named.

For a time no word came from Vincennes, and though the silence ought perhaps to have alarmed them everything at the convent was moving so quietly and pleasantly that their fears died down. There was a general feeling of relaxation and the hope that all might be well. During those weeks there had been no need to consult the bishop and so provoke his anger.

Then word came that interrupted the interlude of calm. Rather, the word came indirectly from a community that wrote to ask Mother Theodore just when she planned to withdraw her sisters from Vincennes; the bishop was asking for sisters of their congregation to replace the Sisters of Providence.

Mother Theodore thought long and hard. The house at Vincennes was doing well; to give it up now would not make a good impression, for it would mean they were being dismissed from their episcopal city. She knew she must take some action, but first she prayed. She spent much of the night before the Blessed Sacrament, and in the morning her face was so radiant that Father Corbe asked her what good news had brought this happiness.

She smiled and answered him with a phrase from à Kempis: "In the Cross is infusion of heavenly sweetness."

No further word came about leaving Vincennes, and no movement on the bishop's part to replace the sisters. On April 19, Mother Theodore set out on her visitation—Jasper, Fort Wayne, Terre Haute, Madison. She planned to leave the house at Vincennes for the last; she had a presentiment that trouble was waiting for her there. Yet it was one of her houses, and if she went to one she must go to all.

She spent pleasant hours with her sisters at the various houses, and when she reached Vincennes there too she had a quiet day with her sisters in the old house where they were still living. Then, after having already engaged the stage for her return to Saint Mary's the next day, she went to call on the bishop.

He had very evidently been expecting her. He hardly waited for her to greet him and kiss his ring before he launched into an accusation that she was insisting on remaining as superior at Saint Mary's when he had some time before very definitely dismissed her from that office.

Mother Theodore collected her wits in the face of this unexpected attack. "Monseigneur, we will present the matter of an election to the sisters," she said. "If they agree and elect someone else that will free me of my charge. Until then I cannot leave my daughters."

"Very well," he said, and his face was red with anger. "Then you will have to wait right here until you obey my orders." He rose from his chair, and turned to leave the reception room. He turned the key in the door and went to his dinner. Only later her sisters, wondering why she was gone so long and fearing she might have been taken ill, came to the bishop's house. He unlocked the door where he had confined Mother Theodore. Very composedly she knelt before him and he blessed her. Then her puzzled and amazed sisters took her home.

Later in the evening, the bishop came to the convent and insisted on seeing Mother Theodore. He was still angry, more so than before. He began shouting at her almost before she came into the parlor.

"Not only are you no longer a superior, but you are no longer even a Sister of Providence," he told her. "I release you from your vows. You are to leave the diocese and go elsewhere to hide your disgrace. You are not to write to the sisters at Saint Mary's. They have no further need of your letters—or of you."

At Saint Mary-of-the-Woods, the community was awaiting their Mother's return. A letter had come asking them to send the carriage to Terre Haute, and they were waiting eagerly when it came in sight.

"Here is Mother," called several, and Sister Olympiade said, "Let us all go to the chapel and thank God she is come back," and they went to say a prayer. Then they hurried to meet the carriage. To their surprise only Sister Mary Xavier, who had been Mother Theodore's companion, alighted.

"Where is Mother?" they asked anxiously. "Is she ill?'

For a few moments Sister Mary Xavier could say nothing at all; then in a burst of grief she sobbed, "*Mon Dieu, mon Dieu*, she could not come. The bishop has expelled her from the congregation and forbidden her to come back to Saint Mary's."

They stood staring at her in disbelief, for what she had said was beyond credence. When she went with them into the house, she told them all that had happened. Mother Theodore had remained at the Vincennes house. There was really no other place for her to go.

While she was still on visitation, a letter had come to Mother Theodore from Father Corbe. "If the thunderbolt leaves you with one cent's worth of life," he wrote, "come back to us. No matter what anathemas you may be charged with, we will receive you with joy. But, despite my confidence in divine mercy, my soul is sad; it is truly tired of this sort of warfare—more and more arguments, no peace, and only a feeble hope for the future. Truly at present we can chant a *De Profundis*."

Now, only a few days later, the worst was known at Saint Mary's, and he wrote again: "What prevents you from returning here since the bishop has released you from all your vows? You could consider yourself as the common faithful, free to go where you please. Could you not take the stage on Monday? The sisters are in deepest sorrow; they indeed excite compassion. They will pray for you. Pray much to Our Lady; she will bring you back to us." He sent her his "unvarying affection and prayers."

Word of what had happened at Vincennes went to Archbishop Eccleston at Baltimore and to the superiors in France. The council sent word intimating that the Congregation was planning to leave Indiana; if Mother Theodore had to leave, they would all follow her. Father Corbe had already offered to go with them.

At a meeting of the sisters, novices and postulants, it had been decided that if Mother Theodore went they would go with her. Not one hesitated. A general resolution was drawn up and sent to Mother Theodore at Vincennes, announcing that although the bishop had sent word that any member who left the diocese would be excommunicated they stood ready to go wherever she would go.

In the meantime Sister Francis had received a letter from Archbishop Eccleston. He had read their news with painful interest and felt for them in their trials. However, situated as he was, he could not with propriety take any active part in their affairs. It would only make matters worse; besides he had no jurisdiction outside his own diocese. However, he felt no hesitation in urging them to be guided by Bishop Bouvier, whom he venerated as one of the most holy and learned prelates in Europe and who still had some measure of authority over the Sisters of Providence in the United States.

After that unhappy meeting with the bishop on May 20, 1847, Mother Theodore felt she could bear no more. She was in anguish over the situation — the accusations, the expulsion, the treatment of her as a rebellious subject, the fear of what might now happen to her sisters. Finally, she fell seriously ill. She had been worn out even before the bishop's attack. She had gone long miles by stage and packet to visit her houses, and now added to the physical fatigue came this mental anguish. What of her own future? She was a deposed religious, dismissed from her congregation. Had she any future at all?

An attack of her old enemy, pleurisy, brought her once again to a dying state. Dr. Baty said it was an acute condition of the disease and at one time he expressed doubt whether or not she would survive. She herself felt that she would not live and asked for the Last Sacraments.

Mother Theodore was actually glad to be dying, feeling that perhaps only her death would save her sisters from ruin. It was an unhappy time for her spiritually, too, for when she requested a confessor she was given her choice of the bishop himself or his nephew, who had just been ordained. She asked for someone else, but her request was refused and so she made her confession to the young priest.

Now a terrible fear beset her: was she to die without the consolations of religion? She had made her confession, but she had not received Holy Communion or extreme unction. The Vincennes sisters managed to send word to Father Corbe, and he made a quick trip, reached her late at night, administered the sacraments and returned home, no one knowing he had been there—so he thought. Mother Theodore, her mind at rest, began to recuperate.

Whether someone had told the bishop about Father Corbe's midnight visit to Vincennes was not certain, but the priest was suddenly summoned to Vincennes and deprived of his office as ecclesiastical superior to the Providence community—"for the fourth time in four years," he said with wry humor. However, deciding to wait before he took any action, Father Corbe returned quietly to Saint Mary's.

Dr. Baty was still refusing to allow Mother Theodore to have any callers. But when, on May 30, Father Bellier, president of the Eudist College, begged to see her for a few minutes because he had important news for her, he was admitted. He had just received a letter from his superior who had been in Rome and who had heard the Holy Father say, "I have accepted the resignation of the bishop of Vincennes."

A few mornings later, as the Vincennes sisters were leaving the cathedral after Mass, the bishop stopped Sister Vincent, the superior of the house. "You will be pleased to learn that you are to have a new bishop," he said abruptly. "I have just written to Father Corbe that I leave you in his hands until my successor arrives."

The official word soon came, and shortly after that Mother Theodore, with Father Corbe's permission, returned to her community at Saint Mary's. She was still so ill that it was feared she could not make the journey, but she wanted so much to go that the doctor agreed she might. She was carried on board the *Daniel Boone*, the Wabash River boat. Though she had been almost too weak to stand, she felt strength returning to her as the boat went along. Happiness gave her strength. She was going home.

It was a lovely day in mid-June. Flowers bloomed everywhere; birds were singing; a warm wind touched her cheeks. The wagon trundled slowly along the familiar lanes, and when it came in sight of the convent workmen fired a volley of gun shots to welcome her. Her sisters came to meet her in procession, Father Lalumière at their head on a white horse, his long white scarf blowing out in the breeze like a banner. Back of the sisters came the academy pupils and the farm workers. Around them all leaped Taillard, the convent dog, barking his welcome.

In the afternoon, Father Corbe gave Benediction in the chapel, and all who were there felt that this was indeed a benediction, a blessed happy end to difficulties, a new opportunity to go ahead with no more hindrance.

Though Mother Theodore had kept a journal ever since she came to Indiana, there was little in it about her difficulties with the bishop. There had always been his reputation to be considered; there had also been her own duty to him under God. She wrote little about him except for the careful letters to Le Mans and Ruillé. Otherwise she wrote little and said less.

But many had followed her troubled course and tried to help her or at least show their sympathy. Father Corbe and Father Martin had, without doubt, aided her most of all. Father Deydier had made vigorous efforts but with little success. Father Lalumière at Terre Haute had once written to Bishop Bouvier, "The poor Sisters are suffering grievously. I was almost exterminated, but I survived. And so have they."

The day after Mother Theodore returned home, a letter came from Father de Saint-Palais at Madison; he wrote sadly of the bishop who had resigned his see: "Poor Bishop, how unhappy he renders himself and with the best intentions in the world…. I was, and still am, like yourself, the object of his displeasure. But his last letter contained only reproaches for ingratitude, mingled with a sentiment of affection…. I only regret that he has not known who are the persons in his diocese who loved him sincerely. I trust that the peace that has been restored to you will continue."

CHAPTER FIFTEEN

Security at Last (1847-1850)

℃

On July 18, 1847, came word of the appointment of Father John Stephen Bazin to the see of Vincennes. He came from Mobile, where he had been vicar general. He was to be consecrated in the Vincennes cathedral on October 24.

The new bishop was French by birth and had come to the United States as a young man. He had a fine reputation as an administrator, and clergy and laity both looked forward to relief from the past hectic days. It was said of him that he had the kindness of a Brué, that he was a tenderhearted and humble man.

Bishop de la Hailandière was still in Vincennes, and Father Corbe heard that he planned to remain there. "He is going to build a fine house on his property at Highland and is telling people that Bishop Bazin will of course have spiritual authority only and that he is reserving the temporal for himself," said Father Corbe, with some alarm in his voice.

Mother Theodore had received an invitation to the consecration ceremonies and had planned to take with her several of the sisters. Almost at the last moment, however, the lung infection from which she still suffered intermittently grew worse, and so Sister Francis, the Vincennes superior, attended as her substitute.

Bishop Purcell came to the ceremonies. Bishop Portier of Mobile was the consecrator; his assistants were Bishop Purcell and Bishop de la Hailandière. Father Badin was among the priests in the sanctuary.

Bishop Purcell gave an eloquent address, and the new bishop spoke at Vespers to the large crowd assembled to hear him. It was evident that he was all but weeping when he ended, and his voice broke more than once during his sermon. Some of those listening knew why: he had been very loath to leave his beloved Mobile and Bishop Portier; he came only because he had been told he was needed.

He promised his new flock all his help. "Dear children, if you are sick or afflicted or suffering, send for me by day or by night," he told them. "Do not fear to disturb me, for I have today consecrated myself entirely to your welfare. My hair is gray, but I am still vigorous, and I shall love you exactly as I loved my spiritual children in Mobile." Many eyes besides his own were full of tears. It had been a long time since such words were spoken by a prelate to the people of Vincennes.

Sister Francis wrote full details of the ceremony to her superior at Saint Mary's. The Vincennes community of four had been invited to the dinner that followed Vespers. It was a very festive occasion, she wrote, except for the fact that Bishop de la Hailandière was there and obviously very unhappy. "It was sad to see him. He was like a man assisting at his own obsequies and discontented with his lot in the other world," she wrote.

When Mother Theodore read the message of the new bishop to his people, she hoped with all her heart that he would be able to make his program come true. He had been very cordial to the Sisters of Providence when they came to call on him, but later, when Father Corbe came to see him, it was clear that his attitude had changed. His manner was noticeably cold when the sisters were mentioned. Father Corbe learned that the retiring bishop had given his successor a full account of his grievances against the sisters, and especially against their superior. It was evident that the new incumbent was wary and waiting to learn more.

Evidently he made inquiries of his own, for when Mother Theodore herself wrote him a letter of welcome in which she briefly stated their past difficulties and her great hope that they would work together for God and in peace his reply was definite and reassuring. First, he told her to bury the past, or to remember it only as crosses sent by God because He loved them. "The future is yours. I shall judge you only by it and your rule," he wrote, and he hoped that nothing would disturb the happy harmony that should always exist between religious communities and the shepherd of the flock, "for it seems to me that if we on both sides seek the greater glory of God we must necessarily agree."

She read the letter over and over. If the Bishop Bazin felt like that, then a new era was opening for the diocese of Vincennes, one of true peace. There was an additional message that she hastened to share with her sisters: the new bishop promised that Father Corbe would remain as their chaplain.

A month later the bishop wrote again, this time enclosing a letter from the bishop of Le Mans: he was certain she would find it as fine a letter as he had. This time the new prelate wrote also that he approved their rule and promised that she would feel his authority only as a support to help her in carrying out that rule: "A bishop should be a lever to a superior to raise her up for her heavy burdens, a confidant to whom she may entrust her troubles and from whom she may draw consolations." He said he was planning to visit the community very soon. As yet he was overwhelmed with pressing duties and busy with the departing bishop about diocesan matters.

"I think that Bishop de la Hailandière will leave tomorrow by the stage," said Father Corbe one day, when he came from Vincennes. "His effects went yesterday by steamboat."

The former bishop had spent some time before selecting the place where he planned to live; he was building a house on his property at Highland two miles from Vincennes, from which vantage point he planned to supervise the temporalities of the diocese. He had evidently been dissuaded from all this, for early in December he left, telling no one his destination.

Bishop Bazin had done his best to be polite to him, but the one thing that Bishop de la Hailandière wanted—an invitation to remain in the diocese—was not forthcoming. During those first weeks at Vincennes, Bishop Bazin had heard many things from his predecessor—that the new incumbent was listening to poor advisers, that he himself was being treated like one driven from the diocese, that he could tell him a great many things he ought to know about the ingratitude of the Indiana clergy and the difficulty of getting along with the men and women religious.

"Like Don Quixote, he tilts at windmills," wrote the new bishop to Father Corbe, and it was clear he was growing weary of watching the pastime.

Mother Mary wrote from Ruillé, happy to know that now all would be better with her American daughters. She hoped that Mother Theodore would forget the past and never allow the person who had caused her trouble to be spoken of badly. At Ruillé everything was going on as usual: "Your best friends are all still alive, but we are growing old." Since her last visit, the congregation had opened twelve new houses. "We do all we can," she wrote, and then added a little wistfully, "we would do more did we enjoy the liberty that is given you in the United States.... Tell all your daughters in Indiana that their Grandmère Marie loves them very much and begs them to pray for her."

At the year's end, Mother Theodore learned that the seminary was demanding Father Corbe's return. He had begged the bishop to let him remain where he was, for the sisters needed him and he was very happy there. He would, of course, be on call to help the bishop whenever he was asked. Though he did not bring it forward as an argument, he knew that at Saint Mary's he could continue to carry on his beloved avocation, the increasing of his collection of butterflies and mineral specimens and shells. He had opened a little museum at the academy to house them. He was still pursuing his other interest, photography, with increasing delight. "If you bring me back some hyposulphite of soda, I shall repay you and daguerreotype you on your return," he wrote to Mother Theodore when she was on a visit to Louisville.

However, there was immediate need for a competent president of the seminary. "Where shall I find the right man?" asked the bishop. Father Corbe said that if Father de Saint-Palais could be persuaded to come, he would be excellent for the position, far better than himself. The offer was made, but Father de Saint-Palais came from Madison with only one intention: to decline the offer. When he was ushered into the bishop's office, he found the prelate in tears at the foot of the crucifix. The priest stood perplexed for a moment and then the bishop became aware of him; he rose from his knees and embraced him. "So you have come—and to stay?" he asked hopefully. "Are you come to help me in my very difficult task?"

Father de Saint-Palais found it impossible to refuse; he agreed to come to Vincennes. Bishop Bazin bought the Eudists' college, making it a combination college and seminary, but retaining the name, St. Gabriel's, and installed Father de Saint-Palais as its new head. The sisters at Vincennes were given the old seminary building to house their school. They were also to open a pharmacy as soon as possible. The new house was a gift to rejoice in, much larger and better in every way than the old tumble-down house in which they had been lodged.

Early in January of 1848, Bishop Bazin made his promised visit to Saint Mary's. He remained for six days, inspecting improvements, suggesting others, giving talks to the sisters and the pupils. They had hardly expected him before spring, for winter had set in early and with its usual rigor, with now and then a warm day to melt some of the snow and then a cold day to freeze it again and make the roads and paths a glare of ice.

"He was like a father to us," wrote Sister Francis in the annals. Before he left he went over small points of the rule with Mother Theodore. The only thing he had not liked at Saint Mary's was not really a criticism at all: it troubled him that their buildings were so far apart, especially hard on them in cold weather.

He was happy that Mother Theodore was pleased with the new house at Vincennes. Sister Marie Joseph, now superior there, told Mother Theodore of the bishop's goodness to them when the superior came on a spring visitation of her houses. She learned that not only had Bishop Bazin come to see that the moving was progressing satisfactorily but also he had helped them put the furniture in place and sent some additional pieces they lacked. Mother

Theodore brought home good news: the bishop had signed the deed for the property at Saint Mary-of-the-Woods. Now the sisters had legal possession of their home. After almost seven years of constant struggle, the congregation would at last know security.

At Vincennes, Mother Theodore had learned that Bishop de la Hailandière had not carried out his plan to sail for France but instead was in Baltimore working on a biography of Bishop Bruté. He had taken all the papers for this from the cathedral files. He wrote to Vincennes that he was planning one more trip to the middle west before he went abroad to live.

Soon after Mother Theodore arrived in Vincennes for the beginning of her visitation, Bishop Bazin had come to call on her, saying he heard she had been ill. "You must take good care of yourself," he said. "Your little congregation is too young to lose you. You have too much work still to do here."

He said he had spoken to Father Corbe about the advisability of holding an election at Saint Mary's. From Father Corbe's statement, and also from her letter of obedience that he asked to see, he learned to his surprise that Mother Theodore already held the office of superior general of her Congregation.

"Then elections do not matter at all," he said. "You are the superior general. I wanted to give you that title because I felt it necessary so that there would be more weight to your authority. I felt we owed you that mark of confidence after all you have suffered."

Mother Theodore wrote of the interview to Bishop Bouvier. "So you see, dear Reverend Father, all the difficulties are removed," she ended, and there was joy in every word.

Bishop Bazin had offered to come back in the summer for their retreat. That promise and others he was not able to keep, for he was taken ill with a heavy cold. When Mother Theodore heard of his illness, she came hurrying from a visitation at Jasper to see if she could be of any assistance, since she was trained in nursing. She found there was great need, and she took the bishop in charge. She was there when he received the Last Sacraments, his priests about him weeping.

He called her to his side and whispered, "Tell all your sisters that I love your congregation tenderly. God knows that if I had lived longer I would have done more for their spiritual and their temporal prosperity. Tell them that such were my desires and my intentions."

She could not speak. She could only nod to show she had understood. Even in his moments of pain and struggle, he was thinking of others and not of himself. After she gave him a drink of water, he said she must go and rest for a while. Later, seeing her on her knees, he smiled. "You and Father de Saint-Palais need not tire yourselves out by praying for me—a few elevations of the heart now and then will do," he said.

Early next morning he called to her. "Please—stay with me," he said, and she did, after calling the doctor. She and Father de Saint-Palais and Father Chassé were with him when he died, at six o'clock on Easter morning, after a brief illness of only eight days.

People who came to pray for him as he lay in the dim light of the funeral candles found it impossible to realize that he was really gone from them. In those six months he had healed many wounds and shown himself a man of love as well as one of high administrative ability. No doubt his death was at least in part due to the winter in Indiana, cold and harsh after the years of mild weather in Alabama. The deed he had signed for the Sisters of Providence had been the last of his official acts.

The former Bishop of Vincennes was not far away. When he learned of the death of Bishop Bazin, he said that though he was planning to sail for France he would be happy instead to return as bishop of his old diocese. To some people this was a startling offer indeed, and to none more so than those at Saint Mary-of-the-Woods, where there was a feeling that this would be much like Napoleon's return from Elba.

However, before long, Archbishop Eccleston settled the matter by writing directly to Bishop de la Hailandière: he did not think his offer to return to office was wise, but perhaps "from your local knowledge and experience you might facilitate the selection of suitable names to be sent to the Holy See regarding a successor to Bishop Bazin."

In May Bishop de la Hailandière sailed, after suggesting the name of Father de Saint-Palais for the Vincennes see.

When Mother Theodore came home after the funeral, she spoke to her sisters of the bishop who had left them for heaven.

"He loved us—he told me so—and do you know why? It was because he thought that love and concord reigns among us, and he who was all charity loved this virtue in us," she said. "So let us say again and never tire of saying it—'Little children, love one another.' For we cannot love God and not love our neighbors. The two loves are inseparable. I think the bishop would say they are even more—they are one."

The community began to make plans for a small memorial for the late bishop. It was to be the project he had asked them to establish in Vincennes, a small pharmacy for the poor people of the town. He had seen much suffering in the hard winter there—his first experience of such weather—and he could do little to help his people. But he knew that the sisters could, since some of them were nurses.

Sister Olympiade selected from her store of herbs a fine supply; drugs were also ordered from Baltimore. In the late spring the little pharmacy was opened in a room in the Vincennes convent as a memorial to the bishop who had stayed with them so brief a time and yet had made himself greatly loved.

Bishop Bouvier had written Mother Theodore to console her for her loss; he wished with all his heart that he could gather all the sisters about him and comfort them. He also wrote that he was getting old and would be asking for a successor soon. As for the political situation in France, it was far from good; it was, in fact, rapidly growing worse. Louis-Philippe, at first hailed by the people as one who would work for their good, was growing more and more illiberal, so much so that he now had arrayed against him many royalists and Bonapartists, as well as all the people of the left to whom the doctrines of Marx and Engels offered great appeal.

Only a few months later came word that Louis-Philippe had been forced into exile in England, following another revolution in France, which was now a republic. The bishop wrote that he feared for the safety of the religious houses.

This fear prompted Mother Theodore to write immediately to Ruillé to offer Mother Mary the hospitality of their convent at Saint Mary's if it became necessary for the community to leave France. Mother Mary thanked her for the offer but said that matters were not as bad as it had been at first feared they would be. The word "republic," of course, naturally alarmed them all, for it brought back the unhappy history of 1793 and memories of outbreaks in later years, but so far there had been no bloodshed

During that summer of 1848, Mother Theodore decided the time had come to organize their administration more closely. The Congregation had a considerable number of members now and there was need of a division of duties, since during all those years Mother Theodore had been functioning not only as superior but also as assistant and mistress of novices. When she called her professed daughters together to elect these officers, Sister Mary Cecilia was chosen assistant and Sister Francis as novice mistress and second assistant.

Father Corbe presided and Father Deydier and Father Lalumière were interested observers of the little ceremony that followed the voting. They brought the white cross which had once been worn by Mother Mary at Ruillé and placed it about Mother Theodore's neck. On the back of the cross was carved, *Supérieure Générale*. Bishop de la Hailandière had never allowed her to wear it.

Not long after the death of Bishop Bazin, a new house was opened at Terre Haute, one which had been planned for some time.

In 1837, when Mass had been said in Mrs. Williams' parlor, only five persons had been present. Three years later, when Father Buteux had been installed there temporarily, only ten signed to contribute to his support. The building of the canal had brought many Irish workers, and a little later German immigrants had begun to come. St.Joseph's Church, ambitiously built when the town had few Catholics, now was filled with parishioners.

In 1842, Father Lalumière came to Terre Haute as resident pastor, and soon afterwards he began asking for Sisters of Providence for his school. In 1848, feeling he at last had Mother Theodore persuaded, he bought a lot for a convent and school site and asked for contributions for the buildings.

Mother Theodore, well aware that he could not pay for this alone, agreed to help with the costs of the building and the furnishing of house and school. "The revenues from this house," she wrote Father Lalumiére, "as from all the others we have established, will be our trust in divine Providence."

The work began rather slowly, but advertisements in the *Wabash Courier* announced that by the beginning of the year "a day school for young ladies" would open at Terre Haute. It was something of a disappointment when only twenty-six pupils enrolled at first, but Mother Theodore was not discouraged. She felt that although this town was not so pleasant a place as Vincennes, it had far more of a future. She was right to be optimistic about the new school, even though it cost a good deal of money at first. St. Vincent's Academy grew rapidly. By the autumn of 1855 there were 140 pupils, and two pianos were needed for music lessons.

One other reason made this mission at Terre Haute of value to the Congregation. The town was on the direct route to their house at Madison and to others that were to be established a few years later. The sisters on their way back and forth no longer needed to go to an inn to spend the night but had a home of their own where they could stay.

After the death of Bishop Bazin, Father de Saint-Palais had been appointed administrator of the vacant see. Archbishop Kenrick of St Louis, Bishop Purcell of Cincinnati, and Bishop Spalding of Louisville, all of whom had been at the funeral, had learned that one of the requests of the dying bishop had been that Father de Saint-Palais he named his successor. After some months, though other names were suggested, his appointment was confirmed in Rome.

The bishop-elect, who had been head of the seminary under Bishop Bazin and also vicar general, was the one whom the whole community at Saint Mary's had been praying to have as their bishop. They knew him well. He had studied and been ordained at St. Sulpice; there he had met Bishop Bruté who persuaded him to come to Indiana where he had now been working for over twelve years. Three of his sisters were Sisters of Charity in France. One of them, the superior at Angers, Mother Theodore had known. She wrote to Bishop Bouvier after the appointment that their new bishop reminded her very much of the bishop of Le Mans—"which renders him still more dear to us."

On January 8, 1849, Bishop de Saint-Palais was consecrated in the Vincennes cathedral. For a time there had been a fear that the ceremony would have to be postponed because of the weather. It had been unusually warm and the melting ice had caused great floods. Bishop Purcell and Archbishop Kenrick were unable to come because cholera was rife in the south, the steamboats were crowded with refugees, and neither prelate felt he could leave his diocese in the emergency. Others could not come because of the floods, but two bishops finally reached Vincennes in time, Bishop Miles of Nashville and Bishop Spalding of Louisville, who came part of the way by wagon and with great difficulty.

On the day of the consecration, a torrent of sleet fell and the winds were of gale strength. Vincennes streets were all but impassable because of this sleet, of which Mother Theodore wrote graphically that "it forms a layer of ice like molten lead or lava from a volcano, covering every object it falls upon and taking its form, and woe to the man or beast exposed to its violence."

Despite the elements and the diminished number who could come, the consecration was held with great dignity, for many nearby clergy were on hand—"a veritable family feast for the clergy of Indiana," wrote Father Corbe of it to Father Martin.

A few months later, cholera struck the midwest, due in part to the many refugees fleeing from the south who brought it with them. The weather had become very cold, and this kept down the number of cases in the beginning. But the epidemic grew worse in the late spring, when the ebbing waters uncovered the low places along the rivers. Mother Theodore sent sensible advice to all her houses: "Do not fast. Eat well prepared food. Keep your children clean, those who are still with you. And pray." In regard to the nursing that many of the sisters were called on to do, she wrote: "Do good to all without distinction of persons. And write me, if only a few lines, about yourselves. Everyone here prays for you, loves you, is uneasy about you. And if you must die, then die for Him who died for you."

By August the epidemic was at an end, but it had left in its wake so many orphans that Bishop de Saint-Palais opened the old seminary for them; he renamed it St. Vincent's and asked the Sisters of Providence to staff it.

The retreat that year was a time of happiness for them all after the terrible winter and spring through which they had lived. None of the sisters had died, but some had been ill and others were worn out from months of nursing.

Sister Francis had escaped the cholera, but she fell ill in the autumn and her nurses for a time despaired of her life. One day Father Corbe said sorrowfully that he must soon give her the Last Sacraments; Mother Theodore was already trying to phrase a letter to Madame le Fer de la Motte to tell her of her daughter's death. It was a letter she did not have to write.

Sister Francis called weakly to her superior, "Could I have a little of the La Salette water? It will cure me." This was a small flask that had been sent her some months before by the M. Dupont—the Holy Man of Tours—who had sat and prayed with her in the stage when she was coming to America.

Mother Theodore saw that her sick sister was burning with fever and knew her little strength was almost gone. She brought the water to her with a prayer rather than with hope, and Sister Francis drank a little.

"What sort of cure shall I ask for, Mother?" she whispered. Mother Theodore, looking at her and hoping for the best, said, "A gradual one."

A few minutes, later Sister Francis sat up in bed to the amazement of her nurses who tried to persuade her to lie down again. "But I'm cured," she insisted, and asked for something to eat. The sisters, who had been called, came and embraced her with joy.

Later in the day, however, Sister Francis was once again close to death. Again they gave her a little of the miraculous water; it revived her, and by evening she was strong enough to speak aloud. Her first words were to tell those about her not to doubt that she would be cured. However, she was still so sick that Mother Theodore and Father Corbe came to kneel and pray for her. When she saw them, she managed a little smile and told them to continue giving her of the La Salette water. "Even if I seem to be dead, sprinkle the water on me. It will bring me back," she said.

Some hours later she asked for more of the water, and it was clear the "gradual cure" was almost complete. Soon she was able to get up and take a few steps, leaning on her nurse's arm. That night she slept soundly for the first time in days. When she woke, she said she was quite ready to go back to work. The doctor who was called to examine her said there was no doubt about it: the dying woman had made a complete recovery.

On December 3, the feast day of St. Francis Xavier, Sister Francis was able to go to the chapel, and that evening her feast was celebrated in the refectory. She was happy and evidently in perfect health. "Mother had a fine collation served," she wrote to her mother in France. "I shall whisper to you that they even drank a little wine, something which does not happen every day."

With the coming of Bishop de Saint-Palais, a good era came to Saint Mary-of-the-Woods, one that had begun under Bishop Bazin during his short time in office. The present bishop knew all about the Congregation and the difficulties the sisters had suffered under Bishop de la Hailandière. He himself had suffered under the bishop. He made very clear his own intentions in their regard. Financially, he could do little, for he was himself so poor that the sisters met the expense of his vestments and Sister Olympiade made all his new black and purple cassocks for him.

One day after the retreat of 1850, the councilors sent him a petition without having shown it first to Mother Theodore, and he answered promptly. "Like yourselves," he wrote, "I am sure the good of your community demands that Mother Theodore be retained in the office of superior general during her lifetime. I accede to your desire and confirm with all my heart the nomination made by the Bishop of Le Mans."

This freed the Congregation from something that had long troubled them: because of her continued ill health Mother Theodore might resign her office. No one among them could replace her. They knew this not only because they loved her but because they recognized her ability.

They learned they were not alone in their happiness at the decision of the bishops of Le Mans and Vincennes. When it became known outside Indiana, word came from others who knew of her and her work and all offered congratulations to her Congregation—Bishop Perché of New Orleans, Bishop Timon of Buffalo, Bishop Lefevre of Detroit, and many others. All rejoiced, as did the priests in the area of Vincennes who had worked with her.

From this time forward, there was never any further ecclesiastical trouble for the Sisters of Providence. The past began to seem like a bad dream from which they had wakened to reality. Troubles and problems lay ahead, sorrows and losses that were a part of human life. But these they knew they could bear.

Chapter Sixteen

The World Comes to Saint Mary-of-the-Woods

From the time the Sisters of Providence first came to the New World, the postulants who entered the Congregation were nearly all American born. The small group that came in 1840 from the older Congregation in the Old World had to depend almost entirely on the native population for its members. More than once, Mother Theodore had appealed to France for additions to their ranks, but none was sent; those who came did so for reasons of their own, as Irma le Fer had done, and as her sister Elvire, and later Mother Theodore's own nieces were to do.

By 1850, the Sisters of Providence were receiving many calls for new missions; sometimes it was even from a Protestant group that wanted a school for its daughters. The French academy teaching of both subjects and manners made many settlers, whose material condition was much improved since the early days, anxious to give to their children such an education.

Then, too, travel conditions were much better. Steam vessels were in common use. Railroads and canals were doing away with the long delays necessitated by river travel, and bridges over the Wabash made connections with nearby towns much easier. Mother Theodore said admiringly that in one year as much was accomplished in Indiana with ships and trains as it took the Old World twenty-five years to bring about.

Again and again, she longed for more sisters to carry out the increasing requests for schools. "If we had thirty more, we could use them all," she said, but vocations were not yet very common. Other established congregations were fortunate in that their motherhouses in the Old World kept them supplied with recruits, whereas the Sisters of Providence were completely dependent on the New World for members.

Even so, and with only limited numbers, there were now seven hundred children in their various schools, and well over half were Catholic. Occasionally one of the Protestant pupils was baptized into the Faith; if there were parental objections, however, the sisters followed the parents' wishes and did not allow the ceremony to take place. When there was no objection, there was rejoicing over the new Catholic. Perhaps the greatest excitement in the diocese was the day the Episcopalian minister at Vincennes entered the Catholic Church.

Even by 1850, it was evident that the convent at Saint Mary-of-the-Woods had outgrown its quarters. The academy had been enlarged from time to time, but the motherhouse had not, and it was a very cramped and crowded place. A new house was an obvious necessity. The summer of 1851 was unusually hot and rainy, and the overcrowded house made for great discomfort. The rains endangered the hay crop and the sisters helped with stacking it; then they had to return to a hot and humid house where the dormitory was under the roof. To add to other annoyances, a strange phenomenon known as the seventeen-year-locust made its appearance— "armed with a kind of saw, dangerous to plants and animals," the annals described it.

In her Christmas letter of that year to Bishop Bouvier, Mother Theodore outlined the year's work, its successes and failures, as she did each year. The Congregation now had thirty-three professed sisters and almost as many novices and postulants. At Vincennes, the two orphan asylums, which they had taken at the request of the bishop, were crowded with a hundred boys and girls. The bishop had wanted Father Sorin to send his brothers to take charge of the boys, but the priest said he could do it only if he were given financial aid. The bishop had no money to spare, and so the sisters took on Saint Vincent's for the boys as well as Saint Mary's for the girls.

Mother Theodore wrote that among the opportunities offered them that year was one in Louisiana, but it was very far away and they were really too poor to take it. Besides, the bishop was not willing to help: "His Lordship is deaf in that ear."

She wrote of France, too, for she knew of religious and political matters there from Father Corbe's French newspapers that he always lent to the sisters. "Faith seems to be reanimated and religion more respected there now," she wrote, "but one wonders how long this will last. I am always uneasy about you, my venerated Father, and about our Mother and Sisters there, and in fact about the whole of our dear France. She remains ever our country, ever dear to a French heart, even though for us she is so far away that she seems to be at the antipodes."

At the end of May 1851, Bishop de Saint-Palais departed for France on a quest for funds and also to secure more religious for his congregations, especially for those at Saint Mary's. It had been arranged in advance that any he secured would meet him at Ruillé and then come with him to Indiana. He promised he would be sure to call on Bishop Bouvier.

"You will find him a very kindly prelate," wrote Mother Theodore to Le Mans of their present bishop. "He has been so good to us all. He never makes us feel his authority except by the favors he bestows on us." That was very true. When he had money to give, he saw to it that they had their share; when he did not, he was thankful for all help given him. That was why she had sent sisters to his orphanages though she well knew the number of children there would increase and the funds for their maintenance would not.

The bishop was as eager as she that the Congregation have a new motherhouse, but the decision was that it would not be begun until much of the money to build it was on hand. By the next year they began planning it; Mother Theodore was to get architects' designs for it while the bishop was away. Only a few weeks after his departure, Mother Theodore met with an accident that almost put her beyond plans of any sort. She was saved by what seemed a miracle.

She and Sister Francis were coming home from Terre Haute on a quiet moon-lit night, and they were saying the Office together. The horse was part way across a bridge when suddenly it stepped back. Sister Francis jumped from the buggy to find out what was wrong and saw that the horse was still pushing backwards and the buggy was slipping over the edge of the bridge.

"Jump, Mother, jump," she called, and Mother Theodore attempted to do so, but she was too late. Suddenly before Sister Francis' horrified gaze the buggy, the horse, and Mother Theodore disappeared over the edge of the bridge into the ravine below. Sister Francis stood alone on the bridge. The buggy had overturned. In the moonlight she could see the horse lying on its back with Mother Theodore's head caught between the wheels and the horses's hooves. She was alive and calling for help.

A man passing in a wagon heard their cries for help and ran to be of assistance. He went carefully down the side of the ravine, managed to undo the harness, and untangled Mother Theodore. The horse remained quiet, otherwise Mother would have been killed.

When Mother Theodore was helped from the ravine, she was composed and it was she who comforted the weeping Sister Francis. It was not until she reached the convent that she began to shiver as with a chill. She was put to bed. But though they watched her carefully, she did not seem to have suffered any consequences from her terrifying experience.

No doubt each accident, each such hard trip, took away more of Mother Theodore's diminishing ability to recuperate. Her attacks of pneumonia had more than once brought her to death's door. It was little wonder, for the long trips in cold stages and on canal boats had been very hard on a body that had never really known good health. By this time, Mother Theodore could eat even less than in the past, usually a gruel made of flour and milk or perhaps broth made from a squirrel that Father Corbe shot in the woods. The too frequent use of the lancet, a common treatment of the time, did not help, for it drained from her the blood she needed.

Despite the hard illnesses, one fact emerged again and again; no matter how severe the sickness, Mother Theodore recovered and went to work again. It was as if her entire life was a series of little miracles. More than once, even the doctors despaired of her recovery, but she did recover and went back to work for the Congregation for whom she was heart and head.

The bishop did not return from Europe until the following October, and Mother Theodore went to New York to meet him and the postulants he was bringing with him. She wished to discuss the plans for the new motherhouse with the New York architect she had chosen, but she wanted the bishop to go over the plans before she decided fully on them.

She was delighted to find how travel conditions had improved since she made that trip more than ten years before. She stopped in Cincinnati and saw that the ramshackle cathedral she had seen when she first came there was replaced by a spacious and beautiful building, and a fine new seminary stood high on a hill of the city. In New York, too, there were many changes—more churches and more schools, and Madame Parmentier took her to the great white marble department store of Mr. A. T. Stewart, recently opened.

The bishop and his party had already reached New York when she arrived, and after their first meeting Mother Theodore sent an enthusiastic letter home. He had told her all about his meeting with the bishop of Le Mans—"the two pillars of our house in America were thus happily united." She added that he had brought her wonderful gifts for the missions and especially gifts for the orphanages. He had been at Ruillé, where he said all was prospering, and he was that day taking Mother Theodore to meet the young women he had brought and who were lodged at a convent in the city.

"Has anything important happened since I left?" asked the bishop, and then added that he was certain nothing adverse had happened, not with the diocese in the efficient hands of Father Corbe as his temporary vicar general.

"There is nothing new at Saint Mary's except that the railroad from Terre Haute to Madison is almost completed," she said. Then she smiled—yes, there was one other item of interest. Some Protestant groups at Madison were insisting that the Sisters of Providence pay taxes on their property there.

"We have refused positively," she said, and her eyes were full of amusement, "and I think it embarrasses the gentlemen a little to have women resist them—and quote the law besides."

She did not say that when she had written to Mother Mary about this, she had phrased it a little differently. "Women in this country," she wrote, "are as yet only one-fourth of the family. I hope through the influence of religion and education women will eventually become at least one-half— and the better half!"

The bishop took her to the convent to meet the waiting postulants, four in number. There had been five, but one of them, a German girl, grew so homesick by the time she reached New York that she had gone back again immediately.

Two were Belgian girls, lacemakers from Brussels, Justine Hermann and her sister Nathalie. The bishop had thought that they might start a new industry for his orphans through their craft, and they had brought with them their bobbins and threads and pillows. However, when they were ready to leave they were informed that according to Belgian law they could not sell such laces outside that country. They decided to come anyway.

Mary Marshall, the third newcomer, was an English girl, educated in a French convent, whose school the bishop had visited. He had so impressed the girl with his story of the needs of the religious in Indiana that she had given up her intention of going on the stage and had come with him instead. She had already spent four months as a postulant at Ruillé.

Her family lineage went back in history to an ancestor who had served with King John, and she said there was a martyr in her recusant family background. Mother Theodore listened with deep interest to her story. "How much you will have to tell the community," she said. When she learned that Mary was well taught not only in languages but also in music, she was happy. "You are the answer to prayer," she told her. "Our greatest need is a trained musician at Saint Mary's."

These girls, though welcome additions to the Congregation, were strangers to Mother Theodore. The fourth member of the group was one whose family she knew well and whose sister at Saint Mary's had long been praying for one of her sisters to join her in the Congregation. It was Elvire le Fer de la Motte, Sister Francis' younger sister. Ten years before, when Mother Theodore last saw her in a school in Paris studying voice and taking lessons on the harp, she had not dreamed that Elvire would one day come to New York and go with her to Indiana. Now here she was smiling at her, a dark, pretty girl who looked much like the sister who was eagerly awaiting her arrival at Saint Mary's.

"After eleven years I shall see my cherished Elvire," she had said joyously when Mother Theodore left for the East. When the two met at Terre Haute there was a touching reunion. They ran into each other's arms, and then the older sister held the younger away from her and looked at her, obviously wanting to speak words of welcome, but her emotion was too great. All she could say, stammeringly, was: "We are together again."

The bishop went to Saint Mary-of-the-Woods with them before he returned to his cathedral, even though he knew he was impatiently awaited there. He stayed several days, for there was so much to tell the sisters about their motherhouse at Ruillé, their good Bishop Bouvier, and the friends in France from whom he had brought messages. There were the gifts to examine, the many lovely things sent by friends and relatives. Mother Theodore looked at these with delight; there would be something to send to every house and to the little churches in small settlements that needed a few objects of beauty. Perhaps what Mother Theodore liked best of all was the statue of Our Lady of La Salette that the novices at Ruillé had sent to the American novitiate.

The new arrivals soon adjusted themselves to the community. The three French girls began to study the necessary English; Mary Marshall quickly showed her skill as a musician. Elvire seemed very happy and contented, but a troubled letter had come from Madame le Fer de la Motte: she hoped that Elvire would not suffer from too much poverty and hardship, for she was a delicate child and had always had very good care.

Sister Francis wrote to reassure her, and so did Mother Theodore. "We are not so poor as we used to be," wrote the latter. "As for Elvire, so with Irma, they are for us a treasure that all the gold in California could not equal. We shall take good care of Elvire." The food was ample now, she wrote, and Elvire was apparently thriving on it. "We have good bread," she wrote proudly. "We use beef each week and have good poultry. Each year we cure about five thousand pounds of pork. We have fifteen cows and good red wine from our vineyards."

She did not, however, write of the difficulties she was having with Sister Francis regarding the training of her young sister. "I'm afraid we shall spoil the dear child," Sister Francis said to Mother Theodore, who replied she thought that Elvire was too unassuming and gentle to be spoiled. Sister Francis was so severe with the training of her sister that more than once Mother Theodore had to interfere.

When next she wrote to Ruillé, Mother Theodore mentioned each of her new postulants. "Elvire is a daughter made to order," she wrote, "a gift from the Lord…. The English lady pleases everyone…. The little lacemakers have been quite timid, but they say they are very contented with us. These gifts of France are a joy to us."

Mother Theodore's first mention of the new motherhouse, the building of which began in the summer of 1852, was in her diary: "We have made our first contract for our future motherhouse. O Mary, take it under thy protection!"

It was to be a fine building, one hundred ten feet in length, forty feet high, and sixty-five feet wide. It would cost a dismaying amount of money too. At least forty workmen would be employed on it, and they did not work for nothing, said Mother Theodore ruefully. The Congregation had hoped to have a separate chapel, but there would not be money enough for that, and so it would be incorporated in the new building itself.

On Corpus Christi of 1852, the Blessed Sacrament was exposed in the convent chapel until after Vespers, and after Benediction the cornerstone of the new motherhouse was blessed. Father Corbe officiated and Father Lalumière gave an inspiring sermon before a large audience of religious, boarders, neighbors, and people from Terre Haute. They all entered the chapel in procession, singing the Litany of the Blessed Virgin.

In July of 1853, the new house was ready, and in that month the sisters gathered on the lawn to watch the gilded cross with the globe beneath it raised and placed on the roof. It was just such a one as stood on the motherhouse at Ruillé. Now there was another raised in the New World.

"God grant that it may triumph here too," wrote Mother Theodore in the circular letter she sent to the various houses. "It is with deepest joy and gratitude that we call you once more to your cherished home after a year of labor and trials, to take part in the annual retreat.... A house is ready to receive you. As yet it has only walls and a roof and hardly any furniture, but such as it is, you will be happy, for it is the fruit of your labors and your privations.... When we compare the little frame house in which we were received through charity twelve years ago with this splendid building, we see clearly the effect of the beautiful words: increase and multiply. We have indeed increased and multiplied. Our exterior improvements are astonishing. But does our interior advancement correspond? It is in the silence of the retreat that we shall be able to answer all these questions. Come then, my dear children, to refresh your souls."

By August 2, most of the sisters had arrived. They were present at the examinations of the students and the *distribution des prix*. One of the most prized of these was the premium for good behavior, a crown of artificial flowers made by the clever fingers of Sister Francis. The silver cross that was worn for a week by the girl who the week before had been judged the best-mannered and of "elegant decorum" was put away until school opened again.

On August 6, the feast of the Transfiguration, when Bishop de Saint-Palais blessed the new house, all the sisters were present. When they were gathered in the chapel, Mother Theodore looked over the rows of her Congregation. "Grant that they may love Thee always," she prayed, "and that they may love one another and never forget why they came here. And grant that all who shall dwell in this house in the future may one day be united in heaven."

After the retreat, ten young women received the habit, one of them a daughter of the Thralls family and another, Elvire le Fer de la Motte, who received the name of Sister Mary Joseph.

To the American sisters, the new house and the beautiful chapel were the results of growth and loving work and sacrifice, but to those who came from France with the first contingent it was much more. They remembered their first chapel in the New World—the dim cabin, the planks covered with blue calico that held the pyx whereon rested their Lord.

Now, in the new and lovely chapel there was a plain but fine altar, with beautiful linens spread on it, silver candlesticks sent by the Le Fer de la Motte family, silver bowls full of Easter daisies, and a ciborium worthy of Him. He had been with them in the cabin chapel as well as through the later years. That was really all that mattered—that they have Him in their midst.

One statue was in the new chapel that had for some years been lost to the Congregation, though it belonged to them. Ever since Bishop de la Hailandière had ordered the statue—the one which M. Bertaudière had sent the Congregation—taken to the new village church, Our Lady had remained there. Now she was brought home again and placed in the new chapel.

"She will come back to us some day for her hand," said Mother Theodore on the day she was taken away. And so she had. The treasured hand that had been dropped by the workmen in moving the statue was carefully put back into place.

A considerable group had assembled at Saint Mary-of-the-Woods for the retreat of 1853. There were about fifty sisters in the Congregation now and a large group of postulants. In their various schools were more than a thousand pupils, and every sister was needed. This new motherhouse would accommodate many more than the present number of religious. It had been built for the future.

Sometimes Mother Theodore worried about the new building. "I find it too elegant," she wrote to Bishop Bouvier. "It looks more like a castle than the dwelling of poor little Sisters of Providence. I think it might have been built cheaper and less sumptuously."

It was true that she had wanted only simplicity and a solid structure, but in spite of her intention "elegance has crept in," as she phrased it, "and I really don't know how." She felt it would be sad indeed if through her example extravagance were introduced among her sisters. When she came into the chapel, however, she was happy that the Lord had so beautiful a home; she felt no scruples about that and could take comfort in telling herself that the house and chapel, which together would cost fifteen thousand dollars, were already two-thirds paid for.

When Bishop Bouvier wrote to answer her unhappy letter about elegance, his words removed any lingering scruple from Mother Theodore's heart. He said forthrightly that the requirements of the age demanded such a building, that it had been adapted only to the actual needs of the Congregation and could in no sense be considered an infringement on the vow of poverty.

As a matter of fact, though the house was a substantial one, it was also very plain. Coal oil lamps and candles furnished the lighting; a few fireplaces and small stoves provided all the heat; water was still brought from outside and carried to each storey, as was the firewood. It was very true that the exterior of the house was extremely attractive, its design very good, its roof painted a warm gray, the shutters a dark green and the bricks a soft dull gray.

Mother Theodore had written a full description of it to Ruillé and had promised to send pictures of the chapel—"the prettiest little chapel I've seen since I left France"—and a picture of the new motherhouse—"said to be the most beautiful building in the state."

When Mother Theodore's own room was ready, she moved into the small apartment that was to be hers. Her first prayer was that all who would come to dwell there in the future "may be always animated by Thy spirit, be devoted to the Mother of Sorrows, and die in Thy love."

The orphan asylums at Vincennes, which Mother Theodore had taken charge of at the plea of Bishop de Saint-Palais, were projects to which she gave much attention. This work was entirely a free will gift, and her sisters there received no salary; it was the one thing she could do for the prelate who had done so much for them.

Bishop de Saint-Palais constantly expressed a desire to see Sisters of Providence in every possible locality in his diocese, and when Mother Theodore could do so she aided him in this endeavor. It was easier now, for the Congregation had more well-trained members for such missions.

In the autumn of 1853, a mission was opened at Evansville, where Father Deydier had for a long time been asking for one. The bishop, two years before, had bought a house in that town and now he offered it to Mother Theodore.

In earlier years, when Bishop Bruté sent priests to serve the few Catholics, mostly German, at Evansville, there had been little reason for a school. Now, with a great influx of settlers, many of them Catholic, Evansville had more than doubled its population. Father Deydier, pastor there since 1838—two years before the Sisters of Providence from France had looked with sorrow at his shabby cabin and his neglected clothing—was still resident there. By 1854, his pleading for a school was successful. On August 19, Mother Theodore and four sisters went down the Wabash by canal boat to Vincennes and thence overland to Evansville to open a school.

The high hope with which they came, however, was slightly dashed when they faced the reality. For one thing, the Catholic attitude proved one of indifference to their coming, a thing that did not too greatly trouble Mother Theodore, who had come there at the bidding of the bishop and intended to remain. But it was distressing to find that no preparations had been made for their coming. The Griffiths house that had been given them was not only not cleaned; it was entirely without furniture. Parishioners took them in for the night, and next day the sisters went to work to clean their house. For a week they slept on straw ticks on the floor.

Before Mother Theodore went back to St. Mary's before school opened on September 5, leaving a modestly furnished house for her new community, the Catholic attitude had changed. The high school—named St. Joseph's Academy—soon rivaled the best in private schools, and before long Protestant parents were sending their daughters there.

When Mother Theodore came on visitation in June of the following year, even she, who was not exuberant as a rule in her remarks, spoke of the academy's "surprising progress" and promised for the next year six sisters, a number fully justified by the increased enrollment.

For some time the two Le Fer sisters, Sister Francis and Sister Mary Joseph, had wished to send a personal gift to their mother in France. It was Mother Theodore who thought of the best thing of all: a daguerreotype of Sister Francis herself. This delighted Elvire, but not her older sister when it was proposed. In fact, it was not until Mother Theodore and the two sisters were driving to Terre Haute one pleasant day that she suggested it, only to have Sister Francis object immediately and strongly. She was still refusing to consider it when the horses were crossing the Wabash bridge.

Mother Theodore finally won her over. "Forget about yourself, Sister. It is to be made for your family. Can't you see the delight of your mother when she opens the package?" she asked the reluctant nun. "Think of the joy you will be giving to her. It will be like having you with her again."

On the basis of the happiness for her mother, Sister Francis finally agreed. They went to the little studio in Terre Haute, with its skylight in the roof, and Sister Francis submitted to not one but two pictures.

On the way home she had a counter proposal to make: Mother Theodore must have her own picture taken soon, for it would give her daughters great joy, even as she had said how Madame le Fer would be delighted with one from her daughter.

At first caught unaware, Mother Theodore began objecting in her turn, even more strongly than had Sister Francis. The subject was dropped, but Mother Theodore had an unhappy feeling that it would come up again and that it would be difficult to justify her own refusal. As she feared, it was proposed and she resisted. Eventually she yielded, but only after she had written to Mother Mary to ask her permission and had received it.

During 1853, there had been an unusually severe cholera epidemic in the area. The Congregation of the Sisters of Providence suffered the loss of one member, Sister Lawrence, one of the postulants whom Mother Theodore had brought with her from France on her second journey; the sister who had nursed her and been her companion on the trip home from New Orleans.

There had been so many ill of the plague at Fort Wayne, where Sister Lawrence was stationed, that Father Benoit had called on her for help with nursing, and she wore herself out until she fell a victim herself. When Father Benoit told Mother Theodore of her death, he said, "First she asked me to tell you that she had no regrets in this life—none at all. Then she said to me, after I had given her the Last Sacraments, 'Thank you a thousand times, Father—you are good to the very end.' But it was she who was good to the very end, Mother. Her last moments were like the evening of a beautiful day."

Mother Theodore's tears fell fast as she listened, and in part it was because she had been away from the bedside of this beloved daughter in her last illness. She knew the young religious had been in good hands. "Now we have a martyr of charity to pray for us in heaven," she told Father Benoit.

As with all the others before it, the 1854 report of the Congregation's year was sent to Bishop Bouvier. Mother Theodore wrote of the public school system now established in Indiana, which had closed many schools for private pupils throughout the state. Catholic schools were continuing, but fewer children attended them. Their own schools had lost few. At Saint Mary-of-the-Woods there were now seventy-eight boarders and at two newer schools, Evansville and North Madison alone, there were over two hundred children.

Prosperity accounted in part for the increase in the number of boarders among Catholics, of whom there were now many in the academies, whereas in earlier years the schools had had chiefly Protestant pupils. Some years before, there had not been ten Catholics in Indiana who could afford to pay room and board for their daughters; now there were many.

Mother Theodore felt a great joy in having more Catholic children at the academies, but she wrote the bishop that she liked the others, too, both for themselves and because these students became friends of Catholic students and also because they learned there Catholic truths and often became their advocates when they heard doctrines laughed at or falsely stated in their own circles in the world.

She wrote of a community of Benedictines who came to the forests of Indiana in that year to serve the German population, very numerous there—"and difficult to manage. I think they are even more headstrong than the Bretons!"

At the end of her letter she voiced a hope she had held for a long time and had spoken of often: that Bishop Bouvier come to visit America. The great difficulties of travel were over now. When she had first crossed the Atlantic, the trip had taken sixty days. Now a steamship from Le Havre to New York made the crossing in nine or ten days. It had taken three weeks to come from New York to Saint Mary-of-the-Woods at that time; now it took forty-six hours.

She wanted very much to have Bishop Bouvier come to visit them and see how the six daughters he had sent into the New World had grown in numbers. She wanted to show him their schools, with over a thousand pupils in them now. Bishop Martin of Louisiana—to them he was still their Father Martin—was going to Europe soon. Perhaps Bishop Bouvier could return with him for a visit?

In October of the same year something new and exciting came to disturb the quiet of Saint Mary-of-the-Woods.

Ever since the sisters' arrival, the forest had been silent save for the sounds of birds and animals, of children at play, of the convent bell, and the occasional whistling of the steamboats on the Wabash. Now came a new sound—the shrill puffing and whistling of a steam engine. The train cars had come at last to Saint Mary's. There would be a little station where the trains would stop to take sisters to other towns and bring pupils to St. Mary's Institute. It was true, of course, that at first there were frequent breakdowns, and sometimes the old stagecoach had to be dusted off and brought to serve until the new mechanism functioned again.

The trains would bring great changes to their little town, for much of its isolation would now be a thing of the past. Parents could bring children from longer distances—something which proved true even before the end of that year. The school was so filled that already there was discussion about utilizing some of the rooms at the convent as bedrooms for the pupils.

All thought of moving elsewhere, as had sometimes been discussed, had been forgotten or set aside long since. And now this—a train that stopped at their very door—banished such ideas forever. The world had come to Saint Mary-of-the-Woods.

CHAPTER SEVENTEEN

Another Teresa (1855)

Through all the years of changing prelates and priests, one priest had remained constant—Father Corbe, their spiritual director, their never-failing friend. He was a busy man who had other tasks to carry out in parish and diocese, but always the Sisters of Providence were his first care. During all the years since he had come to Saint Mary-of-the-Woods, he had watched over them. Sent away several times by the unreasonable attitude of one bishop, he had been hailed and admired by two others. His small church—when he first came his parlor had held all his parishioners—was now filled with more than four hundred parishioners every Sunday. He served as theologian to Bishop de Saint-Palais on several occasions and was administrator during the latter's absences. He had many visitors, some of them from far away, for he was well known, but during the past few years he had himself gone no farther than Vincennes; he had been too busy.

For years he had had one ambition: to visit once more his dear Brittany. Every time he had the money saved up, St. Mary's village church needed something—repairs or vestments—and the fund for Europe went for those. He still had his avocations; he still collected flowers and minerals and took a deep interest in photography. Everything he shared with the sisters; they were all allowed to read his weekly copy of *L'Univers* from Paris and his scientific magazines.

There were still quite a few non-Catholic girls in the Academy, and Mother Theodore was pleased with their scholastic achievements; but the great desire of her heart was to see these beloved girls become interested in the Faith. Many came with no religion at all; when they left, they had at least an understanding of the Christian faith, but the majority went no further.

Some did, however. It was a happy day for Mother Theodore when five of her pupils received their first Holy Communion after they had been baptized the evening before. She felt that good results would come from this small group, results that would one day be of value to Saint Mary's. She was right. Later two of the five entered the Sisters of Providence and became Sister Mary Ursula and Sister Mary John.

No doubt Mother Theodore did not realize how much she had herself contributed to such results, both by her very life and by her talks to the students. Her conferences were never long, but there was always about her an air of contagious happiness that held them. Despite her almost constant ill health, she always radiated love of life and confidence in God.

With her sisters, the one virtue she was fond of emphasizing was charity; the one person who entered her every talk was Our Lady, the model of charity and love. Every spiritual meditation brought mention of this virtue and of the Mother of God.

Of charity she would say that it was no cloistered virtue. "And so let us continue to impress its value on our students," she would tell them. "Don't let them think that giving alms is all there is to it, either. It may be charity to refrain from saying anything unkind about one of the other students." She often quoted the phrase from the Canticle of Canticles: "He hath set charity in order in me."

In her talks both with her pupils and her sisters, Mother Theodore spoke always with complete informality. She was always on the alert lest her sisters become introspective by too much meditation. As she told them, there was more than one kind of recollection. Merely to be occupied with God's business was recollection, and referring one's actions, all the work of one's day to Him, was also a form of prayer.

"We are surely more acceptable to our Lord when we form and teach the little ones who have been given into our charge than if we prayed fervently on our knees all day long—even before the tabernacle." If some of the sisters in other houses felt they ought to hear from her more often, she would say gently: "Prayer is our postal service, our telegraph, our surest means of communication," and they all knew that she never failed them in that.

When young Sister Josephine died (who had been a pupil in the school and greatly loved), Mother Theodore, despite her grief and her willingness to admit that it was the Lord's will, yet took occasion to speak to the sisters of the fact that Sister Josephine had been very careless about her health; it was the only cause of trouble she gave her superior in all her short life. "You must not forget this, my children," she said. "Health belongs to God and you must take reasonable care of yourself so that you can work for Him and for souls."

It made her impatient, too, when a sister tried to conceal her sufferings and pretend she was well. "There is no real merit or humility in not complaining when one is really suffering," she told them. "I cannot admire that sort of virtue—if it is a virtue. When we are ill, we should say so and get help to become well again so that we may give our best efforts to our work."

Mother Theodore was a practical woman who knew that to direct a school well demanded money, but she never wanted this emphasized to the exclusion of other things. "All we teach our children must be for the glory of God and for the love of the children," she said. "The profit that the community derives from its school is a secondary consideration. Believe me, my dear daughters, there will always be money enough at Saint Mary's if the religious are good religious."

When she spoke of prayer, much of what she said was what she had read in her patron's writings, the great St. Teresa for whom she had been named. What she most often held before her sisters, when she spoke of that saint, was not her raptures but what she called the "commonsense piety of Teresa." Mother Theodore was practical herself as well as prayerful, and she often warned against aimless musing and dreaming that were not really prayer at all nor even meditation.

"It is a waste of time," she would say, "and it produces nothing. That devotion is not solid that flits about from thought to thought like the bee sipping honey from the flowers. It may be the bee's nature, but it is not ours. The bee sips and then goes to work. If we try that method, we shall sip and then dissipate and be empty-handed as well as empty-hearted. And then we shall have no gift to offer Him at all. In fact, we can hardly find Him then, for we shall have wandered so far from Him."

Once a Jesuit, visiting at Saint Mary's and himself a deeply spiritual as well as a scholarly man, heard Mother Theodore talking to the sisters. He had heard her say: "Soul vagrancy—what a futile thing it is for us, and in the end it produces only bitterness and weariness and even disgust, for it is the product of our unpractical devotion.'

He had been passing by when he stopped to listen to this, and she did not know he had been there at all. He was so interested that he stopped at the door to hear the rest of her remarks, and then he said to Father Corbe: "I'm not sure there is any reason for my speaking to these sisters when they have such a Mother to instruct them. And I am inclined to say to you that I think you have here another Teresa!"

In October of 1854, word came that Bishop Bouvier was ill, and Mother Theodore wrote him that she hoped his illness would not prevent his attending the Council at Rome, where the decree of the Immaculate Conception was to be promulgated; the whole Congregation was praying that he might be well enough to attend.

She knew that he always liked to hear news of her community and every letter carried some. This time she told him that despite the storms again arising against the Church because of bigots, the sisters were still advancing in numbers and their schools were constantly growing. There were now about sixty sisters clothed in the Providence habit, and as he perhaps knew two more future members were on the way from France, her own nieces, the daughters of her sister Marie. One of them, Sister Mary Theodore, named in honor of her aunt, had been for six years a religious at Ruillé. With her was coming her younger sister Frances, was still living at home and would be a postulant in the community in America.

With the new recruits there would now be sixteen postulants at Saint Mary's, Mother Theodore wrote. The house was filled. Father Gleizal, who gave their retreat that summer, had told Mother Theodore that in his opinion he knew no community in the land where the members loved each other as they did at Saint Mary's. She felt there was perhaps a measure of truth in this kindly remark, and she thought much of this affection was due to the wisdom of the rule that Bishop Bouvier had helped write for them. "If only we observed it perfectly, it would make great saints of us all," her letter ended.

That autumn another mission was opened, at Lanesville, where the pastor had made arrangements with the bishop to secure women religious for his school. This town in southern Indiana had once been an important stage stop. Mass had been said there in earlier years by Father Badin each time he passed through on his annual middle west visitation. By 1843, so many Catholics had settled there that a pastor from a nearby town came each Sunday to say Mass. In 1854, Father Munschina, who had been made its first pastor, realized the immediate need of a school. He visited personally the hundred and twenty families in his predominantly German parish and found them as eager as himself about their children's education. He began begging the bishop and Mother Theodore for sisters.

When the priest knew they were really coming, he vacated his little rectory and had it made into a house for them. When the three sisters, with Mother Theodore and Sister Basilide, came to Lanesville, they were escorted to their new home by a procession of singing parishioners, who made it very plain that they were thankful to have in their midst these teachers for their children.

On their return trip, Mother and Sister Basilide planned to stop at the house in Madison. As the river boat on which they were traveling would reach that town at night, they had left word to be awakened. No message reached them, and before they realized that they had been forgotten the boat had already left Madison. Mother Theodore appealed to the captain, who offered to have the two religious rowed ashore in a skiff.

Unfortunately, as they stepped from the ship to the small boat, the man who was rowing it pushed away too soon and both sisters were thrown into the water; at that point the Ohio River was at least twenty feet deep. Sister Basilide was reached and pulled to safety quickly, but Mother Theodore was left in the water for several minutes, clinging with one hand to the steamer's side, before she was rescued.

Another skiff was brought, and the sisters completed their journey. They were shivering when they reached the house and Sister Basilide, who seemed really ill, remained at Madison where she was local superior, while Mother Theodore, after a short visit, went home to St. Mary's alone. Once there she said nothing about the accident; in fact, no one knew about it until a week later when a pupil whose father had been on the steamer brought the news.

Mother Theodore tried to shrug the matter off, but at last she said: "Yes, it is true. But, Sisters, it was so terrible that I cannot speak about it. Don't remind me of it—let me forget it. And let us thank God, who sent his angels to help me."

The fright and the exposure had bad results later on. They doubtless accounted for the illness from which Mother suffered soon after she came home and from which she did not recover for more than a month. Then she was so quickly and unexpectedly well that the rumor sprang up that she had been cured by a miracle. This Mother Theodore took pains to deny and tried to disillusion those who thought so.

"You are in error if you think I am cured, my children," she said. "Far from it. But God will not take me away until He wishes to use this poor instrument no longer."

In a letter that Mother Theodore wrote to the bishop of Le Mans that was to be waiting for him when he returned from Rome, she had said that her greetings would await him when he came from his long journey.

By that phrase she did not mean what the words came to mean, as if they had been a sad prophecy. For the bishop was taken ill again before he could leave Rome, and his last journey was not to Le Mans from Italy but to another world.

Bishop Bouvier died a few days after he had heard the decree pronounced for which he had hoped and prayed for many years. "It would be good to die now," he said when he heard the pope speak the words; it was as if he had a prescience of what was at hand.

The Holy Father, who was devoted to the aged prelate and knew well his learning and his virtues, had wished to be his host while he was in the Eternal City. In the Quirinal Palace, a suite of rooms had been made ready for Bishop Bouvier on the ground floor, since he had great difficulty in climbing stairs. When he reached Rome, he had been faint with weariness, but by the next day he was able to be at the Council with the others. His joy was so deep that perhaps it took some of his waning strength, for afterwards he felt so ill that he went to his rooms and to his bed. He was never to leave it again.

Some weeks later, when he learned that the end was near, Pius IX, putting aside court etiquette, came to see the old bishop. When he saw the pope entering his door, the sick man joined his hands as if in prayer. His face full of joy, he said, in Latin: "What a great grace is given to me!" The pope answered him in his native French. "Do you place yourself in the hands of God, my son?"

"I do, Holy Father—and in yours," he said. They were alone together for a long time and when the pope came from the old prelate's room he was weeping. "Oh, how good, how very good this man is," he said.

Bishop Bouvier died four days after Christmas. When his secretary was asked about his last hours, he said he had already tried to tell the Holy Father but that tears interrupted his speech, and the pope had said comfortingly: "Do not weep. He died the death of a saint. He is in heaven."

The blow to Mother Theodore was great, even though she knew the bishop of Le Mans was very old and very tired. She felt as if her own father had died, for since the beginning he had been friend and supporter, a father in every sense of the word.

She sent a circular letter to all the houses: "Our beloved bishop of Le Mans has gone to a better world. He died in the Eternal City, after having heard spoken the decree of the Immaculate Conception. His heart was filled with gratitude, but it was a gratitude to heaven that filled it. The world had nothing worthy of his great soul. He was in our days of darkness what the luminous cloud was for the Israelites in the desert, a shelter and a light. Saint Mary's owed him its very existence and preservation.

"Only five weeks before he set out for Rome, he wrote that he would send us his picture, a promise made at my request, and with it a regret that he could not come himself to bless the community whom he called his Daughters of the Woods."

Mother Theodore wrote to his former secretary, Abbé Sébaux, that the community had nothing at all to remind them, and to show those who came after them, of the bishop and what they owed to this venerated father whose generous heart never knew the forgetfulness that distance sometimes brings. The promised portrait had not arrived—would he have another copied for them?

The Abbé sent a picture and with it an alb that had belonged to the bishop and that Mother Theodore decided the community would use at the four great feasts and at the close of the annual retreats. Ten photographs of the bishop were also in the parcel, and these she sent to the various houses. A medallion containing a lock of his hair was kept at the motherhouse as a treasured relic.

In January of 1855, word came that the Immaculate Conception of Our Lady was now declared an article of faith. At Saint Mary's a commemorative jubilee was held, with Father Corbe presiding at both the exercises in the village church and those at the convent. The community assembled in the chapel and chanted the *Te Deum* and planned to sing it again at Benediction.

Mother Theodore's two nieces, carrying out the promise they made her a decade earlier, had left Ruillé, so a letter informed her, but she heard no more until a telegram came announcing their arrival in New Orleans. Again there was no word for two weeks, and by the beginning of the third week Mother Theodore was seriously worried. Then one day Sister Mary Joseph came hurrying to her superior.

"I hear the carriage coming," she called and they hurried out to greet the travelers, who were weary but happy. They reached Saint Mary's on Christmas Eve, and they were as wonderful a Christmas gift as Mother Theodore had ever received.

The two nieces had had a hard trip. They had come from New Orleans by river boat. As the water was low in the Mississippi, they traveled no more than ten miles a day. There had been much cholera in New Orleans, and evidently some of the passengers were infected; twenty-one had died on the ship. Then, too, there were a depressing number of vessels in the river, burned out or stranded by the low water. The travellers were happy when at last they left the boat for the train cars.

Since they spoke no English, they found it hard to understand directions given them. In fact, when they reached Vincennes, they did not get off the train, for they had not understood the American pronunciation of the town when the conductor called it out. But they had managed to get there at last, thanks to kindly people who patiently listened and managed to understand them and get them going in the right direction. They were especially delighted because some of the passengers on boat and train had taught them a few English words. Already, they said, they felt like Americans.

Mother Theodore had been ill for some time when her feast day came in 1854, but her sisters had gone ahead with plans for celebrating it. On that day, she was much better and a throat condition that had for some time caused the complete loss of her voice had greatly improved.

"Your voice is better than ever," said Sister Maurice admiringly. "It is as good as the time you took us out to burn stumps and you had to shout to make us all hear you." She was busily painting a scene on a card, while Mother Theodore admired those already completed. Sister Maurice was a very talented artist, who had come to Saint Mary's some years before from Germany. She usually painted little scenes, and many had a close resemblance to one another. When people asked her what place it was she painted so often, she would say, with a sigh and in a voice still accented, "Inspachen, where the Moselle enters the Rhine."

During the winter and spring of 1855, Mother Theodore was ill for much of the time, and even by summer, when the sisters came home for the retreat, she could not make it with them. She was still so ill when they left for their missions that she could not come to the door to say goodbye, as was her invariable custom.

Father Gleizal, who had come to Saint Mary's to give the retreat, was greatly worried about her, and the sisters said they thought it chiefly due to the fact that she had insisted on making a spring visitation; they had not been able to dissuade her. Father Gleizal said there were many things she could easily delegate to others, such as reciting the public prayers and writing so many letters.

"I would consider, had I the authority, what is beyond her strength and veto her doing it," he said firmly to Father Corbe, who could only say sadly that he had suggested this himself more than once but with no success.

A month later she was able to take up again the general work of supervision of the motherhouse. And now she embarked on a project that she had had in mind for some time—a new chapel for Saint Mary's. This was no rash idea, for the motherhouse was almost paid for and they had no other debts; besides, she already had a nucleus of several thousand dollars put aside towards a chapel building fund.

She had very definite ideas about this building. It was to be in honor of Our Lady—"nothing that is good but has come to us except through Mary," she often said—and she had sent to Ruillé to ask for plans of the new chapel they were building: she wanted to have their own at Saint Mary's follow the Gothic architecture used in the Providence chapel in France. She still had in her the desire to reproduce in the New World that which she loved dearly in the Old, the material as well as the spiritual.

In October, she signed a contract for bricks for the new building and workmen began hauling the logs to be used in firing the bricks. All that autumn she was so much better that her sisters worried less about her. She was up all day and seemed once more her unwearied self.

She wrote many letters during those months, especially to her daughters in difficult posts and to those who were new in positions of authority. In a letter to Sister Gabriella, one of her first postulants in the New World whom she always called her "good little Easterner," she told her how pleased she was at her success in a very difficult task and that she was praying for her. She added that she felt in much better health than she had for some time; then she qualified that statement: "But in reality all my better health means is to feel a little stronger than I did."

One letter went to Sister Mary Magdalen, a new superior at Fort Wayne and young for the office she held. She was praying for her, wrote Mother Theodore, and she told her to remember that the two virtues she must concentrate on were abstemiousness and kindness.

A long letter went to Sister Basilide at Madison to say how happy Mother Theodore was that the sisters would soon be in their fine new home in North Madison. "I know you will find the first parts of my letter very serious," it ended, "but I wanted to write it to you so that you may make use of it, before or after my death, according to your wishes." Evidently she had changed her mind about this, for she added last of all that she had decided to save that portion of it and send it to her on a later day: "You will have it from me some other time if you so desire. It concerns France."

When Sister Basilide wrote, anxious to know immediately what this message might be, Mother Theodore sent it to her. It was that she thought Sister Basilide might, after her superior's death, wish to return to France, and she wanted her to consider it very seriously. Mother Theodore's own feelings were that Sister Basilide would be unhappy if she went back and would soon wish herself at Saint Mary's again, and she chronicled her own feelings during those first years away from Ruillé and in the forests of Indiana.

"Since the day fifteen years ago when I first received our Lord in a new land, America ceased to be for me a strange country and became the land of my adoption.... Even in the stormiest days no thought, no desire ever came to me to return to stay in France." At the same time, she realized that Sister Basilide had never quite lost her desire to return. If she really decided to go, she was at liberty to do so, wrote Mother Theodore, for she had promised that to all her daughters even before they disembarked in New York. If she wished to return, money for the voyage would be provided.

Later the sisters were to realize that never had she, in so brief a space of time, written so many letters to her daughters, so filled with instructions for the future and with memories of the past. One long letter to Sister Vincent said that she had been reading St. Francis de Sales and was especially intrigued by the statement that a person with a melancholy turn of mind could love God as much as a happier man, but that he could not have as much joy and satisfaction, even though he had equal merit. Mother Theodore felt that was very true. This letter was very long, she wrote, so long that it had been fatiguing to pen it; she would not write again for a while—"but on this day I wanted to write, so important a day in my life—in our life."

It was the day, fifteen years before, when the little group of religious had come to their home in the forest and had knelt in the poor little cabin of Father Buteux. "How many graces since then, dear Sister!" the letter ended.

Christmas that year was a very happy one, even though the weather was very cold, so bitterly cold that the wine froze in the chalice during Mass, as it had done only once before years ago. Three days after the holiday came Mother Theodore's feast day, and the sisters planned a celebration. Despite the weather, the sisters from Terre Haute had managed to come.

In the community room, the statue of St. Anne was wreathed with flowers. The portrait of Bishop Bouvier was hung in a prominent place. There was a table loaded with gifts and an entertainment of music and a little play.

Sister Francis had written a song in Mother Theodore's honor, and they all sang it for her.

"Pour ta fête, Mère tendre et chérie,
Des seraphins j'envie les harpes d'or,"

"For your feast, dear and tender mother,
I envy the angels' harps of gold,"

it began, and their hearts were in every word to the very end:

"Par toi conduites en la Sainte Patrie
De tes enfants quel sera le bonheur!"

"By you will be carried into the holy homeland
children who will be your happiness."

There were tears in Mother Theodore's eyes as it ended. Her voice shook a little when she thanked the singers and the author of the song. Then, since this closed the evening, they all gathered about her and she kissed each of her sisters on both cheeks—"two kisses for the feast," she told them.

CHAPTER EIGHTEEN

Home in Mary's Month (1856)

𝒞

Almost from the day that Sister Francis had come to them, her community worried about her health, and only a little less than they worried about Mother Theodore's. Sister Francis had always been fragile, that was true, but it was equally true that she never allowed her delicate health to interfere with her large amount of work. When, at the beginning of 1856, she was very ill, no one thought it might be fatal, for she had so often recovered from equally serious attacks. But before long it was clear there would be no recovery this time. She died after a brief illness of a week.

Two days before her death, on the eve of the feast of St. Francis de Sales, Sister Francis had suddenly announced that she was better. She had been feverish all day and sometimes had spoken incoherently. At times she seemed to be carrying on a conversation with our Lord with great energy, but no one could understand her words.

"Be quiet, Sister Francis," said the infirmarian gently when the sick religious called out loudly, but she did not hear her. She was smiling and suddenly her words were clear. "Oh, Love—oh, heaven," she said, and fell asleep.

That evening the fever was gone and Sister Francis looked up with a smile when Mother Theodore came to her bed. "Our Lord showed me heaven," she said. "What beauty, Mother—what beauty!"

That night she would speak sometimes rationally and sometimes wildly. Now and then she slept a little. At five in the morning, she asked for Mother

Theodore: she wanted to speak to her alone.

"I must tell you one thing, Mother, and right now," she said. "It is getting late and my thoughts are confused."

"Are you worried about the postulants?" asked Mother Theodore, for Sister Francis was still in charge of the novitiate.

Sister Francis shook her head.

"Is it for me, then?" asked Mother Theodore, and this time Sister Francis nodded. "Yes, Mother, that is it. I want to tell you that I heard our Lord calling me by name, Irma. I thought that I had died, Mother. But then He said, 'Not yet!'" Mother Theodore looked happy. "So He will leave you with us for a while longer."

"Yes, for a day or two—then heaven. And oh, my beloved Mother, you are coming there soon to be with me." As her sister came into the room, Sister Francis looked at her and added, "You too, Elvire, you will be with me through all eternity—but you will come later."

She died very quietly the next day. Her weeping sisters were all about her, and Mother Theodore, who had been sitting beside her, roused herself from her grief to say, "Sisters, we have a sacrifice to make. Let us make it generously and not yield to immoderate sorrow." But, even as she spoke the tears were rolling down her cheeks. It was clear she had never felt a loss, even that of Bishop Bouvier, as she felt this.

She told no one of Sister Francis' last word to her except Father Benoit at Fort Wayne. "She told me, and I entrust it to you, as a secret," she said, "that I am to follow her soon. Oh, if I could really follow her—but I shall never have her virtues. I shall never love as she loved."

When she wrote the sad news to the other houses, she spoke of the "saint of the congregation who has died. The deep wound it has made in my heart will be healed only when I shall be reunited to her in the heaven she beheld so beautifully when she was dying."

It was a death that saddened everyone—the girls whom she had taught, the postulants and novices she had cherished, the priests among whom she had worked. Mother Theodore reflected the general feeling about her when she wrote to Mother Mary in France: "We almost reproach ourselves for praying for her.... Love caused her death—no, not her death, but rather the beginning of her life.... I am talking in this letter of nothing but her, but since I lost her it seems impossible to talk on any other subject."

When Father Corbe told Mother Theodore comfortingly that perhaps Sister Francis was even now acting as a guardian angel for them all, she tried to smile. "I am sure that is true, Father, but I feel as if I have lost part of my life."

They both knew that it was true that during the fifteen years of her religious life Sister Francis had never relaxed in discipline over herself, had never spoken of having good days or bad. "You know how I was obliged to hold her back with the curb of obedience, Father, that virtue which she practised most perfectly of all," said Mother Theodore.

He understood. "I find myself speaking to her and it seems as if I really hear her answer—an illusion, of course, but an illusion productive of good, for the remembrance of her excites one to the love of God and the desire for heaven."

In the weeks following Sister Francis' death, Mother Theodore did not recover even a small measure of health, but she continued at her post, and during those weeks of late winter and early spring she did an incredible amount of work. She was not able to go from the convent but people came to her. Builders came to discuss the plans and building of the new chapel. Circular letters were written and sent to an the houses with an account of Sister Francis' death. Mother Theodore selected, after long thought and much prayer, a new novice mistress, Sister Mary Cecilia. The bishop of Vincennes came several times to see her despite the bad weather. "You must not think of dying until all your debts are paid," he had said jestingly to her more than once. He did not say it this time, for he knew they were almost paid. He discussed with her the proposed new mission at Indianapolis; he wanted it begun on a large scale, since it would be their first house in the state capital.

Mother Theodore continued her daily five o'clock conference with the community; any sister who wished to consult her found her always accessible. She was always at Mass during those weeks. It was one thing she insisted on: to be taken to the chapel each morning. One day, when she felt unusually ill, the infirmarian protested but Mother Theodore said, "How could I bear what I have to if I did not go there for grace?"

Sister Mary Joseph was with her a great deal and helped her with the community devotions that she was still able to perform. Her crucifix was always in her hands; often she held it pressed to her lips. Once, after the doctor had gone, she said it was as well: there was nothing more he could do for her.

"But why do you say that, Mother?" protested Sister Olympiade, who was her nurse. "He is doing all he can to help you."

"I know—I know. He does his best for me, and I am grateful. But I am in the hands of God now, Sister. Give me my crucifix. I prefer that remedy to any other."

On March 16, she wrote to Sister Anastasie in Evansville that she was feeling a little stronger. That was her only mention of herself; the rest of the letter was full of advice. Sister Anastasie was to speak firmly and yet with charity to "that person" and to remember that it was not by pride or selfishness that we could please the Lord. As to the four new pupils who were coming, she was to take only eighty dollars a year for each of them and that was to include needlework. She sent her love to the Evansville community and asked them to pray for her.

The next morning she became ill at Mass and had to be taken to her room. Sister Rose, coming in to clean the room, found her, to her surprise, in bed.

Mother Theodore looked at her. "*Ma fille*, I had to leave Mass. It was my last."

Later that day she wrote in her diary: "I am obliged to keep my bed.

What a beautiful week to be on the cross. O good cross, I will love thee with all my heart." They were the last words she wrote, as her letter to Sister Anastasie had been her last written word to any of the sisters.

Each day after that she grew steadily weaker, but even yet no one was unduly alarmed. She had so often been very ill and each time something had brought her back to work with them again. Several times it had been the Last Sacraments that gave her strength to return. More than once her sisters were certain that she had been miraculously saved. There was the time when she had cholera at Vincennes and Father Corbe asked her to recite the *Memorare*; by the time she had finished the words, she was well. There was the day the angels had saved her when her carriage had overturned in the ravine, and the night she fell from the skiff into the river and was saved from drowning after an incredibly long time in the water.

Yet they felt a growing uneasiness, especially when they remembered how Sister Francis' death had affected her; once Sister Gabriella spoke their uneasiness aloud. "Sister Francis is gone—and who will keep Mother now?" she said. Then, too, Dr. Baty had told them that Mother Theodore had a heart condition that could prove fatal at any time, because she no longer had the resistance that had carried her through so many illnesses.

Mother Theodore had always been cheerfully disposed; her face had reflected her happiness of spirit, just as reverence, adoration, praise of God and His providence, love of Our Lady, had always been the staples of her conversation.

She was changed now. She was withdrawn and silent often, as if she were making a meditation that lasted a long time, and it was this, perhaps more than anything else, that made her sisters realize that here was an illness different from the others. Clearly it was not material things that made her so withdrawn and thoughtful, for she did not speak of temporal matters at all, nor did she give any advice, save very occasionally, as when young Sister Gonzague came to consult her about a matter of conscience. Sometimes she made a few recommendations about prayers that she wished said for her.

It was not in any way that her long silences were at all depressing; it was rather as if she were meditating continuously and deeply. There was little doubt that she was often in pain, but she never spoke of it. When someone came into her room, she smiled the warm loving smile she had always given people.

The days dragged on. All through April she was better one day and worse the next. May came, the lovely May of Saint Mary-of-the-Woods, with trees in flower and birds in their branches building nests. By the second week in May, when Dr. Baty called to see her, he found her so low that he said he considered her beyond human help. On May 11, Father Corbe gave her the Last Sacraments. "Do not let me die without the sacraments," she had told Sister Olympiade more than once.

All that day and the next, she grew constantly worse. The sisters came into her room and went from it continuously. About midnight it was clear that she was dying. From the academy the sisters came to join in the prayers in the candlelit room where Sister Mary Cecilia sat at the head of the bed and Sister Mary Ambrose knelt at its foot.

Mother Theodore had not spoken for some hours, but now it was evident that she was trying to say something; however, the power of speech was gone. Father Corbe had been sent for, and he gave her final absolution and recited the prayers for the dying. She lay quietly, completely absorbed in God. Her breathing had been labored, but now it grew very light. She gave a little sigh and was gone.

Bishop de Saint-Palais spoke at her Requiem Mass, a tender and loving tribute to one he had known long and well. His eyes were tear-filled more than once while he spoke. To the weeping sisters before him he promised that even though they had lost their mother he would be more than ever a father to them. Father Chassé, rector of the seminary, sang the Mass, for Father Corbe knew he would break down if he tried to officiate.

The sisters carried her coffin to the little cemetery on the knoll at St. Anne's, where three of the five who had died at Saint Mary's were buried.

She was laid beside Sister Francis. All about the mourners, the flowers of spring were blooming and the birds were singing as the sisters looked once more upon their beloved Mother Theodore before her coffin was lowered.

Sister Mary Cecilia, her assistant, sent to the houses the letter that told of her death and burial. "Her example is our most precious legacy," she wrote. "We shall follow the path she traced out for us; with this prospect before us, even in our tears we are happy. We saw the hope in her face when she lay dying; she smiled on us with that heavenly look that seemed to say: I will watch over you, so that where I am you may also come."

Bishop Bouvier's former secretary, Abbé Sébaux, wrote that he was happy to know the bishop's alb had been used at her funeral. Father Corbe wrote to Madame le Fer de la Motte of the two deaths, that of her own daughter and that of the other, whom she had loved as a sister, the two who had died within so short a time of each other, just as they had lived close to each other and were now lying side by side.

He had loved them equally, he wrote—Irma, the highspirited girl who all her life had gathered for others flowers along life's highways, and Anne-Thérèse Guérin, the woman who removed briars and thorns from the path of those who must pass there.

Their natures had been very different, he wrote, but they had always worked together and with one purpose. And their deaths had been alike in that they had both been holy and beautiful to witness, their faces so bright that both looked as if they were fallen into a pleasant slumber. "The evening of a good life touches the aurora of Heaven," he ended. "Those for whom we sorrow deeply are not lost to us. They are praying still for their Saint Mary-of-the-Woods."

Mother Theodore Guérin had been all her life a builder, and she built well, not only the houses for her religious and for her pupils but also the house of the spirit without which the others would have had no importance or value or effect. The words on the white cross over her grave in the little cemetery of the religious gave in one sentence the essence of her life: "I sleep, but my heart watches over this house that I have built."

In the more than fifteen years of her life in Indiana, Mother Theodore had gone through many trials and sorrows. "I feel as if I were carrying on my shoulders the weight of the biggest mountains and in my heart the thorns of its wilderness," she wrote on one occasion to Father Benoit. "Pray for me so that I may not lose courage—nay more, that I may have enough to hold up the others who sometimes falter."

That prayer had been granted, not once but many times in the difficult years when only her faith and her trust in Providence sustained her. To anyone who considered the many serious illnesses of her life—there was hardly a year in which she was not at some time critically ill—the amount of work she accomplished was all but unbelievable. Three times within six years she had received the Last Sacraments; each time she came back from the very edge of the grave to take up again her round of duties. She was, as she herself said on one occasion, "never really well—just a little less sick." She was a truly indomitable invalid.

Father Corbe was in that year of loss the community's great comfort. He was to remain spiritual father and devoted friend for many years to come, until his death in 1872. In the early years, there was little doubt that it was he who had kept the community in Indiana; in the days when life there was made almost too difficult for the long-enduring women religious, it was he who urged them to be patient, to wait, to endure.

As for Bishop de la Hailandière, who had caused so many difficulties for Mother Theodore, he remained quietly in retirement in France. He had never received another ecclesiastical appointment, and he signed himself always, *"Ancien évêque de Vincennes"* (former bishop of Vincennes). In later years he sent money to Vincennes for the orphan asylums and occasional sums for the needs of the diocese. When he died, at eighty-four years, he was buried in the parish church of the town where he lived, but it was only a temporary burial place. In the autumn of the same year a hearse came to the cathedral at Vincennes. In it was a great travel-stained box. Bishop de la Hailandière had come to be buried, as he had so earnestly requested, in his old cathedral. He was laid to rest beside Bishop Bruté and Bishop Bazin.

Even before her death, cures and favors had been attributed to Mother Theodore's prayers. Only a few years after her death, Father Corbe had written that she was exhibiting indubitable marks of her power with God. Mother Theodore Guérin, who sacrificed all of herself for God and for souls is still—as the cross over her grave promised—watching over the house that she built.

Afterword

ℰ

On October 15, 2006, His Holiness Pope Benedict XVI solemnly declared Mother Theodore Guérin to be a saint. Saint Mother Theodore is the first saint from Indiana and the eighth saint to have served a ministry in the United States of America.

As a graduate of St. Mary-of-the-Woods College, I feel a personal connection to Mother Theodore. I was very aware during the three years I studied there that I was walking on the same ground Mother Theodore walked. Her vibrant spirit is evident throughout the peaceful woods and in the classrooms, dorms, church and motherhouse.

The canonization held in Rome, Italy, was a very emotional event for alumnae, current students, friends and neighbors, and employees of "the Woods." Most of all, it was the ultimate honor for the Sisters of Providence in the United States and across the globe.

During the canonization, pilgrims from all over the world sat shoulder to shoulder throughout St. Peter's Square and far out into the streets of Vatican City. It was an amazing experience for all assembled to see the banner with Mother Theodore's image hanging on the basilica and to listen to several Sisters of Providence read to the dense crowd from Mother Theodore's journals and from the Scriptures.

I was moved to watch the sisters present to Pope Benedict a stone from Mother Theodore's birthplace, her rosary and white cross, a letter from her journal, a medallion that had been awarded to her for educational excellence, and hand bones from her remains. Only the evening before, at a vigil in anticipation of the canonization, I had the privilege of placing my hand on that very same rosary.

Sister Marie Kevin Tighe, vice postulator for the cause for canonization of Mother Theodore, and Philip McCord, the beneficiary of a miracle attributed to the intercession of Mother Theodore, approached the pope during the offertory of the Mass. Both have invested countless hours in promoting the sainthood of Mother Theodore over the years. I wondered if they had thought the day would ever come when they would kneel before our Holy Father, look into his eyes, and hear him whisper a message for their ears alone.

It was humbling to hear the pontiff speak of Mother Theodore during the homily. The pope said she had devoted her ministry to serving and had trusted completely in the Lord. He added that the Church rejoices in Mother Theodore; she is a source of inspiration, guidance and encouragement to all people.

But by far the most awesome moment came when Pope Benedict pronounced Mother Theodore a saint. Everyone applauded wholeheartedly, and many of us had tears of joy streaming down our face. It was a moment of great pride, and I was honored that I am a follower of Mother Theodore, a graduate of one of the schools she founded, a Catholic, a woman, and an American.

A parallel celebration took place the following weekend, October 21–22, 2006, at Saint Mary-of-the-Woods. It was fitting that the festivities surrounding the canonization also coincided with Foundation Day, the 166th anniversary of the day Mother Theodore and her companions first arrived at Saint Mary-of-the-Woods in 1840.

A Eucharistic liturgy of thanksgiving was held at the Church of the Immaculate Conception. More than a thousand people attended the service in the church and watched by satellite remote at other locations on the campus. An open house, brunch, and self-guided tours of the sacred places related to Mother Theodore followed. Many said that the celebration in the Woods was even more personally meaningful than the one in Rome, because it was held where Mother Theodore's spirit is most felt.

The Catholic Church defines saints as individuals who lived holy and exemplary lives. A very strict and in-depth procedure is carried out in determining someone's qualifications for sainthood, including an investigation into the person's personal history. Evidence of at least two miracles attributed to the candidate's intercession also is required. Both miracles must occur after the person's death—one before beatification and one before canonization, which is the Church's official recognition of a person as a saint.

The process of recognizing Mother Theodore's sainthood began nearly 100 years ago with the miraculous healing of Sister Mary Theodosia Mug. Sister Mary Theodosia, a Sister of Providence, had a number of serious health ailments, including neuritis in her right hand and arm, damaged nerves and muscles in her left arm from a mastectomy for the removal of a malignancy, an inoperable massive abdominal tumor, and poor eyesight. She suffered considerable pain, dizziness, and continuous vomiting.

After praying for another ill sister at the tomb of Mother Theodore on the evening of October 30, 1908, Sister Mary Theodosia was surprised to receive complete healing for herself. She arose the next morning without pain, the abdominal tumor had disappeared, her vision was clear, and she had complete use of both arms. Physicians conducted extensive medical examinations and determined that there wasn't any natural explanation for the healings. Sister Mary Theodosia lived thirty-five more years to the age of eighty-two, and she always gave credit to Mother Theodore for her miraculous recovery.

Bishop Francis Silas Chatard, the bishop of the Diocese of Indianapolis, granted permission to open the Informative Process of the Cause for the Beatification and Canonization of Mother Theodore in 1909. Numerous meetings and studies were conducted in St. Mary-of-the-Woods, Indianapolis and Rome. Mother Theodore's life, work and writings were examined in great detail.

On July 22, 1992, Pope John Paul II granted Mother Theodore the title "Venerable," indicating that she had lived the "heroic virtues." The heroic virtues include the four cardinal virtues of prudence, justice, fortitude and temperance and the three theological virtues of faith, hope and charity.

On October 25, 1998, based on the miracle to Sister Mary Theodosia, Pope John Paul conferred on Mother Theodore the title "Blessed," indicating that she was worthy of honor and veneration. All that was needed for sainthood was one more miracle, which occurred three years later.

Philip McCord, a civil engineer and the Director of Facilities Management for the Sisters of Providence, had developed severely diminished vision and a droopy, swollen, irritated right eye from cataract surgery. After months of tests and procedures, an eye specialist in Indianapolis recommended a cornea replacement as the only option that might restore McCord's sight. That surgery at the time was considered to have only a sixty percent success rate after a recovery period of more than two years.

Depressed and anxious about the surgery and subsequent therapy, McCord asked God for guidance and courage in early January of 2001. He also prayed that if Mother Theodore had any influence she would intercede with God on his behalf. The following morning he realized that the outward appearance of the eye had returned to normal, although his vision remained impaired.

When McCord visited his specialist the following week, however, the doctor knew immediately that he had been cured. All that was needed for perfect vision was a quick laser treatment to remove a tissue mass that remained from the cataract surgery. A cornea transplant was miraculously no longer required. There followed years of medical exams and church investigations until finally McCord's healing was declared a divine miracle resulting from the intercession of Mother Theodore.

Even before her death, Mother Theodore was believed to be responsible for cures and answered prayers. Friends and colleagues went to her because she was a compassionate and powerfully effective woman who accomplished extraordinary things by trusting in God.

At a Mass of Thanksgiving on October 16, 2006, at the Basilica of St. Paul Outside the Walls in Rome, the archbishop of Indianapolis, Daniel M. Beichlein, OSB, said Mother Theodore is a witness of God's love for us. God so loved our little part of the world that he blessed us with her, said the archbishop, and she is a model of faith as relevant to today's society as she was during her ministry in the 1800s.

Those of us who have lived, worked, studied, taught and prayed at Saint Mary-of-the-Woods claim Mother Theodore as our own. We feel privileged to have such a close, immediate connection to her. But with her canonization, Mother Theodore now officially belongs to the world. Her canonization tells us all that we certainly have another friend in heaven, a young woman from France named Anne-Thérèse Guérin who had the courage, perseverance and love to cross both the Atlantic Ocean and the American frontier to help bring the good news to the New World despite many obstacles, both natural and man-made.

Faith was truly the substance of Mother Theodore's life.

Mary K. Doyle
October 23, 2006

MORE BOOKS ON SPIRITUALITY

Three Saints
Women Who Changed History
by Joan Williams

Short biographies of three of the most influential women in history. Genevieve of Paris, Catherine of Siena, and Teresa of Avila all made real contributions in public life, as well as exhibiting personal holiness. Perfect for those exploring the role of women in Church and society. 160-page paperback, $9.95

The Rosary Prayer by Prayer
How and Why We Pray the Christ-Centered Rosary of the Blessed Mother
by Mary K. Doyle

An invaluable resource and aid to praying the Rosary, both for those familiar with the devotion and those seeking to understand and practice it. A treasure chest of information about the history and benefits of the rosary, suggestions for meditation on the mysteries, exquisite artwork, and references. 224-page hardcover, $19.95; paperback, $14.95

Midwives of an Unnamed Future
Spirituality for Women in Times of Unprecedented Change
by Mary Ruth Broz, RSM, and Barbara Flynn
with photographs by Jean Clough

A book for women who are passionate about exploring their role in shaping the "unnamed future," this unique series of reflections and rituals can be used by individuals or groups of women coming together to deepen their own spirituality and uncover new life in age old spiritual truths. 208-page hardcover, $14.95

Running into the Arms of God
Stories of Prayer/Prayer as Story
by Father Patrick Hannon, CSC

Stories of prayer in everyday life by a Holy Cross priest, tied to the traditional hours of the monastic day: matins, lauds, prime, terce, sext, none, vespers, compline. Winner of the 2006 Catholic Press Association Book Award for first time author of a book. 128-page hardcover, $15.95; paperback, $11.95

Allegories of Heaven
An Artist Explores the "Greatest Story Ever Told"
by Dinah Roe Kendall
with "The Message" text by Eugene H. Peterson

Contemporary English artist Dinah Roe Kendall offers a vibrant visual retelling of the full scope of Jesus' ministry through her figurative and narrative paintings, accompanied by Eugene Peterson's widely acclaimed contemporary rendering of the Bible. 100-page, four-color hardcover, $14.95